CW00538769

DAVID MA)

David Maxwell-Scott has been in the drinks business for sixty years, from wine trade trainee to managing director of a major Scotch whisky company, and currently chairman of the UK's leading brewpub company. His travels have inspired him to write about the curious places and the colourful characters that he has had the good fortune to encounter. David lives in London with his wife, Isabel. He has two sons and two grandsons.

BOGOTÁ TO BEIRUT

Halcyon Days in the Whisky Trade

DAVID MAXWELL-SCOTT

For Anthony & Valerie
with all good
wishes
David

PULLINGTON

This paperback edition first published in Great Britain in 2023 by
PULLINGTON

Copyright © David Maxwell-Scott, 2023

A CIP catalogue record for this book is available from the British Library.

ISBN 978-1-7391162-0-0

Cover created by Paul McPherson Design

Typeset Born Group

Printed and bound in Great Britain by Clays Ltd, Elcograf S.p.A.

www.pullington.co.uk

For Isabel

Preface

The police will tell you that two witnesses will remember the same incident quite differently, and that older people's memories can become quite distorted. So, my own recollections may not be accurate, but this is how I remember them; and because I had such fun, I thought I should record them anyway.

For thirty years I was involved in the pursuit of exporting whisky. This book attempts to look back and give some light sketches of how we in the whisky trade worked and travelled in those times. Along the way you will see that we also created a very successful global brand. That too is a good story; but my principal objective in this book is to illustrate the warmth, humour, diversity, and not infrequent eccentricity, of the people that I was fortunate enough to meet while visiting over a hundred different countries between 1970 and 1996. It is distilled from a blend of memory and legend.

I wrote this book during the COVID-19 pandemic. It gave me something absorbing to do during the various lockdowns. At the same time, I was conscious that I was doing nothing practical to help combat the effects of the virus. In an attempt to make some amends for that, all royalties that I receive from any sales of this work will go to CAFOD's Humanitarian Appeal for Ukraine.

David Maxwell-Scott
September 2022

CONTENTS

CONTENTS

CONTENTS

1

In the Beginning

The interview was not going well. I was trying my best, but Dorrien Belson, chairman of J&B and my interviewer, did not seem impressed. There were lengthy pauses. He seemed bored. I was being interviewed for a job in J&B Export. At the time J&B Rare, the whisky brand of Justerini & Brooks, was going gangbusters in America and the company wanted to build a team to exploit the brand's potential in markets beyond the USA. I was one of the candidates.

Eventually Dorrien asked me if I could speak Spanish. I confessed that I could not but added, in desperation, that my wife could. Another long pause followed. I was beginning to think that my suggestion was a particularly inane one when, brightening unexpectedly, he said:

'Well, I suppose you could learn it at home.'

A few days later, and much to my surprise, I got a letter from Dorrien offering me the position of area manager for Latin America. The salary was to be a princely £1,450 per annum. The letter was dated 27th November 1969.

PART 1

~ BY WAY OF BACKGROUND ~

1962–1969

2

A Wine Cellar under Charing Cross Station

When I left school, I did not go to university. That was not so unusual in those days. Today 50 per cent of school leavers go on to a university, but in the early 1960s that figure was under 4 per cent. After I left school, I had no clear idea what I wanted to do. One option that sounded attractive was 'the wine trade'. After firing a few blanks which failed to secure any interviews, my mother responded to an offer 'to help if he could' from our Cousin Bernard. This led to an interview in the Bond Street offices of Justerini & Brooks.

In 1962 UWT (United Wine Traders) had merged with W & A Gilbey (Gilbeys) to form IDV (International Distillers & Vintners Ltd). UWT was a small group of London-based wine merchants. Its principal members were Twiss Browning & Hallows, Corney & Barrow, and Justerini & Brooks (J&B). But with the exploding success of their whisky brand (J&B Rare), J&B had become the giant within the UWT group. The IDV merger was therefore very much a J&B–Gilbey affair.

IDV wanted to recruit management trainees for the new group. Together with three other candidates I was interviewed by an august panel of three: Freddie Hennessy (chairman of the group), Ralph Cobbold (joint managing director of J&B), and Arthur Gilbey (export director for Gilbeys). Of the four candidates interviewed, three were selected. Peter Waugh, whose father Alec had written a history of Gilbeys and who was a friend of the Gilbey family; Simon Pilkington whose godfather was Eddie Tatham, the man who launched J&B Whisky in America; and me. I have to admit that Cousin Bernard, as a customer of J&B and known to Ralph Cobbold, was also a duke. I suspect that Cousin Bernard's pedigree may have given me the edge in the tie-break for the third slot.

I spent the first three months of my thirty-six-year employment at IDV working in the Justerini & Brooks wine cellars. In those days, the J&B cellars were in Hungerford Lane, a grimy Dickensian alleyway under the arches of Charing Cross Station. The last time I walked up Hungerford Lane I noticed that the old J&B premises are now occupied by *Heaven*, a gay night club.

A lot of J&B's wines were bottled in those cellars. I was put to work with Sid and Ernie, two stalwart cockneys who showed me the ropes. Barrels of wine, pipes of port, and butts of sherry would be fined (to clarify the wine), left to rest, and then, once rested, tilted at an angle, and tapped. The bottling was done by hand through a rudimentary asbestos (yes, asbestos) filter.

The atmosphere in the cellars was busy but convivial. There were many cockney characters of the old school. For example, George the van driver who had perfected the art of feigning breathlessness when carrying heavy boxes of wine up to smart Mayfair flats. He would ring the bell, and then lean weakly against the door post mopping his brow. When asked solicitously if he was alright, he would mutter darkly about his 'dodgy ticker'. This invariably did the trick. With a little prompting from George, and not wanting to run the risk of a heart attack victim on their doorstep the grandees of the apartments, or their servants, invariably came up with a nip of the right stuff. Brandy was George's favoured remedy for restoring the equilibrium of his heartbeat.

Fred was another character. We used to bottle a lot of South African sherry, and Fred was partial to the stuff. So, when it was being bottled, Fred would sidle up and scrounge a mugful. He was an accomplished darts player and would monopolise the dartboard in the tearoom. He could hit a triple 20 with ease – especially after the mugful.

And then there was Edith, a stout lady who reigned supreme in her tearoom. The language around the cellar was pretty free and easy but woe betide anyone who used a naughty word in her presence. I did once and got the most awful wigging from our Edie while Sid, Ernie, and the rest of them just sat there, in silence, smirking sanctimoniously. I found this a bit galling, especially after I had discovered that in the summer, when the weather was fine, Sid and Ernie would go outside and eat their lunchtime sandwiches at a spot under the footpath of Hungerford Bridge. The bridge runs from Charing Cross Station across the Thames towards Waterloo. The footpath was then a fretwork metal affair and as this was the era of the mini-skirt Sid and Ernie, the latter almost toothless, would gaze aloft as leggy girls in their platform shoes would clatter past overhead.

3

Camden Town

In January 1963 I was sent to Camden Town to start my two-year management training course. The IDV merger of J&B with Gilbeys was a marriage of contrasts. Apart from the fine wine business, J&B had their own brand of whisky that was growing exponentially in America. The whisky itself was sourced from the broking market, and the blending and bottling was done by outside contractors. Financially, it all worked because Scotch whisky was in short supply and demand was high. Consequently J&B, thanks to the whisky, were stuffed with cash. Conversely, Gilbeys had a broader and more secure wine and spirit business with their own brands of gin, whisky, port, sherry and so on. They had vineyards, production plants, gin distilleries, whisky distilleries and distribution companies ranging across the major Commonwealth countries. But they were not profitable. Indeed, during the first years of IDV's existence, J&B made 110 per cent of the group's profits. So, putting the two companies together created an entity that had a stronger and more cohesive structure.

Camden Town was where Gilbeys had their HQ, gin distillery, bonded warehouses, and bottling plant. The Roundhouse was one of those warehouses. It had been built in 1847 and originally featured a turntable for railway engines but had become redundant. Gilbeys used the Roundhouse to store barrels of rum; nowadays it is a performing arts venue. Camden Town today is a much trendier area than it was in the sixties.

Peter Waugh, Simon Pilkington, and I all spent several months at Camden Town moving from one department to another: an experience that varied from boring, to fascinating, to eye-opening. We spent time in every department from accounts, purchasing, sales, quality control, and production through to export.

In those days anything involving the movement, storage, and production of anything alcoholic was monitored by on-the-spot officers from Her Majesty's Customs and Excise. Every warehouse door had two locks on it. One for the warehouse owner and the other for the Excise. Neither could enter without the other. There was a full team of Customs and Excise officers at Gilbeys in Camden Town. In truth, their role was far from strenuous, consisting mostly of checking and rechecking all the records to make sure that nothing could escape from the bonded warehouse system without paying the full and correct amount of excise duty. They had an office high up and towards the back of a bulk storage warehouse; the 'bulk' consisting of large wooden vats that held whisky or rum. Normally, you were not allowed into the C&E office, but on one occasion I had to go there on some particular mission. Entering their office was a surprise. The tobacco smog was spectacular. Then through the gloaming I spotted four of Her Majesty's finest playing gin rummy, a dartboard, a makeshift bar, and precious little evidence of normal office paraphernalia. It was more speakeasy than office. I was told that if an officer fancied a splash of rum in his tea a junior officer would be sent off to the vat room armed with a milk bottle which had a length of string attached to its neck. He (C&E officers were always 'he') would lower the milk bottle into the vat and haul back a generous sample of over-proof rum. The rum could then be added to the tea. The tea was not an obligatory part of the mix.

4

Speyside Distilling

After the stint at Camden Town, Simon, Peter, and I were sent off in separate directions to learn more about life in the Gilbey empire. In early 1964 I was sent to Scotland and Ireland (North and South). Gilbeys had three malt whisky distilleries on Speyside, and I particularly enjoyed my time there. The manager in charge, Bill Thompson, was extremely kind and lent me his car at weekends. Even though it was February I was able to explore the wonderful scenery of the Scottish Highlands.

In those days malt whisky distilling was a truly arti-sanal affair. Each distillery had its own malting floor where the barley was laid out after being steeped in spring water. The barley had to be turned regularly with wooden shovels and then, once the germination process had reached the right point, dried in a kiln that was fired by coal plus a dash of peat. The copper stills had open fires underneath them and the stillman would deploy a ball that was suspended on a chain from the top of the still. He would periodically whack it against the side of the still; he could then detect from the timbre of the echo whether the batch was being distilled too fiercely or not fiercely enough. Depending on the verdict, the poor sweating stoker below would be told to shovel the coal on faster or slower. Nowadays the whole process is automated, which is less charismatic, though the end product is much more consistent.

I stayed at hotels that were within walking distance of whichever distillery I was visiting. The Station Hotel in Rothes was one such. To be honest my room was not impressive: positively damp when it rained. But the food was wholesome country cooking at its most sublime – which is pretty surprising given the low standard of cooking that pervaded the hotel business in the 1960s. On my last night at the Station Hotel several of the lads from our nearby Glen Spey Distillery promised to come round and have a drink after 'they'd had their tea'. Ginger, the cooper, came together with Jimmy, an Irishman who looked after the washbacks, and a couple of others whose names I forget. Washbacks are very large vat-sized fermentation vessels. Those at Glen Spey were made of Oregon pine.

In the 1960s malt whisky was produced, almost entirely, to mix with grain whisky and thereby create blended whisky. At the time Haig, Teacher's, Johnnie Walker, and Bell's were typical well-known brands of blended Scotch whisky. Very few people produced what we know today as single malt whisky. One exception was Glenfarclas, a distillery situated a little upstream from Rothes, where they produced a very good 10-year-old. Locally, it was establishing quite a reputation. So, Glenfarclas is what we drank. All of us, that is, except Jimmy, who liked Bacardi.

We were having a very convivial evening when towards normal closing time I offered to buy them a last round. My offer was met with some surprise.

'But you're staying here, aren't you?' said Ginger. And when I replied in the affirmative:

'Well then, we can go on for as long as we like, can't we?' was his reply.

He was right. Under the licensing laws, anyone staying at a hotel could order a drink whenever they wanted. And so we did, until the wee small hours.

At around two in the morning on that cold February night, the High Street in Rothes, lined as it was with its grey granite-built houses, wore a cloak of sombre sleeping respectability. But as I walked along it, accompanying my guests back to their distillery cottages, our mood was neither sombre nor cold. Warmed by the glow from Glenfarclas's best, or in Jimmy's case, rum from the Caribbean, we were a cheery gang. After disturbing the good folk of Rothes with an Irish sea shanty, Jimmy decided that we should all go to his place for 'one last one'. He assured me that his lady wife would be delighted to see us. I had grave misgivings about the wisdom of accepting this offer, but Jimmy was having none of it. Then, as we advanced towards his front door, the decision was taken from us. His portcullis was flung open to reveal his wife: a very robust lady in curlers who was looking extremely angry. I'm afraid we pushed Jimmy into the arms of his missus, then turned and fled.

Looking back on it, I feel that the men who worked at the distilleries were craftsmen who were highly skilled in their particular trade. Bill Thompson and his three distillery managers were, in their quiet Highland manner, very good at their job. They were respected by the employees and committed to making high-quality malt whisky. They were also forward thinking. On one occasion, when he was driving me from Keith to Rothes, Bill pointed to a place which he said had a very good source of spring water. He said it would be a fine place to build a distillery. A few years later we opened the Auchroisk Distillery on that very spot. Auchroisk has been producing fine Speyside malt whisky ever since, perfectly fulfilling its original objective, which was to give IDV a better supply of malt whisky to satisfy the growing demand for J&B Rare.

After the distilleries, I went to Inverness. In those days 'off-licences' did not really exist in Scotland. Under the stern eye of the Kirk, it was not considered quite respectable to go into a shop purely to buy a bottle of whisky. However, it was quite acceptable to go to a grocer for a pound of butter, and then add a crate of wine or whisky to your order. So, most of the 'take home' trade was done through licensed grocers. Gilbeys owned D Cameron & Co, and it was the manager of their branch in Inverness who explained this custom. He told me that he had one customer, a minister of the Kirk no less, to whom he provided a regular supply of whisky. But his reverence's monthly orders had to be discreetly delivered out of sight to an outbuilding. Gilbeys' flagship store was Lang's of Perth, a wonderful emporium filled with all manner of delicacies, a veritable Fortnum's of the north.

The still room at Glen Spey Distillery, 1964

Jimmy, amongst his washbacks, the morning after

5

Ireland, North and South

After my stint in Scotland, I sailed from Stranraer to Belfast to spend some time at the Gilbeys branch in Northern Ireland. The branch was purely concerned with sales. There were no Gilbeys distillery or production facilities to see. My visit occurred before the beginning of the Troubles, but I could sense the tensions between the two factions. Indeed, the Gilbeys sales force was divided between a representative for the Protestant trade, and another for the Catholic.

I think that Walter Frampton, the manager of the branch, must have considered me manna from Heaven. He was a sociable type, very gregarious and much addicted to the products he sold, though to be fair I never saw him the worse for wear. As far as I can recall, he used my stay as an excuse to go on a rolling visit to as many of his trade friends and customers as he could. As a callow nineteen-year-old, I found this VIP treatment most gratifying. In other places that I visited I was often given mundane tasks to keep me out of sight.

So, Walter took me to meet all manner of people. The tradition of hospitality in Northern Ireland has always been spectacular. The amount we consumed at these meetings was prodigious. Walter also took me to visit the two whiskey distilleries in the province: Bushmills and Coleraine. Bushmills was the better known. But at Coleraine I remember tasting a very fine malt whiskey. It was triple distilled, in the Irish fashion, lightly peated and somewhat akin to a good Campbelltown from the Mull of Kintyre, which, after all, is not so far away. Although it had an impressive history, going back to 1820, the Coleraine whiskey business has followed a rather haphazard path. It was only operating part time when we visited and closed for good in 1978: a great shame.

The Bushmills Distillery is only a couple of miles from the Giant's Causeway, so I was able to visit this magnificent landmark well before it became a UNESCO World Heritage Site. Whisky, or whiskey as it is spelled in Ireland, was first distilled in Ireland not Scotland. The Scots have, of course, been rather better at developing it. The Irish have always been a bit sore about that. Legend has it that Finn MacCool, a mythical Irish giant, was the one who had started to build the Causeway near Bushmills. His objective was to create a route across the North Channel, so that he could attack Benandonner, a rival giant, in Scotland. Mythology is unclear about the motive for the quarrel, but I like to think that MacCool (and what a great name) wanted to get at Benandonner because Benandonner had nicked his recipe for *uisce-beatha*, his water of life, or more simply his recipe for making whiskey.

From Belfast I travelled to Dublin. Gilbeys were a leading wine and spirit merchant in the Irish Republic. They even had their own brand of Irish whiskey, called Redbreast. The whiskey for Redbreast was sourced from Jameson and aged by Gilbeys for ten years before bottling. It was very good. For many years Redbreast was a neglected brand. Recently I was pleased to see that it has been resurrected: now as a 12-year-old and part of the Jameson stable which is owned by Pernod Ricard. I find it reassuring that some of these old brands that have changed hands can spring to life again.

On one of my Sundays in Dublin I went out to Portmarnock to see if I could get a round of golf on the famous links. When I went into the pro-shop to see if I might be allowed to play, the pro behind the counter was very welcoming.

'To be sure,' he said, 'I'm going out in a few minutes with two of our members. You'd be welcome to join us.'

On the first tee he introduced me to the two members. His own name, he said, was Harry. As the visitor, they gave me the honour to tee off first, always a nerve-tingling moment with strangers at a foreign club. Then at the top of my backswing the penny dropped. Harry must be *the* Harry Bradshaw, the renowned Irish pro who had won countless tournaments; the Harry Bradshaw who had played several times in the Ryder Cup and who might have won The Open at Sandwich in 1949 had his ball not got lodged in a broken beer bottle and caused him to drop a crucial shot. And, in that split second, I remembered that he was currently the resident pro at Portmarnock and was watching me take my first shot.

The shore of Balydoyle Bay runs close to the first hole at Portmarnock. The tide was in and that was where my tee shot went, splat off the toe of my club into the water. This caused my hosts a good deal of friendly merriment. But they very kindly invited me to take a Mulligan, which I did. Fortunately, I played reasonably well thereafter and did not disgrace myself. Harry, with his quiet jovial twinkle, fully lived up to the Irish expression of being 'a lovely man'. At one point I asked him how many children he had? 'Four' was his reply, 'it's the perfect number. You can't go wrong with level fours': which is a golfing expression denoting a very good performance.

6

Oporto and the Douro

In the summer of 1964, I was due to spend time at Château Loudenne, the Gilbeys' vineyard in the Médoc north of Bordeaux. Instead, I got appendicitis and had ten days in the cottage hospital at Haslemere in Surrey. Back then, it was quite normal to spend such a long time recuperating after a minor operation. My timing was rather good because England were playing Australia that summer and I was able to tune in to the mellifluous voice of John Arlott commentating on the Third Test Match. There was also the Open at St Andrews, which that year was won by the swashbuckling Tony Lema. He was popularly known as Champagne Tony. The other patients in the hospital seemed to be long-term residents; mostly they suffered from problems with their personal plumbing. They were friendly and taught me to how to play cribbage, but then got a bit shirty when, somehow or other, I started to beat them.

Once I had recovered from appendicitis, I flew to Oporto to catch up with my training programme. Here I joined up with Peter Waugh, and together we spent the next few weeks learning about port and sherry. This was quite splendid because, apart from being the delightful person he was, Peter arrived, via Château Loudenne, in his brand-new

Lotus Elan – a rugged but magical sports car that he had just acquired having previously owned and rejected, in quick succession, an E-Type Jag (too heavy) and an Alfa Romeo Spyder (too slow). In his Lotus we were to travel from Oporto up the Douro valley to Croft's Quinta da Roêda, then across into Spain and down to Jerez. Eventually we drove home via Rioja and Paris. Peter was some six years older than me, having done National Service and a stint at Oxford. Travelling with Peter was like being in the company of a mischievous elder brother.

Croft was the port house owned by Gilbeys. Established in the year of the Armada (1588), it is the oldest actively trading port company in existence. Peter and I stayed at the English Club in Oporto, a stylish but somewhat faded old building which served as guest house cum club for English wine trade visitors. Every morning at breakfast the waiter would ask us what we wanted. We would tell him, and despite whatever we told him we would get what he called, 'eggs-ee-bakey': and rather greasy it was too. Mind you, the excellent, thick, grainy Brazilian coffee made up for it. Like rocket fuel, it got us off to a racing start. There was consternation in the club one day when the water gave off a queer smell. Then one of the kitchen staff found a dead pigeon in the tank. It was that sort of place: slightly chaotic but with its own charm.

Oporto was, and still is, a delightful historic city. Croft's lodges, or cellars, were across the river from Oporto in Vila Nova De Gaia, alongside those of many other port shippers. Our week in Oporto was hectic. We spent much of our time at the lodges in Gaia. To get there, we crossed the river by the magnificent Dom Luis Bridge. Conceived by Eiffel, and built of iron, it was opened in 1886. One day we were taken to lunch at The Factory House, an imposing Neo-Palladian building, back over the river in Oporto. The Factory House still operates for the port wine trade in Portugal much like a livery company does for its specific trade in the City of London.

At the weekend we bathed from the beach at Foz and drank fizzy vinho verde out of ceramic mugs in local *tabernas*. And we met a great many of the Anglo-Portuguese fraternity who were engaged in the port wine business. In short, we were given a sharp but full immersion into how the very traditional port trade lived and worked in Oporto.

My lifelong friendship with Peter Waugh, or just Waugh as I came to call him, began in Oporto. At the time he had a spectacular psychedelic Madras cotton jacket of which I was very envious. With his sports car, his sense of fun and being, as he was, a scion of a great literary family, he became a great favourite with the daughters of the port barons. He reciprocated by writing poems about them that he would try out on me over the eggs-ee-bakey at the English Club.

It was a Sunday when we drove to Quinta da Roêda: the Croft vineyard in the Douro. As we passed through rustic villages the locals looked wonderfully clean and tidy. David Cossart, another friend made at Croft, told us that because it was Sunday, they would have had their weekly wash before going to Mass.

It gives me a jolt to remember that in 1964 neither Spain nor Portugal were democratic countries. In 1910 the Portuguese monarchy had been overthrown. Anarchy and chaos had ensued until a military takeover in 1926. First as Finance Minister then as Prime Minister, António de Oliveira Salazar had ruled since 1932. Salazar was not a typical dictator, but his 'reign' would continue until 1968, and democracy would not properly return to Portugal until 1975.

The Salazar era is often reckoned to have been beneficial for Portugal, but in 1964 the country was still poor. We could see that as we drove the eighty-mile journey up the Douro valley from Oporto to the Croft quinta near Pinhão.

The Lotus Elan had concealed headlights, but if Waugh pushed a button by the gear lever they would pop up, flash, and then close down: a sort of motoring wink. Driving slowly through the villages, he tried this out on family groups. It had an electric effect, especially on small children. A barking dog, jumping around at the end of a long chain, even stopped barking.

The house at Quinta da Roêda was a large, comfortable bungalow set inside the vineyard of the quinta, and on terraces set above the Douro. It was vintage time and Robin Reid and his wife Elsa were in residence. Robin was the managing director of Croft and was doing much to reinvigorate the business. He was a great raconteur and the ideal person to inculcate us with a lifelong love of port. Elsa was mischievous, irreverent, and sometimes quite outspoken: a delightful combination.

After breakfast on the first day, we set off with Robin at the wheel of a battered Land Rover. We went up hill and down dale, and along dirt tracks to visit small vineyards in remote places. Every year these small growers would supply wines to be included in the recipe for various Croft blends. At each stop Robin would be greeted like a long-lost friend. After lengthy pleasantries had been exchanged in, for us, incomprehensible Portuguese, we would be taken to the cellar and shown the vat that was being prepared to take the new wine. Robin would stick his head inside while banging hard on the outside of the vat with the flat of his hand. At the same time, he would inhale deeply and decide whether it smelled clean enough to take the new vintage. If it did, there would be smiles all round. If not, a lot of shouting and gesticulation tended to take place, with Robin promising to return in a few days for a further inspection.

Back at Quinta da Roêda, the vintage was in full swing. The grapes were picked by local peasants. And yes, I'm afraid we did call them peasants. They were sturdy, smiley, weather-tanned, and straw-behatted people. Waugh and I acquired hats just like theirs. They cost us each the escudo equivalent of one shilling and thruppence (that's 6.25p in new money). I still have mine. The pickers were paid the equivalent of twelve shillings and sixpence (62.5p) for a twelve-hour back-breaking day. Elsa also hired a woman plus cow for five shillings (25p) a day so that those of us staying at the Quinta could enjoy fresh milk.

Tua and Tejo were two large Serra mountain dogs that guarded the property. They were named after two rivers: the Tua being a nearby Douro tributary, and the Tejo being Portuguese for the Tagus. Once properly introduced, they were playful and friendly. But the local people were wary of them. Robin said that once he found a woman, who was coming to the house with a basket of eggs on her head, howling with rage and pain because Tejo had got his teeth into her ankle. Tejo was not letting go of the ankle and the woman was not letting go of her eggs: they were too valuable. The cook told Robin that previously the woman had chucked a stone at Tejo. Clearly having 'previous' with those dogs was not a sound strategy.

One evening after dinner we were sent down to the *lagar* to tread the grapes. The *lagar* was a waist-high open tank made of concrete where the grapes were heaped. Together with some of the male pickers (only men were allowed to do this) we linked arms, Zorba style, and in a line started to tread our way into the pile of grapes. Gradually they were reduced to a liquid sludge. It was hard work. Port grapes have formidable pigments. The red stain on my legs took about two weeks to disappear despite vigorous washing. At the time, treading by foot was being phased out and replaced by mechanical crushers. I had hoped that 1964 would be a great vintage so that in the years to come I would be able to offer it to friends and say with due gravitas that it had my footprint on it. Alas that was not to be. I understand that recently some port houses have restarted the tradition of treading grapes. They say that it is a gentler process and avoids releasing some of the most bitter tannins.

One discovery we made in Portugal was the delight of white port: an excellent apéritif. We thought that Taylor's Chip Dry was the best. As for the red variety, no vintage port was served at Roêda. It was too hot for that. Instead, we tried a wide range of tawny ports. Croft Particular was our favourite: a wonderful 20-year-old tawny port that was served lightly chilled after dinner at the Quinta.

In those days, no table wine was made in the Douro. Everything was made into port which, of course, is a wine fortified with grape alcohol during fermentation. The addition of grape alcohol arrests the fermentation process before it is complete and causes the must to retain enough sugar to leave the sweetness in the wine that we expect from port. Robin, however, had been experimenting in the making of unfortified wine. He was ahead of his time. Nowadays there are some very fine unfortified wines that are made in the delimited port growing region of the Douro.

Robin Reid with the locals at a village in the Cima Corgo

Waugh at Quinta da Roêda, larking with Tua
the Serra mountain dog

7

Jerez and La Rioja

From Quinta da Roêda we drove across the border and down through Spain to Jerez de la Frontera, the home of sherry. In the 1960s massive amounts of sherry were shipped to the UK; it was the de rigueur apéritif. Styles varied from finos, like Tio Pepe, to the category leader, Harveys Bristol Cream, which is very sweet. Sherry was shipped to the UK in large casks, called butts, and bottled on arrival. The emptied butts were then sent up to Scotland where they were considered the ideal receptacle for maturing whisky. Today, sherry is bottled in Jerez.

Gilbeys did not own a business in Jerez, but they were very closely connected to González Byass, a major producer. Indeed, at the end of the nineteenth century two Gilbey sisters had married two brothers from the González family. Gilbeys, however, did have their own range of sherries, and González Byass had created exclusive soleras to cater for them. Soleras are used to age the various types of sherry such as: fino, palo cortado, amontillado, or oloroso.

A solera is composed of a stack of butts comprising several tiers. The oldest wine is in the bottom tier, the youngest in the top. When wine is required for bottling, a proportion of the contents is drawn from the bottom tier.

If, for example, the solera comprises eight tiers, wine from the second tier will be used to replace the wine from the bottom tier, then wine from the third tier will top up the second tier. And so on until wine from the eighth, and top tier, has been drawn to top up that of the seventh. Every year new wine will be used to replenish the top tier. It is a laborious process but ensures consistency in style and quality for every brand of sherry.

The bodegas, where the soleras are held, are wonderfully cool cathedral-like buildings. González Byass even have one, La Concha, which was designed by Gustav Eiffel. One morning Waugh and I were sent off into the bodegas with their top *venenciador*. A *venenciador* is a man who can draw samples from the butts of ageing sherry in a particularly stylish manner. He does this with his *venencia*: an implement with a narrow cup at the end of a metre-long bendy handle. An expert *venenciador* can hold several small *copita* glasses between the fingers of one hand then, with the other hand, plunge the *venencia* into the barrel, draw it out and, in a series of swift, graceful motions, fill, at arm's-length, each glass. The Number One *venenciador* at González Byass made it look easy – but it isn't. He did it for us with eleven *copitas* wedged between his fingers. He filled them without spilling a drop. It is as difficult as trying to turn leg-breaks like Shane Warne. I know because we tried and came out of the bodegas feeling damp and sticky from spilled sherry. But also quite merry from what we didn't spill.

González Byass's top *venenciador* in action

One afternoon we were sent off to the González bodega at Sanlúcar de Barrameda, then a small fishing port, by the sea near the mouth of the Guadalquivir. Sanlúcar is the home of manzanilla, the lovely fino that is said to get its salty tang from being grown and aged in the parish. After 'work' we went down to the beach. Silhouetted by the setting sun, the sardine boats were unloading the day's catch. Later we repaired to a nearby *taverna*. It was a noisy, smoky, jostling sort of place with sawdust on the floor, sardines on the grill, and manzanilla on tap: better than a three-star Michelin place any day.

On the way back to Jerez the fields at the side of the road seemed, in the moonlight, to be aglow. To make sure that it was not us that were aglow we stopped and had a look. It was a field of cotton which, on close inspection, we discovered to be small bushes bearing rather untidy tufts of cotton wool. It was these tufts that had caught and reflected the moonlight. Apparently, Franco was encouraging its cultivation in the region.

Sunset over the sardine fleet at Sanlúcar de Barrameda, 1964

González Byass looked after us extremely well. We met several of the González family and visited their vineyards as well as the bodegas. We were staying at the Hotel Los Cisnes, a grand hotel in Calle Larga in the centre of Jerez. Sadly, it no longer exists. We had to share a room. One night I woke up at around 3 a.m. to find Waugh sitting up in bed and looking distinctly seedy. At the bottom of the bed sat a doctor. Waugh had woken in the middle of the night with terrible stomach pains. Thinking he had appendicitis, he had crept downstairs, and persuaded the night porter to call out a doctor from the nearby American military base. The doctor was telling Waugh that, no, he did not have appendicitis. He had probably just eaten something unsuitable. He gave Waugh a prescription that he could collect in the morning. He said it would ease the discomfort.

The next morning the man in charge of us at González Byass just laughed, but not unkindly, when he heard of Waugh's plight. He said he had a much better remedy than the doctor's prescription. A *peón* was sent off to one of the bodegas and shortly returned with a small sample bottle containing a liquid that was completely black. This was poured into a glass and Waugh was invited to drink it. He looked at it with deep suspicion but did so like a man: only to make a horrible face afterwards. The sample had been drawn from a 200-year-old butt of pedro ximénez. Now, all sherry is naturally dry. It is not fortified during the fermentation process like port. So, to give amontillados and cream olorosos the sweetness that they usually have, some pedro ximénez is added to them. Normally pedro ximénez is a very sweet wine, made from the eponymous grape variety. The grapes are dried in the sun on *esparto* mats to concentrate their sugar content. But Waugh's 'medicine' was so old that it had lost all its sweetness and was extremely astringent. It cured his gyppie tummy, just like that.

Pedro Ximénez grapes being laid out to dry on *esparto* mats

In 1978 I discovered a sample that had been drawn from Gilbeys' 'Doña Gracia' oloroso solera in 1964. It had been sitting in a cupboard ever since. On Boxing Day 1978, Waugh came to dinner, and we tried it. The aroma was magnificent, and the flavour was extremely powerful. But, being so concentrated and completely dry, it was too astringent to really enjoy. In short, this was a wine to admire but not to relish. What it needed was an added slug of pedro ximénez to counterbalance the bitterness. Nowadays you can buy pedro ximénez quite easily, but not then.

One tip I learned recently is to pour pedro ximénez over vanilla, or even chocolate, ice cream. Try it. The combination is sublime.

Sherry was at the peak of its popularity in 1964. Now it is not in favour. That is a pity because Falstaff's favourite brew is a wonderful drink. Still, there is some compensation: because it is unfashionable, sherry is remarkably good value. You can buy Tio Pepe for under £10 a bottle and a really good cream oloroso (to go with the Christmas pud: another wonderful combination) for not much more. These are ridiculously attractive prices for such high-quality and well-made wines.

On our return journey we stopped in Haro, a picturesque wine town in La Rioja Alta. There we visited Bodegas Bilbaínas, a well-known producer of Rioja for whom Gilbeys were the UK importer. We were taken down to their cellars, an extensive underground network. Our guide was armed with a contraption that was shaped like a T-bar, with an electric bulb suspended from it by means of a short wire. He was also armed with a rubber tube and some grubby tooth glasses. The ceiling of the cellar was low, and we were advised to keep our heads down, and on no account to touch the live electric wires above us. The cellar itself was dark, damp, and musty, in the way of all good wine cellars. It was lined with barrels of wine at various stages of maturation.

Our guide, a small man, had a simple technique. He would sling the T-bar across the electric wires, and bingo: we had light. He would then knock the bung out of a barrel, insert his rubber tube, bend down and suck; a lovely easy way to siphon wine out of the barrel. The tooth glasses were then filled, and we all sniffed, tasted, and spat in the approved manner. The wines were actually rather good and the whole experience was doubly memorable, charged as it was with the risk of instant electrocution. Since our guide was a small man, we wondered if a process of natural selection by electrocution had resulted in all the cellarmen at Bodegas Bilbaínas being low in stature. Today, Bodegas Bilbaínas is part of the Cordoníu group and, judging by the website, it looks as if health and safety measures are now fully up to EU standards.

We probably did not do so, but as we crossed the border into France, we might have reflected that we had seen Portugal and Spain in almost feudal conditions. Moreover, we had been lucky enough to do so from the privileged end of the social spectrum. And at the time the 'politics' would have seemed to us quite straightforward. Since both Salazar and Franco were adamantly against communism, we did not think too harshly about them even though they were both dictators. They were, after all, 'on our side'. Looking back on it, Franco and Salazar no longer seem the anti-communist white knights that we had supposed. Their reputations are now grey for many, black for some and white for only a few. To be fair, I think Salazar's reputation has probably held up the better of the two.

We stopped in Paris on the way home. Waugh knew it, but I had never been there, so I was looking forward to it. We were also due to meet some of the girls we had met in Oporto: an added incentive. In the end it was my turn to have food poisoning so my first visit to that wonderful city fell rather flat. Strangely, the one thing I remember from that short first visit was the smell. Maybe it was because my senses were a bit delicate at the time, but the multiple aromas of fresh baguettes, coffee, garlic, Gauloise cigarettes, and urine from pissoirs on street corners seemed wonderfully foreign to my English nose. Today Paris smells like any other big city, which is a pity.

8

Bordeaux and Burgundy

I did eventually go to Château Loudenne. The château is a very pretty pink affair, and one of the few in the Médoc that can be seen from the Gironde. It was acquired by Gilbeys in 1875 and has always produced very acceptable claret of its own. But Gilbeys also developed the property as a depot from which first they, and later IDV, could base their Bordeaux wine purchasing operation.

Although the Médoc is flattish country and not exciting, travelling the length of it is a bit like driving up and down a very grand wine list. Although it was some twenty years since the end of World War II, we found that many of the big name châteaux were still scruffy and dilapidated: Château Palmer, I recall as a case in point. But it was still grand to be taken into their *chais*, and to taste the wines from the recent vintage. The smell in those wine cellars is always truly glorious.

Somewhere, in his *Notes on a Cellar-Book*, first published in 1920, Professor Saintsbury grumbles about the cost of Château Lafite: 'now being 5 guineas a dozen'. Today you can easily pay £5,000 for a case of Lafite. In the late 1960s that pricing escalation had hardly begun.

But if you visit the top châteaux today you are in for a treat. They are immaculate. On a visit to Lafite that I was lucky enough to make in around 1990 I noticed that even the gravel on the driveway had been raked into an elegant swirling pattern. As we drove away, I had visions of a little man, armed with a rake, running out of the bushes behind us to repair the mayhem our vulgar minibus had inflicted on his work of art. At Lafite, I was also conscious that the eventual consumer will be paying, not only for a truly wonderful wine, but also for the cost of every little added embellishment multiplied by the mark-up that a First Growth claret knows it can get.

In 1967 I spent a week in Burgundy with David Cossart, whom I had initially met in Oporto. We spent the first day in Chablis at Domaine Raveneau. Chablis was a charming rural town set in soft rolling country; but for the vines, we might have been in the Weald of Kent. Monsieur Raveneau was delightful and showed us everything including the new oil-fired heating system that had recently been installed in his vineyard. It comprised a Heath Robinson series of pipes and cocks that could be deployed and fired up if a late frost threatened during the key flowering period in May. We also tasted some of his superb 1965 and 1966 wines as well as various batches of the still fermenting 1967: all heady stuff.

On the Tuesday we reported to Domaine Chauvenet in Nuits St Georges. Although Gilbeys were the UK importer for their Côte d'Or wines, here the reception was tepid. They seemed a little confused by our arrival and not sure what to do with us. In the event Cossart came to the rescue by saying that he knew a bloke called Tim Marshall who lived thereabouts and who was trying to set himself up with the local growers.

'Why don't we look him up?' said Cossart. So we did just that, sliding out of maison Chauvenet as unobtrusively as we could.

Spending two days with Tim Marshall was marvellous. He took us up and down the Côte d'Or and we visited several producers. In later years Tim went on to become a vigneron in his own right, as well as the international representative for a portfolio of small but top growers. But, back in 1967, he was just starting out, and it was not an easy task for a lone Englishman in Burgundy. So, the deal was that we paid for lunch and his petrol, and he took us to meet the growers. Domaines that I recall visiting include Rousseau (Gevry Chambertin), Gouges (Nuits St Georges), Armand (Pommard), Marquis d'Angerville (Volnay), and Michelot (Meursault). Thanks to Tim we were welcomed by them all and invited to try many of their glorious wines. All those domaines are now widely renowned.

By way of contrast, we also visited the co-operative at Macon Viré from which IDV had been buying some very decent stuff for their Peter Dominic off-licences. At the co-operative they had a tasting bar where anyone could sample the wines for the price of a tip. When we rolled up, a confraternity of village elders were taking advantage of this privilege, and an animated discussion was in full swing. One old man was telling everyone that his daughter had recently been crowned as Miss Europe. He was handing out picture postcards of her to corroborate his story; I still have one and she was very dishy. Unfortunately, nobody believed him on the grounds of excessive physical dissimilarity between the alleged father and daughter: all of which the alleged father was not taking at all well.

Travelling with Cossart was a real bonus. He was very good company, spoke much better French than me and, to be honest, also knew a lot more about wine than I did.

In 1973 he became a Master of Wine; at the time he was working with Michael Broadbent at Christie's.

For the last two days we went down to visit Piat Père et Fils, negociants in Beaujolais. Again, Gilbeys were their UK importers. This time we were very well looked after. We tasted their wines and were taken to visit many of the properties that supplied them. We were told that the normal alcoholic strength for Beaujolais ranged from 9 per cent for straight Beaujolais up to 10 per cent or 11 per cent for a Cru Beaujolais. Surprisingly, we were also told that when shipped to England they were fortified up to 13 per cent. Nowadays, thanks to climate change, the natural strength of most Beaujolais is likely to be between 12 per cent and 13 per cent.

There seemed to be something feudal about the owner-ship system that existed in Beaujolais. Many of the larger growers had vignerons working under them. Often, they were paid in kind. So, when we visited a property's chais, we sometimes found that several cuvées belonged to indi-vidual vignerons.

The countryside in Beaujolais had a rambling charm that was quite lacking in the Côte d'Or. It was wonderfully rustic. One had no trouble imagining that the hilarious antics in *Clochemerle* could really have happened. Written by Gabriel Chevallier, *Clochemerle* was first published in 1934. I read it at school and enjoyed it immensely. The story is set in a fictional village and concerns a conflict between the supporters of the Third Republic and those of the Church about a proposal to build a public urinal slap bang in front of their place of worship. The nearest we got to *Clochemerle* was to taste Beaujolais Villages from Vaux-en-Beaujolais. Vaux is said to be the village on which *Clochemerle* is based.

9

Harlow and Stockwell

My management training programme ended in 1965. After that I spent a couple of years with Gilbeys. In 1963 Gilbeys had moved lock, stock, and many barrels from Camden Town to Harlow, one of the New Towns that the government had been planting outside London since the 1950s. The origins of the Gilbey family go back to the days when they owned public houses and a coaching business in Essex. The move to Harlow was taking them back to their roots.

Perhaps those roots gave them a special privilege because the Gilbey complex, in Harlow's Fifth Avenue, comprising offices, bottling plant, and the gin distillery, was a mere par 5 away from the town centre. I had a job on the production side of the business and was based in the Sample Room where I was a glorified dog's body in the purchasing and quality control department.

For a time, I rented a flat in a tall, ugly block called The Lawn. Recently I was astonished to learn that The Lawn was Britain's very first residential tower block and is now a Grade II listed building. The Lawn still stands, but the Gilbey buildings have gone. Although the complex achieved listed status in 1992, and despite cries of outrage from the Twentieth Century Society, it was knocked down in 1993 and is now a Sainsbury's supermarket. I enjoyed my time at Harlow and learned a great deal about wine, and about production techniques.

During the 1960s our parent company, IDV, had begun to feel vulnerable to the risk of being taken over. The chief suspect was thought to be Showerings, a company that produced and sold Babycham. At the time Babycham was a big success. It was a sweet, fizzy concoction and marketed itself as a 'genuine champagne perry'. It was very down-market. As far as the chiefs at the top of the IDV totem pole were concerned, it was quite beyond the pale. So, to prevent this fate worse than death, a deal was struck in 1968 whereby Watney Mann, then one of Britain's major and most respectable brewers, took a 40 per cent holding in IDV, and thereby made IDV impregnable – or so they thought.

Watney Mann had their own wine company, Brown & Pank. It had recently moved from Chelsea to a new site at Stockwell in South London, not far from the Oval cricket ground. As part of the intercompany co-operation, I was invited to go there and run the bottling hall. I don't recall what my title was: possibly supervisor, probably not manager. It was a well laid out affair with four bottling lines for wine. No spirits were bottled. I was in charge of around thirty employees, mostly female. They were all local, but there was a wide mix of age and ethnicity. And I had a marvellous forewoman called Mary Dobson who managed her 'girls' admirably and stopped me from making a number of really stupid mistakes. The wines that we bottled came mostly from places like Cyprus and Portugal. They were destined for consumption in Watney's pubs. They were not what you could call *vins fins*.

From the 1960s through to the Thatcher era, which began in 1979, the UK was subjected to an endless series of on-off industrial disputes. The antagonistic feeling of 'us versus them' raged between management and unions throughout the land. Nearly every industry was affected by it at some time or other. This made me apprehensive. There were undoubtedly some rough characters (both male and female) in my team, but after a time I got to like and admire them. On the other hand, I thought the production management at Brown & Pank was truly awful. It was prone to much dithering, and a constant changing of plan. I was astonished that the workforce did not go on strike out of sheer frustration.

My mother had always said:

'If you want to complain, go to the top.'

Although it wasn't quite the same as writing a letter of complaint to the managing director of Harrods (a shop that she loved to hate), I decided to write a memorandum to the top brass at Brown & Pank setting out what I, doubtless rather pompously, thought was wrong with the system, as well as making some suggestions on how to put it right. I duly sent it off with copies to all and sundry. Soon after its dispatch I noticed that certain people seemed reluctant to make eye contact with me; and I was beginning to think that I might have made a terrible mistake. Then one day Simon Heneage wandered into the bottling hall. He was a main board director, and therefore part of the renowned brewing 'beerage'. He came over, was very friendly, and said that he had read my paper. He complimented me on my recommendations and said they were extremely helpful.

Phew!

I first met Robert Cecil, now one of my oldest friends, when I was at Brown & Pank. He was in another part of the company, but we used to meet up from time to time to play tennis and drink some of Watney's then-famous Red

Barrel. In the summer of 1969 Robert transferred to J&B and became an area manager for the company's exports to Europe. Towards the end of the year, he tipped me off that J&B were looking for more people. He wondered if I might be interested.

Until that point, I had wanted my career to be in wine. I had taken various wine exams and was beginning to study for the 'big one': to become a Master of Wine. But the wine trade was changing, and interest was switching from sourcing the finest crus, for an elite few, to flogging large quantities of rather bland stuff to the masses – the sort of wine, in fact, that I was bottling at Brown & Pank. And suddenly it seemed less glamorous.

At the time Harold Wilson was the Prime Minister. The economy was in a mess. Our trade balance was £800m in the red, which in those days was an awful lot. We were being exhorted to, not only embrace Wilson's 'white heat of technology', but also to 'export or die'.

Now, at school, my O Level results for anything scientific had been pitiful. 'Goofy' Garman and 'Botty' Allway had both been surprised and disappointed to find me as the dunce of their respective physics, and chemistry classes. They were surprised because my elder brother had been rather good at both subjects. They had expected the same from me.

Simon, my elder brother, had once demonstrated his expertise in this field by blowing up a wasps' nest. Our wonderful gardener, Gilbert (my childhood hero) had discovered its whereabouts, buried in the middle of our lawn, and reported it to my mother. After extracting gunpowder from some 12 bore cartridges Simon demolished it in a spectacular fashion: though Gilbert was not best pleased with the crater left in his nice lawn.

Consequently, I did not feel capable of helping Britain's top man to forge any of his 'white heat'. But the idea that assisting him with his export drive could be patriotic, as well as fun, was alluring.

And so it was that at the end of November 1969 I found myself in that interview with Dorrien Belson ...

Gilbert, our gardener, and my childhood hero
Taken c1955 with my Box Brownie

PART 2

~ EXPORTING ~

1970–1996

10

Latin America

In 1949 when I first went to school, maps of the World had large areas on them that were shaded pink. I was taught that anything pink was part of the great British Empire and that, even when it was nighttime in England, the sun would still be shining on somewhere that was British. As children we were encouraged to be proud of our Empire.

Apart from 'accidental' splodges, for British Guiana and British Honduras, the map for the Latin American mainland had always been devoid of pink. For me this made the region more foreign, more exotic, and therefore especially intriguing.

To be honest, I was horribly ignorant about my new territory, and still unable to speak a word of Spanish, let alone Portuguese. True, I had read Prescott's *Conquest of Mexico* and his *Conquest of Peru*. So, I knew my Aztecs from my Incas. My mother had also lent me a book called *Green Fire*, a wonderful adventure story, set around 1930, relating the author's emerald mining exploits in Colombia. I reread it recently and the book had lost none of its magic.

Looking back, I cannot think why Dorrien gave me that job; but he did, and I am forever grateful.

In 1970, IDV's Head Office was a fine Nash building in York Gate, on the edge of Regent's Park. J&B's export business was on the ground floor. Working from there was quite a change from donning a white coat and patrolling the clatter and rattle of the bottling hall at Stockwell.

Here I should explain that the company, Justerini & Brooks, was customarily referred to as J&B. Likewise the whisky brand, J&B Rare, was also frequently shortened to just J&B. Hopefully, in the pages that follow, when I sometimes write 'J&B' the context of which meaning I intend will be obvious.

Twenty-one countries lie between the Rio Grande on the Mexican-US border and Tierra del Fuego. In time I managed to visit them all. Four of those countries were still colonies: Guyana and Belize (then British Guiana and British Honduras) were British. French Guiana was, and remains, an overseas département of France; and Suriname, which lies between Guyana and French Guiana, was then a Dutch colony. Of the remainder, seven were ruled by dictators, the most entrenched of which were the Somoza family in Nicaragua, and President Stroessner in Paraguay.

Politics has always been a colourful and volatile affair in Latin America, oscillating as it has between Stroessner's style of iron-fist dictatorship, and decades of fragile democracy in countries like Colombia. And let us not forget the typical example of Argentina, a country that should be rich. Instead, Argentina has had the full gamut of military dictatorships, intermittent democracy, and three terms of Peronist demagoguery.

For Europeans, the image of Latin America's military dictators, dripping in gold braid and self-awarded medals, has always been a cause for gentle mockery. And when we learned that Panama's General Noriega also had a fetish for red underpants, that feeling descended to farcical disbelief:

48

something perhaps for a Gilbert and Sullivan operetta but not, surely, something from real life? It is therefore sad to accept that these characters were also hard-nosed, corrupt, cruel, and arrogant as well as just vain. Their countries suffered accordingly. Some continue to do so.

J&B's whisky business was conducted through a network of agents, each one having an exclusive territory. In truth, most were distributors who imported on their own account, but we did have some who worked on a commission basis. However, we referred to them all as 'agents'.

The first agent I met was Alberto Constain. He was our agent for Ecuador, and he breezed into the office one day. He was a very well-turned-out chap, complete with a three-piece suit, and what looked like a regimental tie. He was also completely charming and spoke perfect English. I explained that I was planning my first trip to Latin America and was going to visit Venezuela, Colombia, Panama and Mexico. I had not planned to include Ecuador because, at the time, it was not a very attractive market for Scotch Whisky. I explained this as diplomatically as I could. Alberto seemed not at all bothered but pointed out that he lived in Colombia so he would be delighted to see me if I had time when I came to Bogotá. He told me that he was on excellent terms (*muy amigo mío* was the expression he used) with Harry Davidson, our agent in Colombia; why only last week he and Harry had sat together on the veranda of the Country Club putting the world to rights over a glass or two of J&B Rare.

South America

11

Colombia

When I landed at Bogotá's El Dorado International Airport I was surprised and delighted to find Alberto Constain waiting for me on the tarmac, accompanied by an *azafata* (ground hostess). She was wearing a typical Andean ruana (or poncho). It was charming and stylish. I had never seen one before. Later the ruana, together with the Hermes scarf, became 'must-have' accessories for Sloane Rangers along the King's Road.

Alberto and his *azafata* whisked me through customs and passport control. In no time at all we were outside the terminal building, and I was climbing into his car. This, I thought, is the right way to arrive. But as I got into the car, I half noticed a couple of people who seemed to be eyeing me curiously from across the parking lot.

My schedule was such that I arrived in Colombia on a Saturday. When I had written to our agent, Harry Davidson, giving him the details, he replied saying that he would be returning from New York on the Sunday so regretted that he would not be able to see me until Monday. Knowing that he and Alberto were such good pals I therefore concluded that it would be in order for me to accept Alberto's offer, which was to call on him if ever I had any spare time when I came to Bogotá. I did now have some spare time and so I contacted Alberto, who kindly offered to look after me over the weekend.

One of the good things about working for J&B was that we always stayed at the best hotels. We were selling a premium product and therefore it behoved us to reflect that in the way we travelled. It was just a pity that, in the inflationary seventies, our salaries did not quite match that profile. Anyway, it was undoubtedly a treat to be staying at the Hotel Tequendama, Bogotá's swankiest hostelry.

I was therefore feeling pretty good as I unpacked in my hotel room. Then the phone rang:

'Is that Mr Scott?' a voice enquired down the line.

'Yes,' I replied, 'who is speaking please?'

'Davidson,' came the reply. A bit gruffly I thought.

'Oh, I thought you were still in New York,' I said rather lamely.

'Well, I'm not. I came back early, and I want to know why you were being met by Constain?'

In the ensuing conversation it became clear that as far as Harry Davidson was concerned, he and Alberto Constain were definitely not *muy amigo mío*. It would not be appropriate to repeat just what he said, but he ended the conversation by saying that on Monday he would be expecting a full explanation.

On Sunday I continued, with some degree of apprehension, to follow Plan A. This was to spend the day with Alberto. I could see that the relationship between these two agents of ours was a bit more complicated than I had first thought, so I decided not to mention my call from Harry Davidson.

Alberto had a country cottage at Fusagasugá, about forty miles south of Bogotá, and this is where we went. Fusa, as it is commonly known, was then a small country town. Our road climbed out of the capital before descending into a warm valley. Bogotá lies nearly 9,000 feet above sea level. Fusa has an elevation of less than 6,000 feet and since it's near the Equator, the temperature rises to around 20 degrees every day all the year round. It is sometimes called the Garden of Colombia, and rightly so. Alberto had a delightful place with coffee bushes in his garden; I had never seen a coffee bush. We had lunch al fresco and then visited a friend of his who had a charming colonial villa. It was constructed of timber and surrounded by trees. Orchids blossomed from every nook and cranny, both on the house and from the trees. The villa had a balcony that could have made a perfect set for the famous scene in *Romeo and Juliet*.

Before 1830, Colombia was part of a Gran Colombia that also included modern Ecuador, Venezuela and Panama. Then in 1830 Ecuador and Venezuela broke away. In 1903, helped by Theodore Roosevelt, who wanted to build The Canal, Panama gained independence.

Colombia and Venezuela are very different; whereas Venezuela with its petro-economy, tended to look towards the USA for cultural input, Colombia turned more to Europe. Harry Davidson's wife bought her clothes in Paris, and he wore tweed jackets.

During the 1960s the Colombian government instituted their Accelerated Economic Development programme. The intention was to make Colombia's agricultural economy more efficient. The consequence was to remove some 400,000 smallholders from their properties so that larger, more efficient farms could be established. Unfortunately, the large number of displaced people provided fertile soil for the emerging revolutionary groups such as FARC (*Fuerzas*

Armadas Revolucionarias de Colombia) and ELN (*Ejército de Liberación Nacional*), both Marxist-Leninist by inclination.

Eventually it would serve to provide a profound cautionary tale. If you treat 'the little people' badly, they will come back to bite you – and how.

Although both the FARC and the ELN were founded in 1964, during the early 1970s their activities were of low intensity. They did not become a major threat until the 1990s. But by then they had turned their hand from a mainly idealistic and revolutionary agenda to one driven by the lucrative exploitation of cocaine.

On the Monday morning, as I set out for Harry Davidson's office, I was aware that from time to time, even in Bogotá, there were occasional breakouts of violence between rival gangs of emerald smugglers. I was totally unaware of the FARC or ELN. If I was worried about anything it was about making a good impression on Harry Davidson rather than what future problems were brewing for Colombia in remote Andean villages.

Dorrien had told me that Harry Davidson was probably the best agent we had in Latin America. He had only recently been appointed but the results so far were very promising. If I had, somehow or other, upset him by hobnobbing with Alberto Constain, my career in J&B would be getting off to a very bad start. That was not what I wanted.

Harry was pretty frosty when I got to his office. He repeated a long list of characteristics that he said applied to Alberto; not one of them was complimentary. All I could do was explain in detail how Mr Constain had visited us in London and how he had told me at such length about his splendid relationship with Harry D, and then how recent events had unfolded. After a while Harry began to relent, rather gruffly mind you ... and we got down to business.

Looking back on it I suspect that Harry must have seen the funny side of my faux pas; but he wasn't letting on. So, I had to sweat it out.

J&B Rare is and always was a pale-coloured whisky which, thanks to the high proportion of Speyside malts that are contained in the blend, has a distinctive and elegant taste. With an emphasis on the whisky's superior style, the policy was to ensure that the brand was introduced into any new market via the top bars, restaurants, and shops. The idea was that if you get the toffs to drink it first, the rest will follow afterwards. Eddie Tatham had called it his 'Tiffany trade' strategy. This concept was reinforced by selling at a premium price.

Harry Davidson had followed our strategy and J&B Rare had quickly become one of the leading brands of Scotch Whisky in Colombia.

Eventually I established a good rapport with Harry. On a subsequent visit, he threw a party to which many of the great and the good of Colombian society were invited. One of these was an ex-mayor of Bogotá. A charming chap, I forget his name, but he asked me to do him a favour. He had, he said, a pair of shoes that fitted him perfectly. He had acquired them from a friend who had died. The shoes had been specially made for his friend by Lobb in London. He wanted to know if I could go to Lobb and ask them if they would make some shoes for him but using the lasts that had originally been used to build his friend's shoes. He gave me the name of his deceased friend, which I have also forgotten.

John Lobb is London's top 'bootmaker'. The shop is in St James's Street on the other side of the road and a bit further down from the J&B fine wine business. All the shoes they sell are bespoke. In other words, you have to have your feet meticulously measured so that the shoes can be made to fit you perfectly. You don't want to go in for a fitting with holes in your socks. Once measured, Lobb make 'lasts' to replicate your feet so that future orders can be made to the same exact dimensions.

When you buy from John Lobb you are in good company. They have Royal Warrants from HRHs the Duke of Edinburgh and the Prince of Wales. Their archive of lasts contains the sculptured footprints of everyone from Caruso to Sinatra, from countless maharajahs, dukes, earls and barons to Marconi and also to Mr. and Mrs. Onassis. Maybe they even have a last for Imelda Marcos. If they don't, it must be the only decent shoe shop that she never patronised.

If you go into Lobb's today a pair of their bespoke shoes will set you back over five grand. And if they are made of crocodile, you can multiply that by three and a bit. I think their prices have risen by more than inflation but back in the early seventies they were still jolly expensive.

As soon as I got back to London after that trip, down I went to St James's Street and into the J Lobb emporium. I expected a rather aloof reception to my request for the reordering of a dead man's shoes. Instead, I was met with wonderful old-world courtesy. After explaining my mission, the chap in charge of the shop disappeared for several minutes then reappeared with an old ledger from which he blew a very large cloud of dust. After much licking of forefinger and turning of pages, he located the entry for the deceased man's last order. It was around the time of the Queen's coronation

(1953). He then returned to the Lobb dungeon for another
search and returned, again after another lengthy pause, and
triumphantly announced that he had found the dead man's
lasts and yes, he'd be delighted to make some more shoes to
their specification. It was, he said, some time since they had
received an order from Colombia. He said this somewhat
in the vein of a stamp collector who has just acquired a rare
specimen from an obscure Pacific archipelago.

When I returned to Bogotá, I learned from Harry that
the whole transaction had gone ahead perfectly and that
his friend was now in possession of two new pairs of top-
notch footwear. During this visit Harry kindly took me to
visit one of Colombia's top emerald dealers. I have always
been mesmerised by the green fire of that gemstone. Harry's
friend showed us a spectacular array of cut and uncut stones.
I could not possibly afford any of them, but it was wonderful
to see. Getting in and out had involved a lot of locking and
unlocking of doors. Harry told me of a ruse that, in the early
days of chewing gum, had been employed by an enterprising
emerald thief. The thief would go to a dealer, look at a tray
of gemstones and when the dealer's back was turned remove
one. Instead of trousering it, he would affix it to some chewing
gum that he had surreptitiously applied to the underside
of the table. If the dealer noticed a missing gemstone, the
thief could happily allow himself to be searched. If it went
unnoticed, an accomplice would come along later, posing as
another customer, and remove the stone.

Under Harry's captaincy, J&B Rare did well in Colombia.
Unfortunately, his time was short. I don't recall how his
family came to be in Colombia. I suspect he was a second-
generation immigrant, but he was certainly a member of the
Bogotá 'aristocracy'. When I met him, he seemed a slim,

fit man, and aged no more than fifty. But around 1972 he must have developed a virulent form of cancer because the news of his death, when it came, was a complete shock. The business was taken over by his son, Harry junior.

Colombia was always one of my favourite destinations in Latin America. It is easy to think of the country in terms only of coffee, emeralds – and cocaine. But with the Andean mountains, highland grasslands, deserts, Amazonian rainforests, mighty rivers, and two coastlines, Colombia is the second most biodiverse country in the world.

One of my treasured possessions is a copy of *Acuarelas de Mark*, given to me by Harry junior. *Acuarelas de Mark* was published in 1963 by the Banco de la República. The watercolours (*acuarelas*) were painted by Edward Mark between 1843 and 1856. Mark had been a British consul, first in Santa Marta (on the Caribbean coast) and then in Bogotá. Although he was an amateur, his images of this bygone, almost colonial, age give wonderful snapshots of how life must have been in his time.

Plaza Mayor, Bogotá, 1846
(From *Acuarelas de Mark*)

58

12

André

André Sans was the representative for Hennessy Cognac in Latin America. He was based in Caracas. IDV, our parent company, had a close connection with Hennessy. We were their agents for the UK and for several Commonwealth countries in the Far East. At the time, Freddie Hennessy was the chairman of IDV, and George Bull's mother was a Hennessy. George was a rising star in IDV. He went on to become the creator and first chairman of Diageo.

In the 1960s, Dorrien had made a couple of pioneering visits to South America and at some stage André had been given a role to help and advise us on the selection and management of agents for both Latin America and the Caribbean. It therefore made sense to begin my travels by calling on André.

In 1970 André was 52, double my age. He came from Pau in Southwest France and had been with Hennessy for some time. He and his wife, Georgette, lived in a gorgeous house high up in the Lomas Collinas Bello Monte. Their house had stupendous views, especially at night, down over the city of Caracas. Georgette played bridge for Venezuela, and they had two daughters at college in Boston. Georgette was very disappointed to know that I was married. She had hoped that I might be a suitable match for one of them.

Over the years I got to know André very well. We often travelled together. He was like a guiding uncle and taught me a huge amount. He knew the region like the back of his hand and was very good at assessing prospective agents. I was very fond of him. He was also a great anglophile. He drove a Jaguar, for which I was constantly having to obtain spare parts. Then, whenever I visited him, I always had to take supplies of Colman's Mustard, and Formula 16, an English concoction that stopped his hair going grey, or falling out – I forget which.

Freddie Hennessy had introduced André to his tailor in Saville Row. So, when André came to England for his annual visit there was always a lot of toing and froing with the tailor to make sure that his quota of two new suits could be cut and stitched in time. I must say he was the best-dressed man I ever met. One of our agents once asked me if André remained standing when he took a flight. The agent thought he might do this to stop his trousers from getting crumpled.

When André travelled, he had an extra suitcase just for shoes. He was the only person I knew whose luggage frequently exceeded the first-class weight allowance. Whenever we arrived at a new hotel, I knew that ten minutes after we had checked into our rooms André would tap on my door and ask me if I had any spare hangers because there were not enough in his room to hang all his suits.

André always referred to J&B and Hennessy as his two *bébés*. Whenever we were in a bar or restaurant, he would quite correctly insist on checking whether they were in stock. He took this role very seriously and was not above going behind the bar to ensure a full inspection. He tried this once at the Connaught Hotel in London, much to the consternation of the barman as well as to my embarrassment.

André explained to me that when it came to paying taxes, most governments in Latin America asked for exorbitant amounts. They did this, he said, knowing they would not get the full amount. It was merely an opening bid. So, in André's case, every year he would have a discussion with his tax inspector and after a certain amount of haggling an agreement would be reached on the amount of tax he should pay. I imagine that, in the era of Samuel Pepys, it was a bit like that in England.

André could be very adroit at handling petty officialdom. Just off the Venezuelan coast, the Dutch Antilles, comprising the three islands of Aruba, Curaçao and Bonaire, were popular duty free resorts for the Venezuelan middle classes. They were also a source for considerable flows of whisky and cigarette smuggling into Venezuela. On one occasion when he was coming back from a business trip to Aruba, the customs officer at Maiquetia Airport asked André to open his bag. Shock-horror ensued when it revealed lots of illicit goodies that he had bought for Georgette and his daughters. Now, behind the official's shoulder, and separated by a glass wall, lay the arrivals hall. Through the glass André could see Georgette waiting for him and waving.

'My friend,' says André in a conspiratorial whisper to his interrogator, 'please be discreet. These are all presents that I have bought for my girlfriend, and my wife is waiting for me right behind you.'

The captain of customs slammed his case shut, chalked it with a tick and, with a conspiratorial wink, waived André through.

13

Venezuela

Ever since Venezuela was colonised by Spain in 1522, the country has endured an unhappy history. From early insurrections, in 1811, to full independence in 1830, there followed a kaleidoscope of volatility whose principal colours were: dictatorship, corruption, populism, and massive public debt; all interspersed with occasional glimpses of democracy.

The Venezuelan currency is named after the great liberator, Simón Bolívar. In 1970 the exchange rate was rock solid at around 3 bolivars to the dollar. It had been so since 1934. That was because the country sits on vast reserves of oil. Only the most inept and corrupt of governments could mess that up. In recent years that, tragically, is exactly what has happened. If I could master the statistics of hyper-inflation, I would probably have to add several pages of noughts to the bolivar of today to equal the value of the bolivar in 1970.

Happily, in 1970, Venezuela was democratic, relatively stable, and enjoying its petro-currency status. Consequently, it could afford to be a major importer for Scotch whisky, and particularly for deluxe brands like Buchanan's, Old Parr, Johnnie Walker Black Label, and Chivas Regal. The price for a stiff one in any bar was 6 bolivars (under $2). Since this was the price for any whisky there was little incentive not to order an expensive deluxe brand. Venezuela was therefore a juicy market for Scotch whisky but a difficult one for J&B because at the time we had no deluxe whisky.

Our agent in Venezuela was Walter Weitzman. He must have been one of our earliest agents because he had been appointed before Dorrien joined the company. Dorrien was not one for giving in-depth briefings. Before my first trip he merely observed rather sniffily that when he had been invited to Walter's house, Walter had given him a full tour of Casa Weitzman and taken great pains to point out that the bathroom taps were real gold.

Walter's story was not untypical. He enjoyed telling it. He was an Austrian Jew who, as a young man, had dodged the Nazi jackboot by leaving Vienna just before the Anschluss. He had sailed from England to South America in an old tramp steamer. The destination was not certain. But by taking a circuitous route, during which the vessel had called at many ports (in one of which he had lost his virginity), he had ended up in Venezuela where through hard graft and perseverance he had done well enough for himself to be able to sport gold on his wrist (a chunky Rolex) as well as on his bath taps.

When André took me to meet him, I found him to be short and stocky. He was wearing a kipper tie with sputniks on it. That morning he was perspiring a lot and kept dousing himself from a litre bottle of cologne. All of which added verisimilitude to his story that he had been out, all night, promoting J&B in the red-light district.

During my time in Latin America, I would visit Walter once or twice a year. To be fair to him, the Venezuelan market, with its penchant for dark, deluxe whisky, was not right for J&B Rare. And to give him his due Walter worked hard and sold enough volume to make the market modestly profitable.

From time to time Walter would visit us in London. He always made a point of entertaining the team from the shipping and accounts departments. They were always delighted to see him because he would take them out for a slap-up lunch at the Savoy Grill. This was very generous of him but also sensible, because in those days, when strikes and other disruptions were endemic, it made sense to keep on good terms with the people in the 'engine room'. I occasionally went to those lunches, which were very convivial affairs. They were always washed down with copious quantities of Château Paveil de Luze. Walter was very loyal to Château P de L because on some historic occasion he had won lots of money at a London casino after partaking of it. Being of a superstitious bent he felt that history might repeat itself. It seldom did.

Sometime later I met Bob Albert, an amiable but shrewd American, whose company was our agent for the Bahamas and who sold truckloads of J&B Rare to American tourists. He had for a time lived in Venezuela. He told me that Walter's rags to riches story was all tosh. He said Walter's father had been the number one dealer for scrap metal in Caracas. I honestly do not know who to believe. In truth I always had a soft spot for Walter. His faults were manifest, but his dealings were straight, and he always tried his darndest. I would prefer to believe him: or maybe, somehow or other, both stories could be true.

14

Brazil

'Do you like football?' asked Dorrien one day.

'Not particularly,' I replied rather guardedly.

I was a bit surprised by this question. Dorrien Belson was not what you would call a football type. Classical music, fly fishing, and fine wine were more his sort of thing.

'Well,' he continued, 'you are about to go to Brazil where you will meet our agent. Crebec is extremely interested in football and will want to know which club you support. If you don't have a favourite club, I suggest you acquire one, and mug up on it because he is bound to cross-examine you.'

With that typical piece of Belsonian briefing, I added mugging-up on football to my pre-trip preparations. I cannot remember which club I decided to favour. It may well have been Ipswich Town, which was near where my parents had once lived, and which, at that time, had enjoyed a purple patch.

Edson Arantes do Nascimento was face down on a massage table having his legs pummelled. I, together with André Sans, was inside the team room of the Santos Football Club. We had been taken there by Roger Crebec who, apart from being our Brazilian agent, was also a director of the club. It was November 1970 and Brazil was at the apotheosis of its love affair with the Beautiful Game. In May they had won the World Cup in Mexico. They had also won it in 1958 (Stockholm) and in 1962 (Santiago).

The short man with the legs like tree trunks that were being tuned up for a match against Palmeiras was, and still is, Brazil's greatest hero. Edson Arantes do Nascimento is, of course, much better known simply as Pelé.

Dorrien's brief about Crebec and his passion for football was spot on. Pelé, back then, spoke no English but he seemed genuinely friendly and affable as he allowed himself to be photographed with us. I have still got that photo. Sometimes I carry a copy of it in my wallet. It does loads for my street cred whenever I dig it out if I find myself being served by a young Brazilian in a bar or restaurant. The only difficult bit is explaining that the tall young man in the photo with plenty of dark hair is actually me.

Crebec was French. During the War he had escaped to England, and joined the RAF, flying Spitfires. Later, he had been dropped into France and had done work for the Resistance. After the War he became disillusioned with the way things were going in France and left for Brazil. At some point he decided that importing whisky into Brazil might be a good idea. On a return visit to Paris, he had discussed this with the head barman at the Hotel George V. The barman confirmed that Scotch whisky was indeed becoming fashionable: rich Americans could not live without it, and leading members of French society were also acquiring a taste for Scotch. Importing whisky into Brazil might therefore be a very good idea.

They discussed brands. The head barman suggested J&B Rare; his American clientele were asking for it, and recently Moët et Chandon had been appointed as the J&B importer for France. That was a positive marker. He probably also pointed out that traditional brands like Johnnie Walker,

Haig, White Horse, and Vat 69 were mostly owned by the DCL (Distillers Company Ltd) and would already have established agents in Brazil. On the other hand, J&B Rare, being a relatively new brand, might not be represented.

I can only imagine that in the early 1960s Brazil did not feature as a major target on the J&B boardroom's radar screen. But, spurred on by the advice from the George V, Crebec did apply to be our agent in Brazil, and we probably thought, 'why not?' And so, he was appointed.

It was like that then.

In 1970 Scotch was very aspirational in Brazil. Brands like J&B Rare, which were bottled in Scotland, were subject to towering import duties and therefore very expensive. They cost the equivalent of £11 a bottle and sold in very small quantities. On the other hand, local whiskies (known as admixes because they contained a small percentage of Scotch malt) sold for as little as £2. They sold very large volumes.

In São Paulo I called on John Shuter, a school friend of my brother. He was working for the Banco Bozano Simonsen. He explained to me how the Brazilian market worked from the consumer's point of view. If you wanted to drink proper Scotch, like J&B Rare, in a bar, club or restaurant you had to be careful because some of the well-known brands were sometimes counterfeit, and occasionally dangerously so. But if you wanted to drink it at home you would have a 'little man' who would ring you up every so often and take your order. The order would be for contraband whisky and cigarettes, which would then be delivered to your abode at a mutually convenient time. It was important, John said, to have a reliable *contrabandista*, otherwise you might end up with some of the counterfeit stuff. Smuggled whisky was half the price of legal whisky.

Between 1964 and 1985 Brazil was ruled by a military junta. Today this sounds terrible. But remember that in the 1970s the Soviet Union was very active in trying to undermine US influence in the American Hemisphere. Military dictatorships were obviously not ideal, but they were better than communism – or so the USA believed. Accordingly, the CIA were instigating Operation Condor, a clandestine arrangement with various military governments in the Southern Cone of Latin America, to counteract the threat of encroaching communism. Only three years before my visit Che Guevara had been executed in Bolivia.

In 1970 I had no knowledge of Operation Condor and have recently been quite shocked to read about some of the shenanigans it got up to. But I did know that smuggling was a way of life to which the military often turned a blind eye (if not a helping hand). Most of the contraband whisky and tobacco came from Paraguay and I'll tell you more about that when we get there. But some came from closer to home: for example, there was the embassy of a Central American country with a staff of three that each year imported 200 cases of diplomatic duty free whisky 'for personal use only'.

Crebec was not into smuggling, far from it. He did not import on his own account but acted as a commission agent. Apart from J&B and Hennessy, and some other IDV brands, he also represented Taittinger Champagne and several wine houses such as Cruse in Bordeaux and Ladoucette from the Loire. In 1970 he had a new secretary called Rosine. She said Crebec was very temperamental and that because he had gone through several secretaries his filing system had been in chaos. She spoke six languages and assured me that his administrative ship was now on an even keel. Crebec also had a salesman called Plastino who had a quaint habit of constantly going through washing motions with his hands. Plastino was paid some commission. I expect he also represented other non-conflicting companies. Crebec was very much a one-man band.

Crebec had two sons; at the time both were students. It appeared that Madame Crebec and he had parted company some time ago. Unusually, Crebec had charge of their children.

He was very hospitable, and always took us to the best restaurants. He was a member of the exclusive Jockey Club, a positive indicator of his connections. In the evening he was often accompanied by Angela, an elegant Italian model who liked to dress from head to toe in black leather. Crebec said their relationship was platonic.

But one evening when Crebec said he was tired and Angela said she wasn't, and we had invited her to stay on in the night club with us, Crebec broke into a tirade of jealousy. He and André were at each other using an awful lot of French words I had never heard before. Certainly, they had not been on any of 'Flash' Dow's vocab lists. ('Flash', poor man, had tried to teach me French at school. We had called him 'Flash' because he favoured bright waistcoats and tweed jackets with loud checks.) Angela, deeply embarrassed, had shot off to the loo to await the end of hostilities. I was trying not to laugh. In the end they made up, but in truth, and despite all the 'tutoi-ing' and the 'mon vieux', they never really got on. Crebec's stories and eccentricities were sometimes too much for André.

Crebec certainly was prone to making exaggerated claims, but on one occasion when I met the French Consul in São Paolo and wondered aloud if his wartime stories weren't all made up, I got a very steely look in response and was told, in no uncertain terms, that Crebec's war record was one of great distinction.

69

Years later, in the 1990s, after he had retired, I used to get phone calls. Whenever I heard the guttural 'Daveeed' down the line I knew it was Crebec. He was living in Paris and was usually on the scrounge. He wanted whisky for a Free French veterans' club of which he was a member. I was happy to assuage the thirst of these old warriors. Later, I took up an invitation to visit the club. Crebec, now well into his seventies, proudly showed me around and introduced me to a couple of distinguished, but long retired, senior officers. There were a number of old black-and-white photographs on the walls: chaps standing next to Spitfires, jeeps, and tanks, that sort of thing. And there in the middle of one photo, was someone who was undoubtedly a very young Roger Crebec.

I once visited his flat in São Paolo. It was cool and dark and in an old-fashioned block. Hanging in his hall was a very large tapestry. I am no expert in these things, but it looked to me as if it could be the sort of Arras that Shakespeare had Polonius hiding behind: the real thing.

Crebec was a complex, emotional, and volatile character, probably a bit Bohemian too. This made him an easy target. I was constantly being told by various parties how unstable he was and how they, the various parties, could do a much better job for us than him. One 'party' said that though J&B Rare did quite well in and around São Paolo, in other places, such as Rio, we were weak.

So, on the next trip I spent two days in Rio de Janeiro staying, naturally, at the Copacabana Palace. I checked out all the best bars, hotels, and shops. J&B was in fact very well distributed and well-spoken of. I had not warned Crebec that I was doing this. When I told him, he went from tizz, at the discovery of my sleuthing, to elation at the revelation of my findings.

When all is said and done, Crebec was successful. He was known to all the barmen in the best watering holes, and J&B Rare was often their best-selling brand. He used to give them tips at Christmas; something his competitors had happily not thought to do. He was also well received by the large food and drink importers to whom we shipped. When I had lunched with the Cacex manager in Rio he had told me that J&B Rare was the best-selling brand of Scotch whisky in Brazil. He would know: the Cacex was the government agency that granted import licences for Scotch. A year or so later the Brazilian government lowered the import duties and the amount we shipped to Brazil shot up to 60,000 cases; a very considerable achievement.

Managing Crebec during my four years on the Latin American beat certainly kept me on my toes. In general, I gave him the benefit of the doubt. I think rightly. The results argued in his favour. It was a volatile but stimulating experience.

São Paolo FC, 1970
DMS with Pelé, André Sans, Roger Crebec, and Zito

15

Argentina

In the 1970s very little wine was consumed in Latin America. Scotch was the smart beverage. At first, I was a bit bemused to find myself drinking whisky with food. But when a barman takes a highball glass, fills it with crushed ice, pours a generous measure of J&B Rare over the ice, and then tops it up with soda or plain water it makes a splendid accompaniment to any food – especially in a hot climate. The one exception to this practice of whisky with food was Argentina (and maybe Chile), where they produced wine of reasonable quality. Today, many of those wines are superb.

At the time of my first visit, Argentina had been ruled by the military ever since Perón had been deposed in 1955. First elected in 1946, Juan Domingo Perón had previously served two terms as president. He and his first wife Eva (Evita) had done much for the poor, but the economy had suffered. Although Buenos Aires seemed to me to be prosperous and comfortable, there were underlying tensions. Peronism, though proscribed, still flourished underground. During my first visit, while golf's World Cup was being contested at the Jockey Club out at San Isidro, a two-day general strike was taking place in downtown Buenos Aires.

Buenos Aires is a wonderful city, very European. It is more Barcelona, or even Paris, than any other city in Latin

America. When I first went there in November 1970 it was springtime and the avenues were lined with jacaranda trees alive with clouds of indigo blossom.

The Argentine capital boasted some wonderful buildings, the Casa Rosada and Teatro Colón being the best known. All the greats, from Caruso to Pavarotti, have sung at that great opera house. There was even a Harrods, opened in 1914 on the fashionable Calle Florida. In 1970 it was the only Harrods outside Knightsbridge. Sadly, the Buenos Aires Harrods closed in 1988. The Hotel Plaza, where André and I stayed, wasn't bad either. The hotel had opened in 1909, in an era when Argentina was ranked as the seventh wealthiest country in the world.

The end of the nineteenth century saw a substantial flow of emigration from Europe to Argentina. Many of the immigrants came from Italy. The Brits also came; we built the railways. James Macadam, a school friend, comes from an old Anglo-Argentine family. James was, and still is, a doctor at the Hospital Británico. His parents were each the first in their families to be born in Argentina. When they generously invited me to dine at their house, a splendid Edwardian villa in the Hurlingham district of BA, they used charming old-fashioned English expressions that could have come straight from the pen of P G Wodehouse.

On a later visit James invited me to play golf at the Hurlingham Club. Established in 1888, built with good Victorian red brick, and panelled inside with plenty of oak, it is more English than its counterpart on the banks of the Thames. The club was conceived as a sporting venue for the British community in Argentina, and you can still play cricket, tennis and squash there as well as golf and polo.

Our agent in Argentina was very different from Crebec, and indeed from any other in Latin America. Proviar was the Argentine subsidiary of Moët et Chandon. Under the name Chandon Argentina they had been established in 1959 as Moët's first investment in winemaking outside France. They had vineyards near Mendoza in the Andean foothills and were already selling respectable volumes of very good red, white, rosé and, of course, sparkling wine.

Proviar were not commission agents like Crebec. They were proper importers and had a sales force that covered the whole country. The person in charge was Baron Bertrand de Ladoucette, a charming man. His family owned the famous Château de Nozet, of Pouilly Fumé fame, on the Loire, as well as a ranching hacienda in Argentina. He told me that he and his brother used to interchange every six months between their two interests.

Proviar were doing an excellent job at introducing J&B Rare to the Argentine market. But nothing in Argentina is ever straightforward. When elections were allowed in 1973 Perón returned from exile, for a third term. He died in 1974 but not before banning all imports of Scotch. That put paid to all the good work that Proviar had started.

Perón was succeeded for a while by his second wife, Isabel. But then Operation Condor swung into action and in 1976 yet another military junta took over.

Incidentally, it was in 1971, the year after my visit to BA with André, that Moët et Chandon merged with Hennessy to become Moët Hennessy.

Later, in 1987, Moët Hennessy merged with Louis Vuitton to become LVMH.

16

Uruguay and Paraguay

If the situation in Buenos Aires was wobbly, on the other side of the River Plate, in Montevideo, Uruguay, it was a whole lot worse. The government was weak; firms were going bankrupt; and, if they could, the middle classes were emigrating to Canada or Mexico. The week before André and I arrived, the Tupamaros had raided the state bank, and nicked US$6,000,000. The Tupamaros were a new sort of urban guerrilla group. A couple of months after our visit they kidnapped Geoffrey Jackson, the British ambassador. They held him for nine months.

The Uruguayan economy had been on the skids since the late 1950s. The way this manifested itself to us was with the cars: a wonderful assortment of vintage marques. As they rattled around Montevideo, you could date them from the thirties, forties, and fifties. I even saw a couple of Model T Fords. Many of these vehicles could have qualified for the London to Brighton Vintage Car Rally. Mind you, they would not have looked very good because they were invariably rusty in parts and held together with bits of string. The mechanics in Montevideo must have been very good at keeping those old cars on the road – rather like their modern-day counterparts in Havana.

Ironically, our agents in Uruguay, Miller & Madeiros, also had the agency for Ford, but they weren't selling many new cars. The owner, one of the Millers, had a brand-new Aston Martin DBS. He took us for a spin. Growling its way through the usual wrecks in the thin rush hour traffic, this motoring thoroughbred stood out like Shergar at a Donkey Derby.

Happily, Uruguay is now in much better shape: noted for its liberal democracy, in 2013 it was the *Economist*'s 'Country of the Year'. But in 1970 potential for Scotch whisky was not much in evidence, so our stay in Montevideo was short.

Paraguay was very different. President Stroessner was in the middle of his thirty-five-year tenure. Alfredo Stroessner was not the sort of chap you would think of calling Alf. He did very nasty things to people he didn't like. He was the archetypal Latin American bully and strongman, or 'caudillo'. He gave refuge to Nazi war criminals and is said to have fathered up to thirty children, some by very young teenagers. True, he won eight elections, but usually with around 85 per cent of the vote, which says it all. From 1954 to 1989 the country was under his iron fist.

But the US liked and supported Stroessner – he was anti-communist – and the country was very stable. In Paraguay itself he was not unpopular. It was said that a lady could walk alone around Asunción at any time of day or night without fear for her virtue or her purse. A wag rather spoiled this story by saying that in Asunción there weren't many ladies with either asset.

I found the capital, Asunción, to be a charming, sleepy, rural town; it could have been in provincial Spain. In the square outside our hotel I discovered the best shoe-shine boys I have ever encountered.

André and I went to Paraguay because it was a very big market for whisky (and also for cigarettes, electrical goods, and other perceived luxuries). Sales were divided between the very small domestic market and the extremely large 'in-transit' market. Duties for the domestic market were low. They were even lower for the in-transit market. There was no income tax in Paraguay. Most of the state revenue came from these taxes.

The transit market sold whisky (and cigarettes etc.) to Argentina, Bolivia, and Brazil, the latter being the biggest customer by far. Some went in the form of 'personal duty free' sold to visiting tourists. But in truth the term 'in-transit' was a euphemism for smuggling and barter trading that flourished on a grand scale. The Paraguayan military were said to be actively involved. An Alan Whicker programme of the period reported that Paraguay had more generals than the USA.

Raul Diaz de Espada was our agent in Paraguay. To get some insight into the transit market it was decided that we should visit Puerto Stroessner, a small town beside the Paraná River on the eastern frontier of the country. Today Puerto Stroessner is Paraguay's second city, and it is now called Ciudad del Este. Nearby the Iguazú River flows into the Paraná. The Brazilian, Argentinian, and Paraguayan borders meet at that point. The world-famous Iguazú Falls are just upstream.

Puerto Stroessner was important because of the new Puente de Amistad (Friendship Bridge) which crossed the Paraná between Paraguay and Brazil. Opened in 1965, and with a 300-metre span it was, and is, a very important link between the two countries. It was the perfect conduit for channelling all manner of 'friendship'.

Our plan was to fly from Asunción on the west of the country to Puerto Stroessner on the east, a distance of some 200 miles. We set off very early one morning in a small single-engine Cessna. The south of Paraguay is flat, open country dotted, I noted, with palm trees. It lies between the rivers Paraguay on the west and Paraná on the east. These mighty rivers meet just north of Corrientes (in Argentina) and then flow (as the Paraná) southwards through Argentina to the River Plate. The Paraná is Paraguay's only access to the sea.

It was a lovely morning as we climbed outbound from Asunción. The sky was clear, and you could see for miles. We were chuntering along quite gently when suddenly the engine gave a little cough and stopped: just like that. Knuckles tightened; faces turned pale; and conversation stopped. The plane dropped as if we had hit an air pocket. We all looked at the pilot. I noted that he did not look frazzled, a good sign. He fiddled with something, and the engine, by the grace of God, restarted. Discussion began about what had happened. Then it happened again. And again, the pilot got the engine restarted but he suggested that it might be best if we turned back. We agreed.

We landed back on terra firma without further incident. Our pilot was quite nonchalant about the whole thing. He explained that the plane had two fuel tanks, and that one probably had a bit of dirt in it which would have caused the problem. He had restarted the engine by switching tanks. He seemed reluctant to lose our trade and, seeing that we weren't keen to reboard, offered to take us in another plane. Silence ensued: we all looked at the ground as if for comfort. Finally, and to the relief of the rest of us André said:

'*Yo no voy*,' meaning, 'I'm not going.'

Raul was very keen that we should still go to Puerto Stroessner. So, we went in his Mercedes. It took all morning to get there. We had lunch over the bridge in Brazil at a hotel beside the Falls. The Iguazú Falls rank alongside those of Niagara and Victoria as the greatest waterfalls in the world. Cascading out of a rainforest, down and down into the Garganta del Diablo (Devil's Throat), they are magnificent. When First Lady Eleanor Roosevelt went there, all she said was, 'Poor Niagara.' Go there if you get the chance.

After lunch we visited a number of traders back on the Paraguayan side. One interesting place was a large hangar of a warehouse. Inside was a mountain of loose coffee beans. In those days, the ICA (International Coffee Agreement) set export quotas for all the coffee producing countries. The ICA was the OPEC of coffee. I was told that Brazil sometimes liked to export more than was allowed. This was done by barter trading the surplus coffee for whisky and cigarettes in Paraguay. I've no idea if that was true or not but there were an awful lot of coffee beans in that big shed.

On our return journey Raul's Mercedes broke down. While we were standing by the road wondering what to do, a dilapidated minibus came trundling towards us. Raul waved it down. The bus was going to Asunción and the driver, who was Japanese, offered us a lift. Raul explained that, in Paraguay, there was quite a large community of Japanese farmers. The seats in the minibus were dirty and rudimentary. I retain a vivid recollection of André sitting there rather disdainfully in one of his best Saville Row suits (with his double cuffs shot to the correct half inch) as we rocked and rolled and bumped along the long country road between Puerto Stroessner and Asunción.

There were two Japanese farmers in that minibus. One was driving, and the other seemed to be asleep on the floor. At one long straight stretch of road the driver suddenly got out of his seat. The bus, by some miracle, continued in a straight line. Then the sleeping co-pilot woke up and in one fluid, but casual movement got behind the wheel: much to the relief of us passengers.

We were very happy to get back to Asunción without further incident. It had been quite a day.

17

The Competition

It might be useful at this point to pause for a moment and explain how the whisky business worked when I first joined J&B.

In the 1970s the Scotch whisky industry was dominated by the Distillers Company Limited; or the DCL as it was commonly known. During the War, the production of whisky had been reduced to a trickle. Most distilleries had been closed. Whisky has to be aged in barrels for many years before it can be drunk. Consequently, after the War the demand for mature drinkable whisky outstripped supply by a considerable margin. This situation continued until the late seventies. The DCL owned a large number of distilleries and most of the big brands. Johnnie Walker was their global leader. Haig was then their top brand in the UK; you may remember the 'Don't be vague ask for Haig' advertising. They also owned Dewar's White Label, White Horse, Black & White, Old Parr, VAT 69, and several other brands, all of which had successful overseas markets. With this collection of labels, the DCL had the best network of agents and distributors around the world. Each of their brands had a different importer in every market. There was no consolidation or 'portfolio management'. This was because the DCL was managed as a loose federation of brand companies.

The DCL had a group head office in St James's Square. It was a large old town house and was popularly known as 'The Kremlin'. The Queen Mum had once lived in it. I know that because in the 1990s after the DCL had moved out, it became the HQ for Grand Metropolitan, by then our parent company. We had a lunch there for the Queen Mother. She was well into her nineties but, after kicking off with her customary dose of gin and Dubonnet, was in sparkling form. She had piercing blue eyes, was tiny in stature, and wore a hat whose brim was in the same league as that of the Quangle Wangle Quee. At lunch she told us the story of how, on the evening of her fourteenth birthday, she had been taken to the theatre. On the way back to the house she had seen the billboards for the evening newspapers. They were announcing the outbreak of war. The date of her fourteenth birthday was 4 August 1914.

But I digress.

Each of the DCL's brand-owning companies also had its separate West End office. For instance, Johnnie Walker was in a spacious house near our fine wine business in St James's Street. Leslie Whitton, a director of Johnnie Walker, whom I visited there sometimes with Bob Lisle (our shipping director), had an office about the size of half a tennis court. These were all prestige sites, and the various DCL brands competed quite aggressively against each other. As a junior area manager for J&B, I would occasionally lunch with my opposite numbers in the DCL. The one thing I discovered was that they all hated Johnnie Walker. Johnnie Walker was clearly top dog in the DCL group but was thought of as being arrogant and conceited. I got a lot of information from those lunches.

82

In the modern world, where industries consolidate, where synergies are sought, and where companies strive to market their brands in a co-ordinated portfolio, it is easy to mock the rather loose federal strategy which the DCL deployed back in the sixties and seventies. It seemed to work very well then, but many of those mighty DCL brands have now virtually disappeared.

By owning so many distilleries the DCL had better access to supplies of mature whisky. This was important in the fifties and sixties. Whisky was then effectively on ration, and if a DCL agent could get a good supply of the brand he represented, it was tantamount to being able to print money.

The DCL also held a majority of the members on the Council of the Scotch Whisky Association. The SWA is the industry's trade association and in those days was able, quite legally, to fix prices. So, what the DCL decided was what the rest of us had to do. Years later, when I served on the SWA Council, any form of collusion to fix prices would have landed you in jail: but not then.

All of this explains why the DCL had the best agents. It also explains why it was difficult for a new competitor like J&B to gate-crash this lucrative party. The only way to get into a party when the people inside do not want you to come in is to find someone who will get you in through the back door. This is where people like André, who had such good contacts, were able to help.

18

J&B Rare: The New Kid on the Block

The creation of J&B's new whisky brand happened almost by accident. This is why it was perceived as a bit of an upstart by the likes of the DCL.

Justerini & Brooks, to give the company its proper name, started life in 1749 as a wine merchant. They were, and still are, at the top end of the business. They have held the Royal Warrant to supply every monarch since George III.

In the early years of J&B, whisky did not much feature on the price list. Many of their core customers were landed gentry. So J&B preferred to focus on supplying them with decent port, sherry, claret, hock, champagne, and other classic wines. In those days, whisky was considered a rather coarse form of beverage. So, if J&B had to sell spirits, they tended to focus on Cognac, for which the company had acquired rather a good name. But in the 1930s the country was in recession, and core customers, who were long on pedigree but short on cash, became subject to bouts of amnesia when it came to paying their bills. It was clear that something had to be done.

If America had previously been the Promised Land for a White Russian or a starving Pole, by the 1930s it was also the answer to J&B's prayers. Eddie Tatham, the managing director, who had joined the company after World War I, was on nodding terms with all the right people in America: Rockefellers, Mellons, Vanderbilts, etc. Thus, in 1930, three years before Prohibition ended, he had sailed to America to prospect the market and hopefully drum up some business for J&B.

His contacts were excellent, and he secured a full order book from these princes of industry and barons of banking. Delivery was slightly more complicated because Prohibition still reigned. Nevertheless, he had managed to lay plans to have the stuff smuggled in through some highly unorthodox channels. One of these would require the strategic deployment of his distinguished customers' yachts. Alas, all of this came to nothing when he and his order book were caught red-handed as he was boarding a train for Canada at Grand Central Station.

Prohibition did finally end in 1933. The pending case against Eddie Tatham was dropped, and suddenly a vast and very thirsty market was clamouring for liquor. And by liquor they meant real liquor – man's liquor. Al Capone had taught them that the best liquor was Scotch whisky. So that was what America wanted.

When ET had gone to America in 1930 and tried to sell a range of proper wine to his 'Tiffany trade' contacts, he had been somewhat miffed when many of them preferred to focus on the vulgar end of our price list and insist on ordering whisky. At the time, the house brand was J&B Club: a conventional dark blend. But ET was quick to appreciate the needs of this exciting new market. He could see that the American palate would go for a whisky which was smooth, elegant, and easier to drink than conventional DCL brands.

So, Eddie went to work with a brilliant blender, Charles

Julian, and J&B Rare was created. By 1936 the Paddington Corporation had been appointed as our US distributor, and the American business had really started to grow. The orders picked up. Cash flow turned positive. Or to be more precise, it turned into a positive flood; and despite Adolf Hitler's attempt to screw it all up, J&B's sales to America grew and grew – and grew (until 1978). America became a balance sheet miracle.

The problem was that the directors could neither quite believe it nor understand it. On the day when Charlie Guttman and Abe Rosenberg (the owners of the Paddington Corporation) arrived in London with an order that would take their imports for the year to over a million cases, they were virtually ignored. A duke had just dropped by to order some claret. How could a couple of liquor dealers from New York take precedence over a top-notch peer of the realm? The directors failed to appreciate that pedigree had hit a bear market.

But they were not completely daft. They would not admit it, but they did realise that Britannia no longer ruled the waves. It was increasingly America that set the trends. They could see that. So, if something did well in America, then in time it could also do well outside America.

Put simply, the new strategy was to grow J&B Rare from New York in a westerly and southerly direction across the fifty-two states. After that the idea was to seed J&B Rare in the capital cities of other nations. They would start with the fashionable watering holes favoured by wealthy American tourists in Paris, Rome, Madrid and so on. The man behind this strategy was Dorrien Belson. Dorrien had been recruited as export director from Harveys of Bristol in 1963. He was quick to realise the global potential for J&B Rare.

So, let us return to the small part that I was playing within this grand strategy and move on to the land of the Incas.

19

Peru

From 1968 until 1975 Peru was governed by a left-wing military dictatorship. The president was General Juan Velasco Alvarado. Some of Velasco's intentions may have been Utopian; for example, education levels improved, but the economy suffered grievously. At the time of my first visit, with André, you were not allowed to buy meat on Monday or Tuesday.

Our agents in Peru were Rodblu. They were owned by a Mr Katz and Daniel Malamud. Katz was the majority shareholder, but had other interests in Mexico and Venezuela as well as in the Peruvian capital, Lima. It was Malamud who ran Rodblu.

Daniel Malamud was young, intelligent, likeable, and energetic. He had spent several years working in Iquitos on the Amazon – Peru's principal city on the other side of the Andes. While he was there, he had earned enough money to buy his share in Rodblu. He also told me that during that time his wife had given birth to three babies (but not all at once).

Peru in the early seventies epitomised many of the problems that we had in shipping whisky to any Latin American country. Imports of Scotch whisky to Peru could not be made without a licence. It was also necessary to get a permit to buy dollars to pay for the whisky. The two government departments for licences and dollars were not co-ordinated: perhaps deliberately.

And it is not as if everything in the UK was hunky-dory either. Far from it, we had dock strikes, miners' strikes, and industrial action on a wide scale. In 1974 this culminated in the 'three-day weeks', which lasted for two months. None of this was helped by the first oil shock. Between 1973 and 1974 the price rose from $3 to $10 for a barrel of the stuff.

Exporting was undoubtedly fun, but it was also challenging.

You may wonder why most Latin American countries had sizeable armed forces. What was the point? The reason is that, since they had gained independence from Spain, there had been a great many border disputes between the various new nations. In some cases, these had resulted in serious wars. For example, between 1930 and 1935 Paraguay fought the bitter Chaco War against Bolivia. At the time, there was thought (wrongly) to be a lot of oil in the north of Paraguay, and Bolivia had tried to grab it.

And when Pinochet came to power in Chile, he was genuinely afraid that Velasco might overrun northern Chile.

So, throughout Latin America the military usually held privileged positions, if not autocratic power. One way in which they rewarded themselves was through their *cantinas*. These were retail stores where military personnel and their families could buy goods, such as whisky and cigarettes, at duty free prices. Sometimes the quantity that flowed through these stores was quite astonishing, and ended up as a version of contraband on the local market. Such a system existed in Peru, but we asked Malamud not to engage in it with J&B Rare. He was doing a great job on the legitimate market, and we did not want to muddy the waters.

Rodblu had a splendid liquor store in the centre of Lima. I do not know what sort of wood was used in the fittings, but all the doors, windows, shelves, and alcoves were made of delightfully carved and turned wood. It was old fashioned but light in style: more Belle Époque than heavy Spanish colonial. I hope it survives.

Rodblu had another shop in the fashionable Miraflores district. They also had several salesmen, including Efraim, Daniel's brother, who covered the provinces.

This was before the time of the Sendero Luminoso, the Shining Path guerrilla movement that was to wreak havoc for several years in the eighties and nineties. It was therefore possible to visit Cusco and Machu Picchu, the thought of which fascinated me. Daniel was delighted. He had never been, and having a gringo alongside gave him he said, the perfect excuse to go himself. It was therefore agreed that we should go together the next time I went to Peru.

During the time that I covered Latin America I used to do three trips a year. Each one lasted about four weeks, and I would visit about seven or eight markets on each trip. It was jolly hard work. When you arrived at any market, the agent would be all revved up to show you as much of his market, and as many of his customers as possible: the latter often late-night establishments. After two or three days of this he would dump you at the airport and probably go back to bed to recuperate. You, on the other hand, had to face another revved-up agent after a mere three-hour flight.

I had planned my next market visit to South America so that I reached Lima in the middle of the trip, at a weekend. When I landed at Lima, I was met by Efraim who told me that Daniel and his wife were already in Cusco waiting for me. He had organised a ticket for me to fly up to Cusco the next morning (Saturday) at a very early hour. I would spend the day in Cusco. We would visit Machu Picchu on Sunday and fly back on Monday. That was the plan.

Efraim had organised a taxi to pick me up from the hotel and get me to the airport at 5.30 a.m. He had told me that it was important to get a window seat on one side of the plane because the views on that side would be spectacular.

I got to the airport in good time, checked in and went to the departure gate. Parked by our gate was a very dilapidated old flying machine. I did not like the look of it but settled down near the exit from the terminal so that I could be poised to get on board quickly and grab a good seat.

There I was, somewhat drowsily waiting to be called. A couple of times I heard a *falta un pasajero* announcement indicating that we were waiting for one missing passenger. This clearly explained why we had not yet started to board. Eventually I got fed up with the waiting, went to the desk and asked when we would be boarding 'that plane for Cusco' and pointed to the old banger outside.

'That plane,' said the nice *azafata*, 'isn't going to Cusco. It is going to Arequipa. The one for Cusco has gone. It went from another gate. They were waiting for a missing passenger, but he never turned up; so, they left without him.'

In thirty years of hectic travel, I only ever missed two flights. That was the first one. Daniel was very nice about it. I think he thought it rather funny. I was annoyed with myself and disappointed.

Anthony Burnet, a chap I was at school with, once told me that he went to Machu Picchu just after the Falklands War (1982). At the time, he was working for Bell's Whisky. The usual way to get there is by train from Cusco, the wonderful ancient capital of the Incas, which sits high in the Andes, at an altitude of 11,000 feet. The train climbs away from Cusco by means of a switchback railway. After zig-zagging up the hill, the railway descends to the valley of the Urubamba.

With its wonderfully onomatopoeic name, the Urubamba is a truly splendid river. Like a Spey in spate, and on steroids, it hurtles along, gurgling and grumbling as it rages to itself, towards Aguas Calientes which is where the train stops just below Machu Picchu. After Aguas Calientes, the Urubamba charges in an angry loop around the foot of the Inca citadel before crashing onward between mountains and through canyons for hundreds of miles in the central Andes. Eventually it descends to the Amazon basin and, calmly now, meanders into the headwaters of that mighty river just upstream from Iquitos.

Between Cusco and Aguas Calientes, the railway line criss-crosses the Urubamba, so you get great views of the river from the train. It was somewhere along this part of the track that Anthony's train broke down. He was sharing a compartment with an Argentine family who, while impressed by his magnificent Spanish, were beginning to suspect that he might possibly be British. Eventually they asked him outright if he was English. Thinking quickly Anthony said certainly not; he was Scottish. On hearing this news there was a long pause after which Mr Argentina said:

'But that is a province of England is it not?'

'Absolutely not,' replied Anthony with a vehemence of which Ms Sturgeon would have been proud, 'it's a completely different country.'

Then they all got out and took a stroll while the train was being mended. When it restarted the Argentine family got back into another carriage.

I did eventually get to Cusco and Machu Picchu but not until 2003, by which time the Sendero Luminoso had come and gone: or mostly so at any rate.

That time I did not miss the flight; nor did my train break down.

PERU

2003, Machu Picchu in the clouds

Looking down on the Urubamba from Machu Picchu
(the train station at Aguas Calientes is just visible bottom centre)

The Urubamba at Aguas Calientes

20

Chile

Our agents in Chile were Enrique Taverne y Hijos. The Tavernes were a great sporting family. Marcello, who ran the company, used to come to England every summer to play in the seniors' tournament at Wimbledon. In 1948 he had captained Chile's Davis Cup team. At the time of my visit his son, Felipe, was the amateur golf champion for Chile. In 1983 Felipe went on to win the Chilean Open.

In the early 1970s Chile was not a good market for whisky. In 1970 Salvador Allende and his Socialist Party had been elected to power. He introduced several Marxist policies such as nationalising banks and expropriating the important copper mining companies. Naturally, the Americans did not like any of this. With prodding from Nixon and Kissinger, Operation Condor swung into action. A number of destabilising measures were instigated.

The economy then went from bad to worse. Real wages collapsed. When I visited Chile in 1971 many basic items, such as toothpaste, were not available. You could only get meat every other week. Marcello's wife, who was English, said that some middle-class wives were throwing chicken feed over the walls of the army barracks. Their message being, 'have some chicken feed you spineless and good-for-nothing lot'. They wanted the military to do something.

The domestic market was closed for imported whisky, but Marcello's company was able to sell to the various embassies, including the UN Latin American HQ that was in Santiago. He also hoped to get an order from Lan Chile, the national airline. That, then, was my excuse for going to Chile.

While I was there, Marcello took me to a shop where I bought some vicuña material: enough to make an overcoat. It cost me $50. Vicuñas together with guanacos, alpacas, and llamas are South America's camelids. The vicuña is the rarest of these. Some thirty years later I was lucky enough to see these small, graceful, wild animals near Lake Chungará, on the high altiplano in northern Chile.

It was on that later visit that we found a shop in Lima selling the cloth from each of the four Andean camelids. The finest by far was that of the vicuña. The sample we saw and felt was unbelievably light and soft. At $1,000 a metre, its quality was reflected in the price. When I got home after that trip, I dug out my old 'vicuña' overcoat and sadly concluded that it was a bit too heavy; soft yes, but not that soft, and so probably made of alpaca not vicuña. Ah well!

On that first visit to Chile, I was also lucky enough to play nine holes of golf with Felipe at their country club. I may be wrong about this, but I distinctly recall Felipe playing with a set of 'single-length clubs' made by Spalding. He lent me a similar set. Having your iron clubs all the same length was very unusual and still is; though the top American pro, Bryson DeChambeau, uses them and has reignited interest in the concept. I recall liking the ones that Felipe lent me and played quite well – for me. Maybe I should see if I can get some of the modern ones.

In 1973 the military finally 'did something'. There was a coup d'état. General Pinochet took over and remained in power until 1990. It was reported that Allende committed suicide, though some say he was assassinated when Pinochet's forces stormed the presidential palace.

During the Pinochet years the economy improved, and it became a good market for Scotch whisky. In so doing it illustrated just how quickly things can change in Latin America.

Today Chile is a stable, democratic country, and relatively prosperous. Pinochet's reputation has been considerably tarnished and probably rightly so. But let us not forget how well he got on with Mrs Thatcher and how he helped us in the Falklands War. Also, our victory in the Falklands War helped to trigger the downfall of that unsavoury military regime in Argentina.

21

Communication and Travel

In the early 1970s, if I wanted to telephone Crebec in São Paulo it would have been for an important reason. Making a long-distance international call was expensive and complicated, and the line would not be very clear. Before attempting the call, I would send a cable to Crebec telling him when it would take place. Then I had to book the call with the telephone exchange in London. Finally, at the appointed hour, the lady at the GPO exchange, doubtless with earphones on, and wires, plugs, and dialling mechanisms to hand, would, if all went well, put the right plugs in the right sockets, dial the correct numbers and connect us.

In those days, the telex was not much used, faxes were little known, and email had not been thought of. Most communication was therefore done by airmail. It was reliable and sometimes surprisingly quick. I once sent a postcard to my mother from Rio de Janeiro on the day I arrived there from London. She received it in rural Hampshire the next day. During my trips I would airmail letters and postcards home to Isabel, and she also wrote to me at hotels where I would be staying. It worked well. We did not use the telephone unless there was a real emergency.

In 1970 British Airways had not yet been created. So I would fly out on BOAC or British Caledonian. BA was created in 1974 by the merger of BOAC (British Overseas Airways Corporation) and BEA (British European Airways). All were state-owned enterprises. BA was privatised in 1987.

To begin with I had to travel economy. There was no club class in those days: only first or economy. Whenever André travelled with me, he thought it frightfully infra-dig to travel economy. We always had to get seats at the front of the economy section so that on landing we could sneak out of the first-class door, just in case our agent was meeting us. André did not want to be spotted crawling out of the cheap end of the plane.

Eventually, I was allowed to travel up front. The first-class seats were rather like today's club class seats, no better. But the food and drink were excellent. I once flew from Paris to Santiago with Air France. On the way we stopped at Rio de Janeiro, and Buenos Aires. The food and wine – and Romeo y Julieta cigars – were superb; but the quality declined gently as we got nearer to Santiago. For example, between Paris and Rio the champagne was Dom Pérignon. Then between Rio and BA it was vintage Moët et Chandon. But from BA to Santiago, all we got was non-vintage champagne.

The long-range plane of choice for BOAC and B Cal was the VC10: a wonderful plane, British made, and with quad Rolls Royce engines on the tail section. It had been designed not only for long haul but also for its ability to take off from places, like Kampala, that had short runways. Consequently, it was slightly less fuel efficient than Boeing's 707. When oil was $3 a barrel, that did not matter: but when the oil price rose it did.

There were several local airlines in Latin America, some of which were excellent, and others a bit ropey. One splendid airline that flew the region was Braniff, an American airline. The Braniff planes were brightly painted, each in a different colour. While the B Cal air hostesses were kitted out in rather ill-fitting tartan suits, and the BOAC ladies wore prim pinstripes, the girls pushing the trolleys for Braniff were stunning goddesses from various Latin American countries. They were clad, just, in chic uniforms designed by Emilio Pucci. The Braniff pilots spoke proper American, and came, reassuringly, from the airline's hubs in places like Boston, Dallas, and Kansas City.

And of course, in those days there was none of today's security hassle at any of the airports. That all started much later.

Credit cards were not much used in 1970. I used to take dollar travellers cheques. The UK had strict exchange controls in place. If you went abroad on holiday, you were not allowed to take more than £50 with you. If you went on business, you could take more but the amount you took had to be registered on a schedule at the back of your passport. In today's 'global' world this sounds bizarre: but it was so.

22

Bolivia

You may wonder why indigenous women who live in the high Andes wear bowler hats? I discovered the answer in Barbados when I got there in 1972. Our agents in Barbados were Stokes & Bynoe. The company was run by Dick Stokes and his nephew David Harris. Dick was an old man and almost blind. He sat at a big desk holding a huge magnifying glass through which he examined various documents that were put before him. This sounds a bit forbidding, but he was always friendly and could easily be distracted from his paperwork. He liked to reminisce about the old times.

On one occasion we were talking about Old Parr. Now, Old Parr is a brand that belonged to the DCL. It was, and still is, a deluxe whisky like Johnnie Walker Black Label or Chivas Regal. The brand was created in 1909 and its owners, Macdonald Greenless, were acquired by the DCL in 1925. Old Parr comes in a squat, brown, dimpled bottle that looks a bit like a Mills Bomb and is named in honour of Old Tom Parr, an Englishman not a Scot, who is reputed to have lived from 1482 to 1635.

Old Parr Scotch Whisky is still a popular brand in several Latin American countries. Dick Stokes said that its success could be attributed to one man. I cannot remember his name but for the sake of this story let us call him Wilson. This

Wilson was a sales representative for a portfolio of disparate British companies. He lived in Barbados and every year in late February he would set off on a clockwise journey around South America. His tour took ten months and allowed him to get back to Barbados in time for Christmas. He was a true pioneer.

Wilson was greatly respected. It was said that on one occasion, when he was in Santiago, the president of Chile honoured his visit with a public holiday. Wilson was accompanied on his annual circumnavigation (he went mostly by ship) by a faithful retainer. If they were in a meeting with an important client, and if it was very hot, which it often was, there being no air conditioning in those days, the servant would stand behind Wilson and fan him with a big banana leaf.

Dick Stokes told me that Wilson could sell anything: thus, his success in introducing Old Parr. 'For instance,' said Dick, warming to his theme, 'it was Wilson who got all those Indians in the Andes to wear bowler hats.'

The story went that one of Wilson's principals, a firm in Huddersfield who made hats had, at the time, suffered a major production cock-up. A large consignment of bowler hats that should have been made in the standard colour of black, came out brown. This was a catastrophe. The idea of selling a brown bowler was quite beyond the pale. The owners of the hat factory in Huddersfield did not know what to do. Then some bright spark said:

'Why don't we ask Wilson to take them? He can sell anything.' Which they did, and Wilson took them to Bolivia.

Initially he sold them to some Brits who were working on the railways (we were building the railways all around South America in those days). But these unique brown bowlers also took off with the ladies of the Aymara and Quechua tribes and have been fashionable with them ever since. The hats are no longer made in Huddersfield. They are made locally and are called *bombins*.

In 1971 Bolivia was poor and not a good market for Scotch whisky; but, as Mallory might have said, 'it was there', and it was part of my patch. So, I was curious to see it. We did not have an agent in Bolivia, so I went there to find one. Moreover, it was only four years since that iconic figure, Che Guevara, had been caught and executed in Bolivia. This added to the allure of the place.

Che Guevara's strategy of going to Bolivia was quite sound. Unstable as it was, and with a poorly treated under-class, Bolivia was fertile ground for revolution; surrounded too by Brazil, Paraguay, Argentina, Chile, and Peru, it was the ideal base from which future revolutions could be exported. Che Guevara's big problem was that he did not get on with Mario Monje, the Bolivian leader of the Communist Party. Both wanted to be more equal than the other. That, and CIA intervention, led to the failure of the big plan as well as to his own downfall.

When I got there, I found that the ruling, and for once democratically elected, government of Juan José Torres was popular but weak. The US did not appreciate the leftist policies of Torres. So, shortly after my visit, there was a typical CIA-backed military coup d'état, and Hugo Banzer shot up the totem pole from colonel, to general and then president in one swift pugnacious move. He remained in office until 1978.

La Paz nestles below snow-capped Mount Illimani on the Andean altiplano at an altitude of just under 12,000 feet. When I got there from Santiago, which is almost at sea level, I was hit by the altitude and had to walk around rather slowly, and with a splitting headache. But I loved the city of La Paz. There were very few high-rise buildings in those days. The population in Bolivia has a far higher percentage of indigenous people than other South American countries. And on the streets of La Paz there were many native Aymaras with their colourful shawls ... and yes, the ladies were sporting their brown *bombins*. At one point I saw a circus processing through the street. I have never before, or since, seen elephants and llamas in the same troupe.

The Aymaras and other Andean Indians are short, swarthy, and barrel-chested. Being barrel-chested helps them deal with the thin air. Chewing on coca leaves also helps. By contrast many of those who came from European stock were much paler than in other Latin American countries.

I did manage to find an agent for Bolivia and appointed the company on a trial basis. I am afraid I cannot remember who they were, but they did send us some small orders.

The airport at La Paz is over 13,000 feet above sea level. The runway is two miles long. Taking off from La Paz is interesting: the plane lumbers along the runway slowly gathering momentum. It trundles on and on ... and on. Finally, it claws its way up into the thin atmosphere, a bit like an old dog getting out of its basket. But once up, the plane offers wonderful views flying low over Lake Titicaca, which itself is higher than La Paz. When I timed the take-off for my Braniff 707, I noted that it took fifty-five seconds to get airborne from La Paz but only twenty-five from Santiago.

I never went back to Bolivia. But I am glad I went that time.

23

Ecuador

Talking of hats, Panama hats do not come from Panama: they come from Ecuador. They are called Panama hats because when they were first exported, they were shipped from Panama. On a visit to Guayaquil in 2003 I discovered Almacenes Sombreros Barberán. Guayaquil (Ecuador's major port) is a scruffy town and Almacenes Sombreros Barberán was a pretty scruffy store. But I had been told that it was the best hat shop in town, and it did have wonderful old-fashioned signage above its door. So, I ventured rather nervously inside and found myself in a small, narrow establishment, lined with glass-fronted display cabinets. These offered a large, but rather untidy, range of Panama hats. The interior was none too clean, either. Had Mrs Thatcher been with me, she would doubtless have run her finger along the top of one of the display cabinets and been appalled by the amount of dust it had collected.

Behind the counter was a very old man. With wonderful old-world courtesy, he asked if he could help me. I replied rather inanely that I was thinking of buying a hat. Without any sarcasm whatsoever he replied that he would be 'honoured to help' me find one.

As this preamble was going on, I noticed that pinned

to the wall behind him was a very old, yellowing cutting from *The New York Times*. The cutting featured a shot of Himself in his emporium and, judging by the headline, the text was waxing lyrical about the genuine Montecristi Panama hats that he sold. I was reassured to learn that the tip about the shop that I had got from a spiv in the port was underwritten by a man from *The New York Times*.

So, I asked Señor Barberán, because that was he, if $50 could secure me a decent sombrero. Satisfied that I was a respectable customer, he rummaged around for a while and then found me a splendid hat that fitted perfectly. It was more Borsalino than Colonel Blimp, and with a wide rim. But I loved it.

'Hold it up to the light,' he said.

I did as he said but was not sure why. The reason, he explained, was to examine the quality of the weave, which was so fine that only the odd chink of light could be seen through it. As he was packing my sombrero, Señor Barberán explained that it was a genuine Montecristi, handmade in the small town of that name which lies about 100 miles north of Guayaquil. My hat would have taken about two months to make. He went on to explain that he was now eighty-eight and had been involved in this business for over seventy years. Clearly, he loved his trade. He was a lovely old hombre.

After I had paid, Señor Barberán wondered aloud if I would like to see one of his Ultra-Fino Montecristis. I leaped at the idea.

The hat that he passed to me looked like mine but when I held it up to the light, not one chink of light penetrated its tight, but delicate, weave.

'Now drop it,' he commanded.

Perplexed again, I did as he said, and then noticed how ... light as a feather, it floated very gently down to his outstretched hand. He said it would have taken nine months to make that hat. He also pointed out that, though such a work of art would cost $1,000 in his shop, it would cost much more abroad. He is quite right. Today if you go to Lock's in St James's, you can order a 'Bespoke Ultra-Fine Montecristi Panama' for just under seven grand: and that is in pounds, not dollars.

When I first went to Guayaquil in 1971, I did not know about Almacenes Sombreros Barberán, but it must have been there because in 2003 Señor Barberán told me he had owned a shop in Guayaquil since 1940 ... and that is my excuse for this digression.

In the early years of independence from Spain, what is now Ecuador had been part of Gran Colombia. But in 1830 Ecuador broke away. Since then, and in typical South American fashion, various bits of the original Ecuador have been lost in frontier wars to Peru, Brazil, and Colombia. So today Ecuador is a lot smaller than it was in 1830.

At the time of my visit, José María Velasco was serving as president for the fifth time. A great orator, and very popular, he was frequently elected, then in true Latin American style almost as frequently booted out – usually by a military coup. And that was what happened again in 1972.

But in 1971 when I met Alberto Constain in Guayaquil, there was an air of optimism in Ecuador. I was there to visit his company, Mercantil Ecuadoriana, who were our agents. The new pipeline was due to open. In 1972 it would start pumping oil from the Amazonian regions of Ecuador, across the Andes to a Pacific port some 300 miles away.

At a stroke Ecuador then became the second-biggest oil producer in South America.

Alberto also had the agency for some competing brands, Ballantine's, Teacher's and Vat 69 being the principal ones. This was not ideal, but he had a good organisation and did well for us. Normally one would go to Quito, the capital, but on this occasion, I started in Guayaquil and rather than fly up to Quito we decided that it might be more interesting to drive. This we did, with Alberto at the wheel.

At over 9,000 feet above sea level, Quito is higher than Bogotá but not quite as high as La Paz. The journey from Guayaquil was over 250 miles, and took all day. The road was still quite basic in 1971, but there was very little traffic.

As its name suggests, Ecuador has the equator running through it, so as we climbed from sea level up into the Andes we seemed to go through several climates. Much of the country was wonderfully wild and rugged. About half-way up Alberto stopped the car and tinkered with the carburettor. He said that the adjustment had to be made once we got to a certain altitude. Otherwise, the engine would not fire properly.

Quito was another lovely city with fine colonial churches and *palacios*. The few tall, modern buildings that I saw were frequently wreathed in Andean cloud.

Since the 1970s, Ecuador has been one of those countries constantly attracted towards a Chavist style of Marxist-Bolivarian revolution. Often tempted, frequently prevented by military intervention, and constantly indecisive, that diverse and beautiful country has, so far, avoided falling off a precipice.

24

The Guianas

Before we leave South America and head for Panama and Central America, we should pay a brief visit to the Guianas.

The Guianas sit perched side by side, like three monkeys, on the north-east shoulder of Brazil. Guyana is the most westerly and is next to Venezuela. Then moving east and south you have first Suriname and then French Guiana.

Guyana had been British Guiana until it gained its independence in 1966. At the time of my visit, Surinam was still a Dutch colony and did not gain independence until 1975, at which point it added the 'e' and became Suriname. French Guiana remains an overseas département of France and, rather bizarrely, is therefore inside the EU.

These three countries were established as slave colonies with plantations set up to produce sugar and other agricultural products. Consequently, they have populations of great ethnic diversity. Inhabitants of European stock are in a minority to those with African, Indian, Chinese, Amerindian, and mixed blood.

The Guianas were not big markets for Scotch whisky. In fact, their domestic markets were tiny, but since they each have a border with Brazil there was a certain amount of in-transit business to be had. In-transit being mostly, of course, a euphemism for smuggling.

I found Georgetown, the capital of Guyana to be old-fashioned, sleepy, and not without colonial charm. Forbes Burnham had been in power since 1964 and would, thanks to a series of rigged elections, stay there until he died in 1985.

Guyana was part of the territory that Stokes & Bynoe managed for us from Barbados; a useful reminder of how the Guianas were often considered as part of the Caribbean. Guyana was a founder member of CARICOM when it was set up in 1973. CARICOM is a Caribbean trading block for English-speaking countries.

Guyana has played a big part in the great cricketing tradition of the West Indies. When I went there Clive Lloyd, Rohan Kanhai and Lance Gibbs, all Guyanese, were in their prime.

In Surinam they did not play cricket. They preferred football.

Whereas Guyana was famous for rum, cricket and Demerara sugar, Surinam was a significant producer of bauxite, the ore from which aluminium is derived. Despite this, in the 1970s, the country was poor and unemployment, as in Guyana, was high. Our agent, Harry Cabell, was a large, genial Dutchman who spoke perfect American. He explained that over 80 per cent of the whisky that came into Surinam went on to Brazil – much of it, as in Paraguay, in a barter swap for coffee. Since J&B Rare was popular in Brazil, he was doing well for us.

We did not have an agent in French Guiana. Harry said he had contacts there and could do something for us. He agreed to take me there.

We went by car from Paramaribo, the capital of Surinam, to Cayenne the capital of French Guiana: a journey of some 250 miles. There was little traffic. Much of the route was through jungle and along dusty red dirt roads. Harry said they were red because of the bauxite. The Maroni River marks the frontier between the two countries, and we crossed into French Guiana on a rickety ferry, there being no bridge.

As we drove into Cayenne I was astonished to see, walking cheerfully down the main street, a man with a very large snake wrapped around his neck. Later we asked Harry's contact, Monsieur Abchee, a Lebanese trader who specialised in the in-transit market, if it was normal in Cayenne for chaps to wander about town with live snakes around their necks. Monsieur Abchee explained that we had probably seen a well-known snake charmer who had the ability to wander off into the jungle, and come back, every so often, with a prize specimen. When we asked what he did with them, the answer was: 'Turn them into handbags.'

Other than a slight awareness of the Dreyfus Affair, and its association with the infamous prison on Devil's Island, I had little previous knowledge of French Guiana. I imagined therefore that Cayenne would be a grim and forbidding penal settlement. In fact, it turned out to be a small, neat, spacious, and well-ordered French town.

In 1965 de Gaulle instituted the Guiana Space Centre. This is situated by the sea, not far from Cayenne, and just opposite Devil's Island. Today it is run by the European Space Agency.

Devil's Island was closed as a prison in 1953. Now it is a tourist attraction, just like Alcatraz.

I was amused to note that in Guyana most of the cars were British and, naturally, everyone drove on the left. In French Guiana all the cars were French, and they drove on the right. Very logical. But then in Surinam most of the cars were large American beasts that they drove on the left with their steering wheels on the wrong side. Very double Dutch.

25

Panama

It is said that in 1671, when Captain Morgan carried out his famous raid on the Spanish Main, the one thing he really wanted to get his hands on was the famed Golden Altar in the City of Panama.

It is less than fifty miles from Panama City across the isthmus from the Pacific Ocean to the mouth of the Chagres River on the Caribbean coast. This was an important route for the Spaniards. They would ship their gold, silver, and other treasure up from Peru, land them at Panama City, transport them across the isthmus and down the Chagres to the Caribbean before onward shipment, first to Cuba and then to Spain. It was much easier and safer than taking the long way around Cape Horn. But, as a sweet spot on the treasure trail from Peru to Spain, Panamá la Vieja was likely to be worth plundering. Egged on by Charles II, Morgan was attracted to it like a bear to a honey pot.

Dodging mosquitoes and troublesome natives, Morgan and his privateers got from the Chagres River across to Panama City surprisingly easily. They then defeated a Spanish force outside the town. But by then the Spaniards were alert to the advancing danger. They removed many of their treasures and, with a bit of help from some gunpowder, the governor of the city blew up and set fire to as many buildings as he could. When Morgan got to the Church of San José, all he found was a wizened old priest in a scruffy church with a dirty altar. The priest meekly handed over a precious chalice, explaining to Morgan that it was all that he had of any value. Then rather bravely he added that since his parish was a poor one, perhaps the great Capitano could, in exchange for the chalice, spare a few small coins to help repair some of the damage that his men had wreaked.

Morgan, with ill grace, tossed him some pieces of eight, muttering darkly that it seemed to him it was the priest who was the pirate not he. In this he was not far off the mark. Before the sacking of what was left of the city, the clever old cleric had got his parishioners to paint his Golden Altar with a mixture of tar and mud before they vanished into the surrounding jungle leaving him to outsmart the cut-throat pirates on his own.

The narrow isthmus of Panama has always been of strategic importance as a crossroads between Central America and South America, as well as between the Pacific and the Caribbean. After the opening of the Canal in 1915 it became even more important. At the time Panama had ceded a 'Zone' alongside the Canal, five miles wide on each side of it, that was granted in perpetuity to the USA. But under the terms of the Torrijos – Carter Treaties which were signed in 1977 and ratified by the Senate in 1979 – Panama managed to have this rescinded. Panama regained full control of the Zone and the Canal on 31 December 1999.

Panama was an important market for Scotch whisky. The market was divided into three segments: the domestic market for the local population, the Canal Zone, where the duties were slightly lower, and the Colón Free Zone.

In the 1970s, when you drove through the Canal Zone it brought home to you the strategic, as well as commercial, importance of the Canal. There was a strong US military presence, and it was all very American with nice roads, modern housing, and easy sightings of golf courses, tennis courts and other must-have sources of R and R for the modern Yankee warrior: all quite different to Panama City.

Finally, the third segment of the market was the Colón Free Zone: a freeport in the town of that name on the Caribbean coast, and a market of special interest for Scotch whisky.

The first time I went to Panama was in early 1971. I did not go with André so did not mind crawling out of the back of a Braniff 707 after landing at Tocumen Airport. The first thing that hit me was the heat. It was like stepping into a Turkish bath.

Panama is noted for its tropical humidity. They have a garment called the *guayabera*: a comfortable, but smart, loose-fitting shirt which is worn untucked and is acceptable on almost any occasion. It is perfect for the climate.

When I climbed out of that plane, there on the tarmac at the foot of the steps was a very genial looking man, in his fifties and sensibly garbed in his *guayabera*. He seemed to recognise me. He was Alberto Motta and his company, Motta Internacional, were our agents in Panama. I had never met him.

'How did you know that I was me?' I asked as we sashayed past passport control.

'Easy,' he replied, 'by your shoes: very English.'

Alberto was one of the most extraordinary people I ever met. He told me that he started his business career by selling chocolates at school. One of the world's truly great entrepreneurs, charismatically engaging and always loquacious, he was popular wherever he went. Whenever he came to the office in London, he would carry a large briefcase stuffed full of perfume samples: all from the top maisons. Our secretaries had him on a par with Father Christmas.

But Alberto was also extremely shrewd. He was one of the visionaries who helped to create the Colón Free Zone after World War II. By the time of his death in 2006, Alberto had been president of COPA (the national airline), a bank, an insurance company, and a TV company as well as Motta Internacional. He had also established a couple of charitable foundations. He was a major and much respected name in Panama: and rightly so.

The liquor trade in Panama was dominated by two companies: Motta Internacional, and Silvestre y Brostella, or Silbros. These two companies did not like each other – not one bit. In my first report from Panama, I described the relationship between the Brostellas, who owned Silbros, and the Mottas as somewhat akin to that between the Montagues and the Capulets.

Our domestic and Canal Zone business was handled by Felipe Motta e Hijo. The *hijo* adjunct was appropriate because the company was run by Felipe father and Felipe son. Felipe senior was Alberto's older brother and was just as gregarious and convivial as him. I once popped out of their store with Felipe senior to go to the post office which was about 20 yards away. It took for ever to get there and back because Felipe seemed to know everyone in the neighbourhood. And they all wanted to stop and chat with him. It was like taking a dog for a walk when the dog wants to stop and have a sniff at every lamppost. On my first visit Felipe senior very kindly took me on a VIP tour of the Canal's Miraflores Locks. He knew everybody there, too.

I think Felipe junior let his father do all the PR work, at which he was brilliant, while he ran the show on the local market. He did it very well. Every Christmas I would get a wonderful card from Felipe junior. It always featured him, his wife, and their children – the latter neatly lined up with tallest on the left and smallest on the right. Every year there always seemed to be one more than the year before. Eventually there were six, and they were all boys: a wonderful family.

The Colón Free Trade Zone was the richest segment of the market. It held important trading links throughout Latin America. Apart from liquor, Motta Internacional represented a wide range of luxury brands encompassing watches, jewellery, perfume, and fashion houses as well as electronics, toys, and tobacco. At their HQ in Colón, they had a display room. It was a bit like going into Harrods. At the end of every visit Alberto would insist on going there for a spot of 'shopping'. This was very embarrassing because Alberto would grab a basket and load it with various goodies, none of which you were allowed to pay for. And you could not refuse either – he would have been genuinely offended. I still have a couple of elegant Nina Ricci ties from those shopping expeditions.

It was André who recommended we appoint the Mottas. Hennessy were, in fact, with Silbros. Both Motta and Silbros had customers throughout the region. Many were duty free shops; others were embassies or stores for ships passing through. Also, many of those military *cantinas* in Central and South America got their supplies from Panama, this being a form of condoned contraband. The attraction of going to Panama was that a trader could fill his boots from one supplier. It was like being able to get everything from one supermarket rather than having to make separate trips to the butcher, the baker, and the candlestick maker.

To facilitate this, Silbros and Motta also stocked limited amounts of each other's brands. So if you were a Motta customer and wanted Johnnie Walker (for whom Silbros were the agents), Alberto would sell it to you, albeit with gritted teeth, and after trying to switch you to J&B Rare.

Because Silbros stocked J&B Rare, I used to pay a courtesy visit to them. Before I went for the first time, I was warned by the Mottas that Silbros would promise me the earth if only I transferred the agency to them, and that I was not to believe a word they said.

Silbros was owned by Miguel Brostella and his son, also Miguel. Alberto Motta and Miguel senior were poles apart in character. Whereas Alberto had the exuberance of a Frankie Dettori, Miguel senior played his cards more like Aidan O'Brien.

André told me that Miguel senior had started life as a barman in Barcelona. When I first met him, I found an old, rather severe-looking man sitting very upright in a high-backed leather chair. Like Aidan O'B he was very softly spoken but, and again like A O'B, he spoke with authority. And he did suggest that if I switched the agency to Silbros it would prove to be a very wise decision. I explained as diplomatically as I could that being in the same stable as Johnnie Walker was an insurmountable impediment. Eventually he accepted, with majestic dignity, my refusal

116

to accept his 'kind' offer. Over time I got to know Miguel junior a bit better and enjoyed the meetings that I had with him. Indeed, it was he who gave me an introduction to José Somoza who became our agent in Nicaragua. I believe that in later years the relationship between the Motta and Brostella clans improved.

The Mottas went on to do a very good job for J&B Rare. After my first visit they sent in a very large order which did my street cred back at HQ a power of good. In speaking of the Mottas I have to include Alberto's two sons, Stanley and Pancho, both of whom were extremely able and active in the business.

When I went to Panama in the early 1970s the country was under the rule of Omar Torrijos, 'Líder Máximo de la Revolución Panameña'. He was a friend of Graham Greene, who wrote about him in *Getting to Know the General*. Torrijos was a leader who carried out several popular reforms; but he was killed in a plane crash in 1981, in suspicious circumstances. Then the dreadful General Noriega took control: he of the drug trafficking, money laundering, and fetish for red underpants fame. Under him things got so bad that the US invaded Panama in 1989. Bush called the invasion Operation Just Cause. Since then, the country has stuck successfully to a democratic path. The economy has prospered. Panama is now a major financial centre for the region. And in 2016 the capacity of the Canal was expanded by the opening of new larger locks.

The Mottas too have thrived. In the 1990s Alberto together with Stanley and Pancho set up Inversiones Bahía. Stanley and Pancho now manage a swathe of investments that include holdings in a bank, a TV company, the COPA airline and of course Motta Internacional. Moreover, in Panama today, Stanley has nine grandchildren and Felipe's six sons have produced twenty-three grandchildren and three great-grandchildren.

I read that in 1997 the newly formed Diageo gave Motta Internacional the agency in Panama for all Diageo brands. This meant that J&B Rare, in Panama as elsewhere, is now in the same stable as Johnnie Walker. If I congratulate the Mottas for this appointment I do so through teeth that are distinctly gritted.

With Alberto Motta and his prize bull at the Motta's ranch

26

Central America

Including Panama there are seven small countries in Central America. If you fly north from Panama you will fly over Costa Rica then Nicaragua, Honduras, El Salvador, Guatemala, and eventually Belize. Beyond Guatemala and Belize lies Mexico, which is in North America. The climate is tropical with two seasons: dry from December to April and wet from May to November. I took the precaution of always going there in February or March when it was very agreeable. In the 1970s the total population of the region was well under fifty million, and as we had an agent in each country it seemed like visiting seven markets each about the size of Yorkshire.

The region first achieved independence from Spain in the early 1820s, initially as the Central American Federation. But by 1841 the territory had fragmented in typical Latin American style into the separate states of Costa Rica, Nicaragua, Guatemala, El Salvador and Honduras. In 1862 we declared the territory that is now Belize, to be our colony of British Honduras. Panama seceded from Colombia in 1903.

Costa Rica

In 1948 there was a forty-four-day civil war in Costa Rica. There was nothing unusual about that in the Latin America of those times. José María Figueres had led an insurrection that overturned the government of President Calderón. But after the civil war, Figueres carried out a number of reforms such as giving the vote to women ... and illiterates. Figueres himself was subsequently elected on three occasions and served those terms between 1953 and 1974.

But José María Figueres's most astonishing and unprecedented act was to abolish the military. Since 1948 Costa Rica has remained without an army, navy, or air force. Today, Costa Rica remains the most stable and democratic of all the countries in Latin America.

Costa Rica was a small but steady market for J&B Rare. Our agents, ADA, were owned by Miguel Yamuni and his brother Eduardo. Miguel was an impressive entrepreneur and a distinguished diplomat. Among their many businesses the Yamunis had a bra factory and the agency for Cessna aircraft ... a truly uplifting mix of interests. Miguel was himself a pilot. On one occasion he took me up for a spin. We flew out from San José (the capital) to the Pacific coast at Punta Arenas and then back. The country looked gorgeous. I can readily understand why tourism to Costa Rica is now so strong. When not involved in his family business, Miguel served his country as a diplomat. During his career he had several postings, starting with the Lebanon in 1963 and ending with the Court of St James in 1989.

Nicaragua

When you cross the San Juan River from Costa Rica to Nicaragua you pass from a stable, democratic country to one with a very chequered history. Between 1912 and 1933 there was a US Marine presence in Nicaragua. And between 1927 and 1979 it was ruled by the Somoza dynasty.

I first went to Nicaragua in 1971. The country was clearly run on feudal lines. Extremely poor, the economy was based on cotton and coffee. With its reputation as a fascist state, there were not many foreign concerns who were keen to invest in the country. The outlook was not bright.

The market for whisky was small. Most of the whisky available was imported by the military, and on-sold through the Casino: a sort of officers' club. From time to time, the Somoza regime also gave away rewards to their most favoured henchmen. One of the most popular rewards was a 'concession' to import whisky without paying any duty.

Our agent, José Somoza, was a scion of the ruling family. I found him able, energetic, and disarmingly congenial. Dewar's had a huge grip on the market, but José managed to get us a small slice of it. He controlled one of the duty free shops at the airport. He also had the agency for Browning guns.

Just before Christmas in 1972 there was a massive earthquake and 90 per cent of Managua, the capital, was destroyed. I went back in 1974 only to discover that very little reconstruction work had started. The place was a mess. I was told that the president had siphoned off much of the aid that had poured in. It was therefore no surprise when the Sandinistas seized power in 1979. The last of the three Somoza presidents fled to Paraguay only to be assassinated by a member of the Argentinian Revolutionary Workers Party.

The Sandinistas are named after César Sandino, who had been assassinated by the first Somoza. They are led by Daniel Ortega, who has won presidential elections in 1984, 2006, 2011, 2016, and 2021. Accepted at first by Carter but disliked by Reagan, Ortega has held on increasingly like a Somoza. The last election was almost certainly rigged and the country, beautiful though it is, remains wracked by poverty, corruption, and mismanagement.

And as I said at the beginning of this section, when you cross the Río San Juan from Costa Rica into Nicaragua you are not just crossing a river.

Honduras and El Salvador

Landing at Tegucigalpa's Toncontín International Airport was always decidedly hairy. On the approach, the wings of our plane seemed to brush the houses on the side of the hills which themselves formed an aerial chicane through, and around which, our pilot banked and side-slipped us down onto the runway: all with stylish élan. As soon as we touched down, he had to stamp on the brakes, the runway being famously short. André and I were strapped into a rather ancient turboprop airliner, and I was beginning to understand why André had said that Honduras was a very small market, and he hardly ever went there. He did however assure me that he knew Señor Cabrera, our agent, very well. To emphasise the point, he declared that he and Señor Cabrera were on *muy amigo mío* terms.

Señor Cabrera had his office inside Supermercado Tip Top, which was one of the businesses that he owned. So we went into the store and André asked a fine-looking old gentleman if he could direct us to Señor Cabrera's *despacho* (personal office).

'Of course I can,' was the reply, 'since I'm Cabrera that will be easy. And who may you be?'

Poor André was mortified.

The year before my first visit to Honduras and El Salvador the two countries had fought against each other in the famous 'Football War'. The antipathy between the two countries had come to a rolling boil during two legs of a FIFA World Cup qualifying round.

The ensuing war has sometimes been referred to as the '100 Hour War' because after a short time the OAS (Organisation of American States) got the protagonists to see sense and stop the fighting. Unfortunately, a considerable amount of damage had already been done by both countries.

Honduras and El Salvador were both small markets for whisky. Usually about half the market in such countries was legitimate and half was contraband. If duties were increased, there was a corresponding increase in the level of smuggling – and vice versa.

In El Salvador our agents had the wonderful name of Almacen Liverpool; where they got that name from, I never learned. We did small but regular business in both countries, and I enjoyed my short visits to them. At the time they were attractive and peaceful. Despite the airport, I particularly liked going to Tegucigalpa, which in those days was a small, sleepy town set between surrounding hills, and with its own aura of colonial charm. Sadly, in recent years both countries have been beset with problems.

Guatemala

If they had a forty-four-day civil war in Costa Rica, in Guatemala they had one that lasted for nearly forty-four years. It did not end until 1996. To be honest, when I went there in the early 1970s the war was not much in evidence. But I was advised not to wander around Guatemala City at night.

Typically, much of the whisky sold in Guatemala passed through the military *cantinas*. Some, the *ejército* bought through the appointed agents, and some they smuggled in themselves from neighbouring British Honduras. Our agent, a splendid man called Vidal, whose first name I forget, took me to meet the colonel in charge of whisky purchases at a military base that was spectacularly devoid of spit and polish. The colonel kept us waiting for two hours but was charmingly apologetic when he finally deigned to receive us. He told me that he liked J&B Rare, and the brand sold well. However, he could not order any 'now' because his predecessor had bought a large stock of inferior brands, and he had to get rid of those first. Vidal explained the obvious implications.

On my second visit to Guatemala, Vidal very kindly took me to visit Antigua. Surrounded by volcanos and set at an elevation of around 4,000 feet above sea level, Antigua is the wonderful old colonial capital of Guatemala. It is now a UNESCO World Heritage site. I recall having a sublime black bean stew there, at a traditional taverna not far from the Plaza Mayor.

Since the end of the civil war Guatemala has been relatively stable. Although several elections have been held, the even flow of democracy has been blighted by some high-level corruption scandals.

British Honduras

Guatemala's attitude to British Honduras (now Belize) was, and is, akin to that of Spain's towards Gibraltar: they think it should belong to them. Therefore, full independence for Belize was not achieved until 1981. As a protective measure Britain retained a small garrison there for many years.

Our agent in British Honduras was the delightful William Quinto. He was Chinese and when I met him in Belize City, I asked him what his real Chinese name was. I could not imagine that it was Quinto. In reply he uttered a sound like a stifled hiccup that he said meant fifth in Chinese; Quinto means fifth in Spanish.

British Honduras is the smallest of the countries in Central America. It is about the size of Wales and has a similar population to Cardiff. When I visited British Honduras, it was a sleepy colony with everything priced reassuringly in pounds, shillings, and pence. William said that the local market for whisky was tiny, but he was doing a brisk trade on the duty free side. He cited the Mexican Army (from Cozumel), and the Honduran Air Force as particularly good customers.

Traditionally British Honduras was famous for its mahogany. More recently the economy of Belize, as the country is now called, has been based on sugar, bananas, and ecotourism, particularly to the Belize Barrier Reef. Unfortunately, Belize City has also gained a reputation as a money-laundering centre for the drug trade.

Comprising as it does a collection of small countries, Central America could be considered a microcosm of all Latin America. In the early 1970s the region was relatively stable. But, with the exception of Costa Rica, that peace was fragile. Today none of these countries has benefited due to being on the migrant, and cocaine, pipeline from South America to the USA. These problems hardly existed in my day.

I was lucky to know the countries of Central America when I did.

27

Mexico

On 18 October 1968 Bob Beamon quite literally jumped into history. In the long jump at the Mexico Olympics, he jumped 29 feet and 2.4 inches. This was 22 inches longer than the previous record, and still stands as the Olympic long-jump record. His feat coined the superlative 'Beamonesque'.

Mexico was the first Latin American country to host the Olympics. But when I got there for the first time in 1970, I do not recall much discussion about the Games. Since 1929 Mexico had been governed by the PRI (*Partido Revolucionario Institucional*). They would not be voted out until the new millennium. Before the Games had started the government had brutally supressed a student demonstration. Ironically, the students had been chanting: 'We don't want Olympics, we want revolution.' Hosting the Games had been a tarnished success for the *Partido Revolucionario*.

Our agents in Mexico were Vinos Internacionales, a small company owned by two shareholders, Juan Sánchez Conde and Piro Ricci. They had been appointed through a contact of Ralph Cobbold. When I began my career as a management trainee, back in 1962, Ralph Cobbold had been the joint managing director of J&B.

The appointment of Ralph as Joint MD in 1959 had been a curious affair. At the time, the behaviour of Eddie Tatham, the real MD, was becoming more and more and more eccentric. In his memoirs, Bob Lisle had some wonderful tales about Tatham. Bob had joined the company as office boy in 1944, aged fourteen, and on a salary of twenty-one shillings (£1.05) a week. He left as a director of the company forty-five years later.

Here is an example of Bob's recollections about Eddie Tatham:

ET, as he was generally known, loved Americans. It was he, of course, who put J&B Rare on the map in the States. Whenever passing Americans came into the shop, he would welcome them with open arms, sit them down and offer them a drink. On one occasion, when talking to a couple from Chicago he was sitting on a stool and making a point when he fell back and finished flat on the floor, but with his legs still across the stool. He continued his conversation from this position. Observing his predicament, I and a colleague lifted him back onto the stool. ET continued talking as though nothing untoward had happened, much to the astonishment of the two Americans.

So, brilliant though ET undoubtedly was, the board decided that a stabilising factor was required and had appointed Ralph to the status of Joint MD. But as far as everyone else was concerned, particularly Himself, ET remained *the* MD. For a time, the company had an MD and a Joint MD.

Returning now to Mexico, Ralph, who also had a brilliant network of contacts, knew a man called de Mier. And de Mier knew Sánchez Conde. Thus, contact was established, and the appointment was made. As I have said before, it was like that then. For the two partners, the creation of

Vinos was a new venture. Their main interests lay in various properties that they owned in Mexico City, Acapulco, and Spain. Ricci owned La Mansión, an elegant hotel resort outside Mexico City. Vinos was therefore something of a prestige hobby.

In the 1970s, legal whisky imports to Mexico were restricted by annual quotas. These were granted every year in March or April. There was also a considerable market for contraband. About a third of the whisky consumed in Mexico was smuggled. Mostly, it came in from the US border, some through Tijuana in the West, and then more from various places along the Rio Grande. In the South of Mexico, more came in from Belize.

The brand leader in Mexico was Old Parr. Vinos decided that since those who could afford whisky were both wealthy and, by nature 'aspirational', it would make sense to position J&B Rare with an enhanced premium price. They were also willing to invest heavily in advertising. Our usual custom was to split advertising expenditure on a fifty-fifty basis with our agents. In Mexico, Vinos paid 70 per cent.

I used to enjoy my visits to Mexico. In time I visited various cities including Guadalajara, Acapulco, Mazatlán, Tijuana, and Monterrey. Vinos had sub-agents in all the principal states of Mexico as well as in the frontier zones.

Sánchez Conde had one of those quirky upmarket nicknames, much favoured by the Spanish upper classes: his was Qui Quin. Working with him and Piro was a pleasure because, although they had no liquor-trade experience, they instinctively understood our marketing policy. Qui Quin spoke no English. But his Spanish was of the purest Castilian. He liked to dine in the Centro Gallego, a delightful Galician restaurant in the smart Zona Rosa. At these dinners he was wonderfully patient with my groping Spanish.

In 1973 Qui Quin and Piro took on a new partner, Fabian Arnauld, who bought a majority shareholding in Vinos. Fabian was even more patrician than Qui Quin and Piro. He was charming and very well connected. I was told that his wife was extremely wealthy. I remember going to his house, a magnificent Palladian affair in a very smart part of Mexico City. Fabian led us across a couple of acres of marble flooring; then, from this grand entrance hall we were ushered into a side room. This, astonishingly, was meticulously decorated as a 'Wild West Saloon'. It was clearly his pride and joy. Happily, he was also assiduous at following Qui Quin's marketing policy. And the brand prospered.

Some years later the partners sold Vinos to Domecq Mexico, a subsidiary of Pedro Domecq in Spain, and a very successful company in its own right. Domecq Mexico was famous for its Presidente Brandy, a local brand, of which they sold massive quantities.

Domecq built on the foundations that had been created by the original partners, and J&B Rare became extremely successful in Mexico.

In parallel to this Mexican story, a similar venture was starting in Spain. Again, it began with a Ralph Cobbold contact. And again, the venture started as a hobby. But this time the result would be truly *Beamonesque*. I shall tell you about that when we get to Europe.

Meanwhile we should take a long jump to ...

28

West Africa

When I was given the territory of Latin America it did not include the Caribbean. At that time J&B Rare was very strong in the States. The Caribbean therefore had some good markets for us, especially in those islands 'blessed' with American tourism. With its inherent glamour, it was an attractive region to visit, for whatever reason, especially during the cold foggy months of an English winter. So, I was itching to add it to my territory. It seemed a natural fit.

In the late 1950s Eddie Tatham had taken a leisurely cruise around the Caribbean Sea. While he was there, he had appointed a number of our agents. I once found an old file containing letters that he had posted from his cruise. His correspondence was colourful, risqué and entertaining.

Dorrien had also made a couple of trips to the Caribbean in the 1960s; but when I joined, the region was not receiving any visits. So, at the beginning of 1971, and after a year in the company, I put up my hand and asked if I could have the Caribbean added to my Latin American territory.

The answer was: 'No.'

I was offered West Africa instead.

Since I had just read a book about West Africa being the white man's grave, I wondered if they were trying to get rid of me. Dorrien assured me that they were not. He said that West Africa was virgin territory for J&B Rare and that the experience would be rewarding. I was not entirely convinced but thought that I had better make the best of it.

In fact, West Africa was not completely virgin territory. A year or so before I joined J&B, a Frenchman had wandered into the office. His name was Cotentin, and he travelled regularly to the ex-French colonies in West Africa. He sold a variety of products. I think most of them were paints and other such – but not booze. He had asked if he could represent us in the Francophone countries.

We had said: 'Yes.'

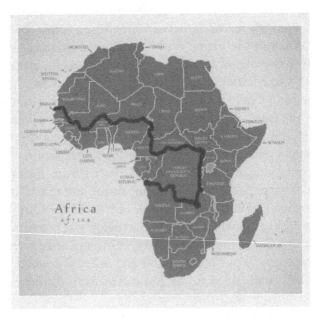

My new territory stretched from Zaire (formerly The Belgian Congo and now the Democratic Republic of the Congo) in the south, to Senegal in the north. I discovered that Monsieur

Cotentin had, in the previous year, secured a few small orders for us. My first task was therefore to make contact and find out a bit more about him and his organisation.

Cotentin had an address and telephone number in Paris. I started by trying the telephone. Most times the phone was not answered. On one occasion when I got through a grumpy lady said that Monsieur Cotentin was not in. She did not seem to know much about him, where he was or when he would be back. Background noises suggested the establishment that I was calling was a bar or café rather than an office.

Fortunately, he did answer my letters, and after a bit of toing and froing he agreed to join me in the Ivory Coast during a trip that I was planning.

I only made the one visit to West Africa. Starting at Kinshasa in Zaire, I then moved up the coast to Nigeria; from there I travelled along the old Slave Coast to Togo and Dahomey (now Benin). Avoiding Ghana, which at the time was particularly unstable, I hopped on to the Ivory Coast, Liberia, and Sierra Leone before ending at Dakar in Senegal.

With the exception of Liberia, which had been an American experiment in colonisation for freed slaves, all these countries had secured their independence from Britain, France, or Belgium in 1960. Looking back now, it is interesting to see how they were being led, and what progress they had made by the time of my visit in 1971. There were some spectacular contrasts. Here are a couple of examples.

In Zaire, Joseph-Désiré Mobutu Sese Seko was at the height of his power. Mobutu was to run Zaire from 1965 to 1997. He was considered the most corrupt African leader of the period. That took some doing. In his youth he had been a very bright, though disruptive, student. His favoured reading had been works by de Gaulle, Churchill, and Machiavelli. Once in power and fully into his klepto-cratic stride he was wont to charter Air France Concordes for shopping trips to Paris.

Consider next Félix Houphouët-Boigny. Known as the 'Sage of Africa', he was president of the Ivory Coast from its year of independence in 1960 until 1993. I always found his name quite impossible to pronounce and so, in my mind, Houphouët-Boigny was reduced to being Humpty Dumpty. This was grossly unfair because, although the various elections that he won were doubtlessly rigged, he was a moderate and relatively benign ruler. When his hand was on the economic tiller the 'Ivorian Miracle' ensued. Less moderately he transformed his up-country native village of Yamoussoukro into the country's capital. He then embel-lished it by building his basilica to Our Lady of Peace. Consecrated by Pope John Paul II in 1990, it is bigger than St Peter's in Rome, but not quite so tall.

I got my first experience of petty corruption in Kinshasa. I was being driven across town by Louis, a white Belgian and a prospective agent. Suddenly, and for no reason, we were pulled over by an angry policeman. Rather strangely, I thought, Louis invited him to get into the car. The policeman got in behind me. Louis got out his wallet and handed the policeman a small banknote. The policeman was instantly all smiles. Louis was now his best friend. He got out of the car, stopped all the traffic, and waved us through as though we had been a Mobutu motorcade. Louis explained that the police were underpaid, and that 'tipping' them like this was the only way to avoid getting trapped into an extremely acrimonious and time-wasting procedure.

In general, I found the ex-French colonies far more attractive, much cleaner, and also better run than the ex-British ones. In Dahomey, Togo, the Ivory Coast, and Senegal the French presence was very strong. The currency was the CFA franc. It was pegged to first the French franc, and later the euro.

Cotonou, the capital of Dahomey, and Lomé, its counterpart in Togo, were attractive seaside towns. I recall colourful open-air markets with tall statuesque women striding around carrying stuff on their heads. They must surely have been the descendants of the Dahomey Amazons, a regiment of female warriors who in days of yore had formed part of the king's formidable army. In the eighteenth century the Kings of Dahomey were of a very warlike bent.

And, of course, the food and lodgings in the ex-French colonies were miles better than in the English ones. The Hotel Ivoire in Abidjan even had an ice rink.

Commerce in these countries seemed to be divided between established colonial trading houses, which had various departments, and dealt in everything from bog rolls to boilers, and smaller independent traders. In the French-speaking countries, the latter were often owned by Europeans, Lebanese or Armenians. The established trading houses tended to be rather dozy and bureaucratic. The independents were more dynamic and entrepreneurial. But they could be risky when it came to getting paid.

Since J&B Rare was beginning to go rather well in France, where our agents were Moët et Chandon, there was much more interest in the Francophone countries. So, I was looking forward to meeting Cotentin when I got to Abidjan.

But Monsieur Cotentin did not show up.

Instead, I was met at the airport by a man called Bart. Monsieur Bart was a friend of Cotentin. He explained that Cotentin could not come and that he had been asked to help me. When I asked why he had not come the reply was a wonderfully expansive Gallic shrug. This told me both nothing and a lot. From it I deduced that Cotentin, in Bart's view, was a lovely chap but probably a bit fey, and whose actions therefore tended to be unpredictable. Bart did not even know where Cotentin was at the time.

Monsieur Bart was not in our business but was very kind and did what he could to help. I visited several traders, and then taking a leaf from the Crebec book asked the head barman at the hotel which merchant gave him the best service when it came to the supply of wines and spirits. The answer was Jean Yezeguelian, an Armenian, who had a company called CAB (Compagnie Africaine des Boissons). He was right, Yezeguelian had a very impressive operation.

When I got back to London, having heard nothing from Cotentin, I decided that we would be much better served by appointing companies, such as CAB, to be our agent in each of the Francophone markets. They were energetic, entrepreneurial, enthusiastic about J&B Rare, and local. It seemed that Cotentin lacked all these attributes. Unfortunately, this meant that Cotentin had to go.

29

Firing an Agent

I had never before fired an agent, so thought I had better get Dorrien's approval before I did so. Now, as I have already indicated, Dorrien was a great delegator. He liked to focus on the big picture which at the time was the American business; and that was going like a rocket. So, as I sat in front of him explaining what I wanted to do he seemed not remotely interested. It was about ten to five on a Friday afternoon, and he seemed more concerned about finding his car keys which he had lost. Eventually, he spotted them under his desk and, while diving below to grab them, he muttered that if that was what I wanted to do I'd better get on and do it. His tone was one of mild irritation – whether for wasting his time on such a trivial matter or the problem with the keys, I could not be sure.

I invited Cotentin to come over to London, which he agreed to do. I then checked the legal position, and discovered that, as a commission agent, he had some protection under French law. He would therefore be due compensation. But this would not be much since he had not achieved a great deal of business. I calculated how much he should get, rounded it up a bit, had a cheque drawn for the appropriate amount, and awaited his arrival.

Monsieur Cotentin said he would be at the office at 11 a.m. By 10.30 I had everything ready and was mentally gearing myself up to face a full-on French tantrum. Colleagues had warned me that agents tended to cut up rough when they were fired. The French were alleged to be particularly volatile.

Eleven o'clock arrived, then 11.15, then 11.30, and still no sign of Cotentin. I checked the flights from Paris. They were all arriving on time. I was getting jittery.

Monsieur Cotentin eventually arrived at around 12.20. He was slightly untidy but a pleasant-looking chap. He was most apologetic for arriving late. He explained that after he had landed at Heathrow, he had had a great need to visit, 'la toilette'.

This seemed rather a feeble excuse. So, trying not to sound sarcastic, I asked him if that had taken a long time.

Much to my surprise he said that indeed it had.

'You see,' he said, 'I got locked dans le cabinet.'

At this point all I could think of saying was:

'Golly how did you get out?' Or words to that effect in my best O Level French.

Apparently, once installed inside the loo, the door of his 'cabinet' had jammed solid. Cotentin, who spoke no English, had felt unable to call for help. After considering his predicament for some time he decided that the only way out was for him to climb out over the top of the door while at the same time leaving his briefcase on the floor in a position from which it could be extracted from underneath once he had escaped. He said that climbing over the door had been very difficult, but he had eventually succeeded: 'Et voilà', here he was, even if a bit dishevelled. That at least added veracity to his tale.

While he was explaining all of this, I was finding it extremely difficult to keep a straight face, but I did my best.

It was also not easy to get the agenda back on course which, of course, was to tell him that we wished to dispense with his services. Eventually I managed to do this, and as diplomatically as I could.

Cotentin could not have been nicer about the whole affair. There were no tantrums. He accepted the cheque for compensation most gratefully. At the end of the meeting, he was looking a bit forlorn. On the other hand, I was feeling relieved: and strangely, rather hungry. So, on the spur of the moment I asked him out to lunch. He accepted, and we went out and had a very convivial *déjeuner* in a jolly restaurant just off Marylebone High Street.

30

The Caribbean

In 1972 Dorrien relented, and I was given the Caribbean.

Imagine, if you can, a large oval bowl filled with mine-strone. The Caribbean is rather like that. In the middle, lying like misshapen carrots, are the larger islands of Cuba,

Jamaica, Puerto Rico and Hispaniola (which is divided between Haiti and the Dominican Republic). Then swirling around the outer reaches, like a stream of peas, beans, spring onions and lentils, are the lesser islands.

Over the centuries the Caribbean islands have been colonised by various countries: Spain, France, and Great Britain being the most obvious. But the Portuguese, Dutch, Danes, and Swedes were also there; and at one time the Duchy of Courland colonised Tobago. More recently the USA has, with Puerto Rico and the US Virgin Islands, acquired a considerable presence in the region.

The ownership of many islands has ebbed and flowed, mirroring the results of various European wars in the seventeenth, eighteenth and nineteenth centuries. Many different languages are spoken across the region: Spanish, English, and French being the principal ones. In the Dutch Antilles they speak Papiamento, which is an extraordinary mixture of languages based largely on Portuguese, Dutch, and others that can be traced back to West Africa. If you hear someone speak Papiamento, you will also recognise the occasional English, Spanish, or French word that will fly out of the conversation, rather like multi-coloured tracer bullets from a machine gun.

Many of the island nations had already gained independence before I got there. Haiti and the Dominican Republic had been independent since the nineteenth century, and Cuba since 1902. In the early 1960s, Britain was engaged in the process of handing independence to several islands. Jamaica and Trinidad became independent in 1962, then Barbados in 1966. These were followed by the Bahamas in 1973 and Grenada in 1974. Other small islands would be granted independence after 1978, culminating with

St Kitts and Nevis in 1983. All these island nations are members of the Commonwealth. Other very small islands such as Montserrat and the Cayman Islands have remained as British Overseas Territories. In 1972 the French islands were, and still are, overseas departments of France. And the Netherlands Antilles also remain as part of the Kingdom of the Netherlands. So, the Caribbean was, and always will be, a real 'minestrone'.

In the 1970s, during the ongoing independence programme, attitudes varied from island to island. In some there was a fair amount of animosity against white people including tourists. In others, such as Barbados, which was already independent, I found the atmosphere much more friendly.

American tourism was also getting going. In the Bahamas it was mostly of the cheap variety. It was said that the American tourists arrived, for their one-week all-inclusive package, with one shirt and one ten-dollar bill, and that during the week they did not change either. By contrast, down in Barbados, if you stayed at Sandy Lane in the high season, you could rub shoulders with the great and the good from anywhere; and for breakfast you could enjoy sublime Wiltshire sausages flown in twice a week by BOAC.

All the American cruise ships went to the US Virgin Islands. This was because the US government had decreed that when you came back to the States you could bring one gallon of duty free liquor if it came from the US Virgin Islands, but only a quarter of that amount if it was bought anywhere else. An American gallon is, of course, smaller than a British Imperial gallon but it is still the equivalent of five ordinary bottles.

Because J&B Rare was so strong in the States, we sold massive quantities in these tiny American islands. Our agent in the US Virgin Islands was Henry Eliot. The company had been founded by Henry Kimelman and Eliot Fishman; by 1972 Fishman had sold up, and Henry Kimelman was in charge. Kimelman did an amazing job for J&B Rare. He also succeeded in making the brand as popular with the local community as with visiting tourists. He enjoyed creating unusual promotions to build the brand in the local, or 'over the hill', market. As part of this campaign, we shipped him London taxis in J&B colours. We also provided him with a suitably branded Rolls-Royce van. I believe it may have been the only van Rolls ever permitted to be made. It had originally been built to transport evening gowns for the Susan Small fashion house. Once, when Henry was in London, after we had had a very convivial lunch at the Mirabelle and were on our way back to the office, we spied a whole line of double-decker buses proceeding down Oxford Street.

'What about a J&B bus?' I suggested to Henry.

'Great idea,' was his reply.

So, we got an old double-decker bus from London Transport, decorated it in J&B colours and shipped it to St Thomas (the principal of the US Virgin Islands). For a while, our double-decker J&B London bus was a huge success. But only for a while.

Until, that is, someone tried to drive it under a low bridge.

Henry Kimelman was also active in politics. In 1972 he was the finance chairman for George McGovern's presidential campaign. He was very optimistic about it, and told us that if elected, McGovern had promised him that he would make him the US Ambassador to the Court of St James. Unfortunately, McGovern was badly beaten by 'Tricky Dicky' Nixon. That was a great shame; I had been looking forward to being invited by Henry to the US Ambassador's grand residence at Winfield House in Regent's Park.

Instead, in 1980, President Carter appointed him as the US Ambassador to Haiti. Not quite the same thing as the Court of St James, but at least he did not have to travel so far to get there.

I was directly responsible for the Caribbean for only three years. I greatly enjoyed all my visits to the region. In time I managed to visit twenty different islands, including some of the smaller gems such as Grenada and St Lucia. St Barthélemy, a tiny French island, was another such. To get there I flew in a small plane from nearby St Martin. I was allowed to sit next to the pilot, a splendid man known as Monsieur Pipe on account of a pipe that, à la façon de Popeye, seemed to be glued to his teeth. As we chugged along towards St Barts (as St Barthélemy is usually known) we were confronted by a large puffy white cloud and flew straight into it. As we bounced around inside the cloud, I asked Monsieur Pipe why he hadn't gone round it:

'Waste of fuel,' was his terse reply.

We came out unscathed from the other side of the cloud and began our descent to St Barts. I could see no landing strip until we skimmed over a hill and there it was, right below us. Monsieur Pipe did a very neat side slip as we dived for the runway that was no longer than a short par 4, and which ended at a beach. Monsieur P landed us with cool dexterity, and we pulled up well before the sea. I was told that during the War he had flown Spitfires in the RAF.

Next to the landing strip in St Barts was the house of Monsieur Hippolyte Lédée, a grand old man and a

144

well-respected trader. St Barts had not been 'discovered' when I went there, so Monsieur Lédée supplemented his meagre local trade by selling whisky to boats from Venezuela.

One important island that I never visited was Cuba. I was sad about that but since Castro prohibited the importation of Scotch whisky, I was unable to contrive a reason to go there.

The Scotch whisky business in the region was another minestrone. The local markets were divided between varying ethnic tastes, all overlaid by Hispanic, American, British, French, Dutch, and other cultures. And in addition to the local markets and the tourist business there was also a lot of smuggling conducted from various islands towards the mainland of South and Central America as well as to Mexico. So quite different brands had pockets of strength in different market segments. On top of that, the traders themselves varied from the dynamic and honest (rare), to the lackadaisically supine (not so rare), and to some that sailed close to the wind and who, had they lived in the seventeenth century, could easily have been pirates. I enjoyed it all.

And there was a wonderful island-hopping airline that covered the territory. It was LIAT (Leeward Islands Air Transport Services). At the time they were flying BAC 1-11 aircraft from the British Aircraft Corporation. The BAC 1-11 was a small jet, powered by two Rolls-Royce rear-mounted Spey engines. It particularly appealed to me because of the natty steps which could be lowered or retracted automatically from the forward section of the fuselage. This was quite a novelty, and particularly useful in the Caribbean where the vigour of the ground crews could not be relied upon. Sometimes you had to wait ages in the midday heat for someone to finish their rum punch before wheeling out the steps and letting you off. LIAT also employed stunning hostesses. They were all from the islands and wore the tightest of uniforms in hot tropical colours. Travelling on LIAT was always a pleasure.

31

Hispaniola

Hispaniola is the second-largest island in the Caribbean and comprises the two countries of Haiti in the west and the Dominican Republic to the east. I found both markets intriguing, and for different reasons.

Haiti was a very small market for Scotch whisky, but I had read *The Comedians* by Graham Greene and was fascinated. Their supremely malevolent dictator, Papa Doc, had died the year before my first visit. He had been replaced by his playboy son, Jean-Claude, better known as Baby Doc.

François Duvalier was called Papa Doc because he had trained as a doctor. But once he became president, the Hippocratic Oath is something that must have slipped his memory. You will recall that it was he who had the head of a rebel put on ice and presented to him. He had wanted to commune with the spirit of his victim. Papa Doc ruled Haiti from 1957 until his death in 1971. During his 'reign' a great many people disappeared and were said to have been killed by his *Volontaires de la Sécurité Nationale*, otherwise known as the Tonton Macoute.

When I got to Port-au-Prince, I was met at the airport by our agent, Najeeb Indonie. In the taxi on the way to his office, I stupidly asked him if the Tonton Macoute were still in operation. Putting his finger to his lips, Najeeb signalled to me that it was best not to raise such subjects anywhere remotely public. Later he told me that after the death of Papa Doc, the Tonton Macoute had morphed into the Léopards who, he said, were just as bad.

Najeeb was a lovely man from a Lebanese family. He explained that the market for Scotch whisky in Haiti was extremely small because duties were high and the country very poor. The market was limited almost entirely to the diplomatic corps, though the Haitian military and police did like to smuggle in further quantities from the Bahamas or Miami. He represented a wide mix of overseas companies, mostly from outside the liquor trade. They included Johnson & Johnson as well as a margarine company, a jewellery range, and cheap shoes from the British Shoe Corporation. Apparently, many of the supermarkets were run by Lebanese. Najeeb was trading, as best he could, in very difficult circumstances. For J&B Rare, he certainly did as well as could have been expected.

My memory of Port-au-Prince is now dimmed by time, but I remember an extraordinary mixture of dirt, poverty, and colour. Bougainvillea was in flower everywhere, especially at the Hotel Oloffson. In *The Comedians* the hotel had been portrayed as the Trianon. It was where I stayed.

In 1973 Najeeb visited us in London. He was only here for a day. In the morning he had an appointment with the British Shoe Corporation. I was due to see him in the afternoon. But at about 11.00 he called sounding upset and at a loose end. So, I invited him out to lunch. He had been to meet his contact at the mighty shoe company and given them an order for a full, twenty-foot shipping container of shoes. To me that sounded like an awful lot of footwear: something for which they should have been ecstatic, and then taken him out for a slap-up celebration lunch. Instead, they gave him a cup of lukewarm tea, and a stale biscuit; then they sent him on his way. He was understandably underwhelmed by the British Shoe Corporation's interpretation of Harold Wilson's exhortation to 'export or die'.

So, I gave him a decent lunch, and hopefully managed to redeem our nation's reputation for hospitality. On our way back to the office, we passed the window of Charbonnel et Walker in Bond Street. I told him that they sold the best chocolates in town, at which point Najeeb stopped in his tracks and said he wanted to buy some. So, in we went. There was a truly enormous box on display in the window. It was a round box, and about a yard wide. To my astonishment, Najeeb said, quite nonchalantly, that he wanted to buy it. The pretty assistant said that he could not have 'that one' because, in all honesty, the chocolates in it were not fresh. She indicated that if he came back later, Monsieur Charbonnel and Mister Walker would spend the intervening time working tirelessly to fill another one for him, just like it, but with super-fresh chocolates. Najeeb agreed to come back and collect it after his meeting with me.

'What on earth are you going to do with a box of chocolates that size?' I asked him as we left the shop.

'Oh, I'm going on to Switzerland tomorrow,' he replied rather airily, 'I have a sister there.'

Of all places, I thought Switzerland a distinctly odd place as a destination for chocolates. I put it down to some sort of Haitian Lebanese eccentricity. Like a Geordie suddenly getting an urge to buy a wagon load of coal in Wales and cart it home to Newcastle.

That evening Isabel and I took Najeeb out to dinner. When we picked him up, he was carrying what looked like a cartwheel, except that it was wrapped, and swathed in ribbons and bows. It was, of course, Messieurs Charbonnel et Walker's biggest and best. Najeeb presented it to Isabel.

I believe it was Eddie Tatham who appointed Victor Jorge to be our agent for the Dominican Republic. Both André and Dorrien would have recoiled aghast at the idea that either of them might have made such an appointment.

Victor liked to live life to the full, especially if it involved sailing close to the wind. If he had been living in the seventeenth century, he might have been a pirate. He had a drooping moustache, rather in the mode of Che, was bandy legged, usually wore cowboy boots, and sometimes carried a revolver. Everybody disapproved of him, but they enjoyed his company.

Rafael Leónidas Trujillo had ruled the Dominican Republic from 1930 to 1961. His 'reign' had been relatively stable. But he was a despot of the unenlightened variety. He bled the country to enrich himself and his cronies. He was brutal to opponents.

Trujillo is infamous for the 1937 'Parsley Massacre'. At the time there were a large number of very poor Haitians living in the northwest of the country, near to the border with Haiti. Trujillo deemed them unruly and disruptive. He was probably right, but he decided on a vicious programme of ethnic cleansing. The problem in getting rid of them was that it was difficult to distinguish whether they were local or from Haiti. They didn't have things like 'papers' in those days. Unfortunately, the Haitians (who speak creole French) found great difficulty in rolling their Rs. So, a sprig of parsley would be held before a suspect and he, or she, would be invited to say what it was in Spanish. If they could not roll the R in *perejil* (the Spanish word for parsley) they were condemned. Estimates of those who were brutally killed in the Parsley Massacre vary between 12,000 and 35,000.

For many years, the Americans supported Trujillo. They considered him the lesser of two evils, the alternative being a communist takeover. But in 1960 Trujillo tried to have President Betancourt of Venezuela assassinated during the annual Army Day Parade in Caracas. The attempt was unsuccessful. For the Americans this was the last straw, and they withdrew their support for Trujillo.

In 1961 Trujillo was himself assassinated.

There followed four years of unrest and a civil war between leftist factions and the right-wing military. In 1965, after a leftist revolt, Lyndon Johnson launched Operation Power Pack. He sent in the Marines and 82nd Airborne Division. 'We don't,' he said, 'propose to sit here in our rocking chair with our hands folded and let the Communists set up any government in the Western Hemisphere.'

He did not want a second Cuba.

The US occupation lasted until fair elections could be held. In 1966 Joaquín Balaguer was elected as the new president.

I do not know when Victor Jorge was appointed, but I suspect it was back in 1959 before the troubles started. Anyway, by 1962 Victor had signed a five-year contract to supply the armed forces of the Dominican Republic with alcoholic beverages. The sales would be made to the military *cantinas* which, as I have explained elsewhere, were a common feature in many Latin American countries.

For a while everything went well. Shipments were made and payments were received. Then the payments began to slow up. Victor reassured us that everything was fine and sent in more orders. We shipped these orders. They amounted to some 8,000 cases of J&B Rare, a considerable volume in those days, and with a commensurate value. As a precaution, these consignments were shipped on payment terms of cash against documents. This meant that the *cantinas* could not obtain the documents that would be needed to withdraw the whisky from the custom's warehouse in Santo Domingo (the capital) until it had been paid for. So, there should have been no problem. Should have been ...

The consignments were shipped at the end of 1963. Several months later they were still lying in-bond in Santo Domingo. Presumably, the forces' *cantinas* were short of cash. This, of course, was during the period between the assassination of Trujillo and the arrival of the 82nd Airborne Division: a time of considerable unrest.

At some point in 1964, an enterprising officer from the Dominican Republic's ruling military class gave an unwelcome display of Latin initiative. Ignoring the documents in the bank, he went to the warehouse, loaded up a line of military trucks with our whisky, and drove off with the whole lot. He did at least sign for what had been taken. Unfortunately, the warehouse, complete with all its records, was burnt down during the 1965 April Revolution.

In early 1966, after the new Balaguer government had made some encouraging pronouncements about paying outstanding debts, Dorrien made a visit to Santo Domingo to obtain settlement of our debt. Victor had arranged for him to see the Air Force Colonel who had placed the orders. They were due to meet the Colonel at the Air Force Base, but when they got there the Colonel had just left. Later in the afternoon they tracked him down. In his report Dorrien described what happened next:

Victor drove me to an area, where the houses were very primitive, with native children running about naked. We bumped over the unmade-up roads, full of potholes, and shortly came upon a house behind whose gates there lurked an Air Force staff car. This turned out to be where the Colonel's mistress lived, and I wondered if it was prudent to call just at that moment. Victor, however, had no qualms, and a few moments later, the Colonel appeared, rather dishevelled and in a dressing gown. One would not have thought that the question of the J&B debt was uppermost in his mind, but there was no escape from Victor, who plunged into a long discussion in Spanish, emphasising again and again that I had come all the way specifically to collect our money. The Colonel suggested that we meet the newly appointed General Chief of Staff and said he would try and arrange it. He slipped away and returned shortly afterwards resplendent in his Air Force uniform, complete with pistol and ammunition.

We drove away past signs such as, 'Go home Yankees' and 'Balaguer por Presidente', and back onto the main road, where an enormous brown sow suddenly trotted across the road, causing some desperate braking. These animals are not, however, the only hazards, as traffic lights do not exist, and most drivers feel that the safest way to get across an intersection is at high speed. This probably accounted for two of the three accidents we saw that day.

Dorrien and Victor did see the General who, having kept them waiting for an hour and a half, explained that all Army and Air Force Canteen accounts had been frozen pending a full investigation of the debts incurred. He suggested that J&B compile a full dossier to back up the claim. He said

153

that now that he was in charge, all guilty parties would be hounded down, and everything would be run honestly. He assured Dorrien that J&B's claim would be considered with all the rest. There were twenty-three other liquor debts but ours was the largest.

The dossier was compiled and sent, but no progress had been made by the time I became involved. This, I thought, would be a great opportunity for me. If I could get the debt paid it would be a real feather in my cap.

André came with me on my first visit to Santo Domingo. Victor had arranged an appointment for us all to meet the Chief of Staff, an Air Force General, who was in charge of evaluating all debts incurred by the armed forces.

After a briefing meeting at the British Embassy on the first day of our visit, we set out early on the second morning for the San Isidro Air Force base. The General was in residence and received us in an enormous office. He was sitting behind a vast desk, and the whole place was festooned with flags, signed photographs and model aeroplanes. We sat before him trying to look like Uriah Heep on collection day.

The General listened carefully to our case and promised us that if we could compile another dossier with all the relevant documents, he personally would take it to the president and seek authorisation for its settlement. We felt encouraged. Hopefully, we would at last get paid. Victor could then receive the agent's commission due from those orders, so he too was enthused.

In 1970 Balaguer had been re-elected and the economy was beginning to recover from the traumas of three decades under Trujillo, as well as from the ensuing five years of civil unrest. Happily, the Dominican Republic has remained democratic ever since. Furthermore, I understand that in the past twenty-five years the country has boasted the fastest-growing economy in the Western Hemisphere, much of this growth being driven by tourism, underpinned by gold mining.

But in the early seventies the country was still struggling. We had to impose strict payment terms for all ongoing business. Victor was a tremendous salesman and built a reasonable level of trade for us. But visiting him was always a challenge. He loved taking you out on the tiles to visit as many of his customers as possible. His client portfolio was extremely varied, a lot of them not being the sort of places to which you could go with a maiden aunt in tow.

On my visits to Santo Domingo, I used to stay at the Hotel Embajador, then a rather ugly brick-shaped block. I have an abiding memory of the doorman. He was a giant, and rather lugubrious, though not unfriendly. He wore a crumpled green uniform. It looked as if he slept in it, which he probably did. With Victor in charge, getting back to the hotel at 3 a.m. was quite normal. And whether it was returning at 3 a.m. or leaving at 9 a.m. or 2 p.m., our big friendly giant was always there to see you out of, or into, Victor's old Mercedes.

And what about the debt you may be asking? Alas I did no better than Dorrien. I tried and tried but got nowhere. The experience left me with a profound admiration for the Latin American art of being able to fob you off with a wonderful mixture of false expectation and charm.

32

Dorrien's Boys

I think it was Claude Fourmon who coined the epithet 'Dorrien's Boys'. They did not know it at the time, but both Claude and Dorrien had been in the same German prisoner-of-war camp during World War II. As a young army officer, Dorrien had been captured at Dunkirk in 1940. He was to spend the next five years as a POW.

Claude was a director of Moët et Chandon, who were our agents in France. Within Moët, he was responsible for J&B Rare in the early days of the relationship. It was through this connection that he and Dorrien discovered their shared POW background. In 1963 Dorrien had joined J&B from Harveys of Bristol; and it was from that time that he started to build his team of 'Boys' to facilitate the growth of the brand beyond America.

As the area director for Latin America, I was one of those 'Boys'. The other area directors were Derek Plunkett for Africa, Asia, and the Middle East; Wyndham Carver for France, Spain, Italy, and Greece; and Robert Cecil for the rest of Europe. Henry Crichton-Stuart was the director for Europe, and Malcolm Burr was the managing director.

Neither Henry nor Malcolm had any experience of Latin America, so for a while I reported directly to Dorrien. This suited me very well. Dorrien believed in giving responsibility to his managers. At first his attitude, almost of disinterest, was a bit of a shock. But it taught me a lot: principally to think for myself, and very carefully too, before making any big decision. There was the awkward moment when I reduced the territory of an agent in the French Antilles. This agent then wrote an angry six-page letter, all in French, directly to Dorrien accusing me of being ignorant (possibly true) and arrogant (hopefully not) and of having made an impertinent and ill-considered decision. After reading this diatribe, I was beginning to think I was in the soup until Dorrien's secretary gave me a copy of his reply. It was short and succinct; and smacked the plaintiff's beamer straight back over the pavilion for six.

Later I was asked to report to first Malcolm, and then Henry. Whereas Dorrien was big on strategy and uninterested in the tactics, Malcolm and Henry took more interest in the detail. They were always very helpful and supportive, but when Henry asked for copies of all my letters, I began to miss Dorrien's detached management style.

In 1973 changes took place. First Henry left; then Malcolm moved within the IDV group to take control of all their wine businesses. He was replaced by James Bruxner who had, for the previous three years, been running the Gilbey export business. Before that, James had been with Mather and Crowther, a top advertising agency.

At 6 foot 5, James cut an imposing figure. Happily, his management style was more akin to that of Dorrien's, though he did take a bit more all-round interest than Dorrien had. He was just the right person to take up and direct Dorrien's vision to make J&B Rare a global brand. Dorrien retired in 1978 and James was to remain my boss for the ensuing fifteen years. I could not have been luckier.

After he took over from Malcolm, James instigated a regional reshuffle. He offered Latin America and the Caribbean to Wyndham. Robert was offered Africa, and Derek was to remain in charge of the Far East. For my part, James offered me Europe. Robert was not enthusiastic about Africa. He received an enticing offer to join Berry Brothers & Rudd, who at the time owned Cutty Sark, so, sadly, he left J&B and joined Cutty Sark in 1974.

I remember discussing the offer of Europe with Dick Matthews. Dick was the Latin American area director for Beefeater Gin. We shared several common agents; the Mottas in Panama and Harry Davidson in Colombia are two that I recall. Dick was an immensely congenial contact and we used to get together every so often for lunch and to compare notes about our markets. The gin and tonics they served at the Beefeater Distillery behind the Oval cricket ground were spectacular. I think it was because the usual ratio of gin to tonic was reversed.

Talking of gin reminds me of his story about the old veteran who worked at the distillery. He had lost a leg in the War but would arrive in good and sprightly order for work every morning. During the day, his prosthetic tin leg would start to bother him – or so thought his managers, as 'poor old Joe' limped out of the gates on his way home every evening. Little did they know that he limped because, during the day, his hollow leg had been filled with gin.

Returning to Dick, who simply loved his Latin America territory: he thought I was completely bonkers to even think of giving it up. In truth, the potential for Europe was much greater. Markets like Italy and France were really beginning to catch fire for J&B Rare. It was a head or heart decision. Despite Dick's protestations, and some sadness, I was very happy to accept James's offer.

33

The Port Game

When I joined J&B in 1970, the export office for the whisky business was in an elegant Nash building at 1 York Gate on the south side of Regent's Park. Today the building houses the Royal Academy of Music, but then it was IDV's headquarters, and we were on the ground floor. J&B's fine wine business had already moved from Bond Street to St James's Street in 1964. Although the two sections of the business were physically separated, there remained a strong bond between them; a bond that was nurtured by Dorrien who was chairman of the whole company and had a great love of fine wine.

At St James's Street, J&B have a splendid dining room which they use to entertain important customers and members of the wine trade. One morning, shortly after I joined, they put through an SOS call to us at export. They had an important lunch that day, but a couple of people had cancelled; could we send down reinforcements? I was delegated to go: no hardship, because I knew the food would be excellent and the wines of the best.

The lunch was hosted by Dick Bridgeman, and the guest of honour was Michael Broadbent. Dick, who was a director of J&B, had a huge circle of friends and brought a great deal of trade to the wine side of the company. Michael was one

159

of the earliest Masters of Wine: the top qualification in the wine trade. In 1966 he had moved from Harveys of Bristol to Christie's and had restarted their wine auctions. Michael was becoming famous for his book, *Wine Tasting*, which had been published in 1968. His star was in the ascendant.

Lunches at J&B were, and doubtless still are, famous for the Port Game. At the end of lunch an unknown vintage port was served from a decanter. Only John Kelly, the delightful, soft-spoken Irish cellarman, knew what it was. After decanting the wine, he would have put the cork in a sealed envelope and given it to the host. The cork would, of course, have been branded with the wine's vintage and the name of the shipper.

The object of the game is to identify the port, both the vintage and the shipper. There are over twenty shippers who produce and ship port. On average they 'declare' about three vintages in every decade: these being the years when the best wine is produced and then bottled as vintage port. So, if you are presented with an unknown glass of vintage port, it requires a lot of skill, or luck, to identify the year it was made and who shipped it. But, in the Port Game, that is what you must do. You are allowed to write your answer on a piece of paper, and only have to display it if you get the answer right. If you are completely wrong, you do not have to suffer the indignity of showing how far out you are in your assessment. To play the game you must ante-up some cash. It was ten shillings in 1970. There is therefore a cash prize if you get the right answer. If nobody can identify the correct vintage, the money goes to a trade charity. This happens quite often.

On this auspicious occasion Michael Broadbent was taking the Port Game very seriously. He sniffed and slurped assiduously; then after a while he declared that he had a pretty good idea what it was but would need to check his tasting notes before deciding. He then got up and went off to consult the records in his office at Christie's, just round the corner. This attracted a good deal of banter and ridicule from Dick, all of which Michael ignored and went anyway. After consulting his archives, he returned from Christie's looking quite satisfied and wrote down his answer.

We all awaited the denouement.

Dick now opened John Kelly's envelope and squinted at the cork. He then asked if anybody thought our port was from the fifties. Nobody stirred. He then said:

'What about the thirties?' A couple of hands were raised.

'Bad luck,' said Dick, 'and now what about the forties?' At which point several hands were confidently raised, including Michael's.

'Oh dear,' said Dick, 'I'm afraid not. Anybody left?'

At this point I tentatively raised my hand.

'Are you in the twenties or sixties – or something else?' asked Dick.

'Twenties,' said I, rather nervously.

'Which year?' barked Dick.

'27,' me.

'Which shipper?' Dick.

'Fonseca,' me.

'Blimey,' declared Dick, 'the new boy is spot on.'

So, Fonseca 1927 was what it was. The wine did have the brownish look of considerable age. There was also a distinct whiff of prunes on the nose. Geoffrey Gibbon, who was next to me, told me that this was a characteristic of wines from Fonseca. So somewhat on an eeny-meeny-miny-moe basis I had contrived to arrive at the right answer.

Poor Michael got ribbed mercilessly for his note-book-checking antics, and then being twenty years out on his assessment. He took it very well, and generously congratulated me on my winning coup without once mentioning that it was a complete fluke, which of course it was.

The dining room at St James's Street was to serve us well. Major overseas agents and buyers of whisky did not expect the brands of whisky that they sold to have a fine wine connection, but, when exposed to it, they were impressed by our 'pedigree'. We once hosted the top buyers from a major French supermarket chain at St James's Street. Moët brought them over in their private jet. We served them what they themselves said were the best French wines they had ever had. We did not mention whisky once, but afterwards we climbed aboard Moët's Mystère 20 and flew to Speyside to visit our whisky distilleries – only after playing the Port Game.

Before closing this section and getting to work on Europe, I should tell you a bit more about Dick Bridgeman. Dick was a great sportsman and a champion racquets player. He was also adept at writing humorous verse and carrying out practical jokes. The butt of these jokes was often Ronnie Lambert.

In the 1950s J&B had taken over Chalié Richards, another well-known wine merchant. Colonel Ronnie Lambert was one of the directors who came across to J&B from Chalié Richards. He had been in the Grenadier Guards and had been awarded the Military Cross in World War I. His knowledge of port and claret was said to be unsurpassed. I never met him, but he was remembered with great fondness by those at J&B who did. Polly Preston (née Marriott) who had once been Dick's secretary, has very kindly sent

me the following account of an elaborate prank that Dick
once played on Ronnie:

*THE ex-QUEEN SOPHIA OF SERBIA – I have been
thinking back [writes Polly] about this and how she was
tied up with Ronnie's appearance in a TV programme
called The Name's The Same. Dick created Queen Sophia
in order to expand and nurture the fan mail which had
resulted from Ronnie's TV appearance.*

*Quite a long, and increasingly romantic correspondence
developed [Ronnie was single], using a London address
belonging to a pal of Dick's, as the ex-Queen's abode, and
from which her letters were posted. Of course, it was me
who typed them.*

*As the correspondence blossomed, Ronnie asked for ever
more details about the Queen, her family, and so on. Dick
went to a lot of trouble to give her an impeccably researched
Central European pedigree, well laced with European
lesser royals and aristocrats, which we posted back to him.
Of course, he swallowed the whole thing hook, line, and
sinker and brought it into our office with great pride to
show off his royal conquest's grand parentage.*

*The correspondence progressed to the point at which the
Queen sent Ronnie a formal invitation to a lunch party. At
the bottom of the invitation it said, 'Medals will be Worn'.*

*This put Ronnie in an awful dither as his old WWI
medals were now (early sixties) in a pretty sorry state,
so he had to send them off in a hurry to Garrard's to be
cleaned and re-mounted; all at breakneck speed to be ready
for the occasion.*

*They were returned only for Ronnie to discover that
his MC had been put back on the medal bar in the wrong*

place! Of course, there wasn't any time for them to be redone so we had to convince him that an ex-Queen of a central European state wasn't likely to be bothered about the layout of his medals.

Having created the lunch party, Dick then had the problem of working out how on earth he was actually going to produce an ex-Queen for him to dine with. So, he asked an old actress friend of his to meet us one evening to discuss the possibility of her pretending to be the Queen. I can't remember her name, but she was a delightful, very sprightly, seventies plus old lady whom Dick knew well, and she was tickled pink at the idea of being brought out of retirement as an ex-Queen. I was roped in to go along and meet her, and to discuss 'arrangements' for the party. We, all three, had a very jolly evening discussing how we were going to carry it off.

In the end Ralph Cobbold or ET finally decided that enough was enough and that it really was going too far to actually go ahead with it. I think we decided that the Queen should either be confined to bed with a chill or unexpectedly recalled to her European home in the Swiss Alps, or some such unlikely excuse. I can't remember how we cancelled it, but we did manage to call the whole thing off, much to Ronnie's chagrin.

Dick, usually, but not always, got the better of Ronnie. If he wasn't lunching in, Ronnie would usually go to the Guards Club where he would meet up with other old warriors and, after a slap-up lunch, totter back to the office. If there was a lunch still going on in the dining room, it was not unknown for him to poke his nose in and scrounge a glass of port. If Dick was there, he would always ask him to guess what it was: and very often Ronnie would know. As I said before, his knowledge of port was amazing. On one occasion Dick tried to fool him by mixing two vintages. The two ports in question were from the same shipper but from vintages of differing styles: something like Graham's 1912 and 1917 perhaps.

On being confronted with this 'blend' Ronnie had a good sniff at the bouquet, looked a bit perplexed then took a nice generous mouthful only to look more perplexed. After repeating this routine, he confessed that he was mystified. He felt sure it was from Graham's but could not, he said, make out whether it was a Graham's from 1912 or 1917. At which point Dick had to concede that Ronnie had just clean bowled him.

34

Europe: Beginning with Spain

I took over responsibility for Europe in the autumn of 1974. From here on, the truly *Beamonesque* story is going to be about how J&B Rare conquered Spain. It is a good story, and my plan is to tell you about it at some length. I have previously recorded this story for Diageo in a booklet entitled *Rare Spanish Oak*, so I am able to draw from that script. But in case you get bored or think there is too much about Spain I shall, every so often, take a break and wander elsewhere.

By way of tapas, it might be best to set down how the J&B Rare acorn had been planted in Spain. This was several years before my arrival on the scene.

In the 1960s when petrol stayed down at $3 a barrel, and hemlines rose inexorably to pelmet level, European economies were clambering out of the World War II graveyard and people were starting to think about having a good time. So, fuelled by Carnaby Street, and to the tunes of the Beatles from Liverpool, London became the 'Swinging City'. All of this is true. But what people forget is that while today's affluent throwaway economy was on its way, it had not yet arrived. Mothers still knitted jerseys and darned socks. In England nobody put olive oil on a salad: it was much too exotic and expensive to eat. Olive oil was what granny bought at the chemist in tiny phials, and used to ease the wax out of little Jimmy's grubby ears.

Instead, the new culinary exotica for the British middle classes was the avocado pear. Of course, in Spain the situation was the reverse. Olive oil and avocados were two-a-penny. Scotch whisky, on the other hand, was a real luxury and was something that only the upper classes could afford. In those days Spain was ruled by Franco. The country was poor. The urchins I met in Andalucía, back in 1964, were barefoot, and the well-shod upper middle classes were in a very small minority. Consequently, sales of Scotch whisky were extremely modest. In 1965 shipments of Scotch whisky to Spain were only 253,000 cases. In time, J&B alone would ship over ten times that amount to Spain.

The Spanish government viewed Scotch whisky as a foreign luxury that competed with local spirits, so importation was discouraged. Scotch attracted high import duties, and volumes were contained within a quota system. This all helped to suppress sales. But it worked wonders for the image of Scotch. It was seen as something foreign, something luxurious, something difficult to get – and therefore something highly desirable. Spaniards were beginning to know about Scotch whisky and to want it. The trouble was that for a new brand like J&B Rare it was not easy to find an importer.

We needed a good contact.

I have already mentioned Ralph Cobbold, and how he was a man of many contacts. He had earned a Blue for cricket at Cambridge. He was a true sportsman and an inveterate gambler. He was also a man of military bearing who had had a 'good war'. If ET was the man who opened the door for J&B Rare in America, it was Ralph Cobbold who found the key to Spain.

With his sporting background and wide circle of friends, many in high places, Ralph Cobbold was a man who did not mince his words. And sometimes his contacts did not always live up to his expectations. There was the famous occasion when J&B had been asked to supply a sample of white Burgundy to White's Club in St James's. The man who headed the club's wine committee had an important ceremonial position in the Royal Household at Buckingham Palace. I do not know his name but, for the purpose of this tale, let us call him Freddie.

Now Freddie was well known to Ralph and, since the wine sample was a real cracker, Ralph felt that he was onto a dead cert. So, when his secretary said she had Freddie on the line Ralph got ready to note down a large order. Picture then his astonishment when Freddie informed him that a competitor's sample had been deemed superior to his. Astonishment quickly turned to rage. Taking a firm grip on the Bakelite, Ralph yelled back down the line: 'The trouble with you Freddie is you've been licking the boots of royalty for so long you've lost the taste for good wine,' before slamming the receiver back on its cradle.

I am told that many years passed before J&B got another order from White's.

Fortunately, Ralph's contacts were not always so disastrous. One of his friends was a man called Ralph Sassoon. I do not know much about Ralph Sassoon but, since he was a friend of Ralph Cobbold, I think it is safe to assume that his connections were of the racing and banking sort. I can only surmise that one day over a glass of decent port our Ralph may have asked the other Ralph if he knew of anyone in Spain who could do a good job for J&B Rare. Now Ralph Sassoon happened to know a man called Ricardo Sicre, and he thought that he might be just the man for the job. Although he did not appreciate it at the time, by forging this introduction Ralph Sassoon was giving Ralph Cobbold a golden key.

Ralph Cobbold retired from the company in 1968. He had not found the new world of IDV entirely to his liking.

Ricardo Sicre was one of the world's great contact men. A man of immense charm and considerable intellect, his network of friends took in the worlds of art, cinema, politics, high society, and business. He had the ability to make you feel important and could remember, in detail, the circumstances of previous meetings. Beneath his polished persona there was also a touch of steel. Ricardo liked to get his way. He usually did.

While I was at J&B I had the good fortune to meet one or two quite famous people. Pelé, Ronald Reagan, and the Queen are a few of the names I could drop. While I vividly remember meeting them, I would be amazed if any of them remembered meeting me.

With Ricardo Sicre it was not like that. He knew people as diverse as Prince Rainier of Monaco and Ernest Hemingway. And they knew him. James Bruxner was lunching with Ricardo at the Mirabelle on one occasion when Ava Gardner came up to their table and said:

'Ricardo what are you doing here in London? I haven't seen you for ages.'

When Isabel and I stayed in Ricardo's flat in Monte Carlo, the walls of his apartment were splattered with works by the likes of Picasso and Salvador Dalí, all bearing personal inscriptions to their dear amigo Ricardo. On another occasion when we visited Ricardo on his yacht, Juan Antonio Samaranch, the long-term president of the International Olympic Committee, was a guest on board.

Ricardo was the son of a country doctor in Catalonia. The story goes that at the end of the Spanish Civil War, after fighting for the Republicans in the *Esquerra Republicana de Catalunya*, he escaped with a friend, first to France and then to London. One day the two of them were sitting in a Chelsea pub bemoaning the fact that their money was running out and they did not know what to do. They were conversing in Catalan. They assumed that nobody would understand them. They were wrong. After a while, a man came over to their table. Apologising for eavesdropping, he said that he had been following their conversation; he had a great love of Catalonia and would try and help them if he could. He could and he did – and his name was Robert Graves, the celebrated novelist and poet. Robert Graves managed to find some form of employment for both Ricardo and his friend. However, after a while Ricardo moved to America. On arrival he was detained by the authorities and given the choice of being sent back to Spain or joining the OSS (Office for Strategic Services), which was the precursor of the CIA. He chose the latter.

In 1943 Ricardo returned to Europe for the rest of the War. As an accomplished linguist (he spoke English, French, and Italian as well as Spanish and Catalan), Ricardo was used for espionage work in North Africa, Spain, and France. It was in France that he met his wife, Betty Lussier. She had been born in Canada and raised in the States, and since her father had flown for the Royal Flying Corps in

World War I, she had learned to fly at a young age. In 1942 she came to England and enlisted as an ATA (Air Transport Auxiliary) girl. ATA girls were used during the War to ferry all manner of aircraft from the manufacturers to their squadrons, or back for repairs. After the D-Day landings, disgusted to find that female pilots were not allowed to deliver Spitfires or any other aircraft into France, she resigned and joined the OSS. She met Ricardo when they were both working in the South of France as counter-intelligence agents. As the Germans retreated, they succeeded in uncovering a network of Nazi agents.

Back in Spain after the War, Ricardo joined the World Commerce Corporation, an American import-export company. WCC may also have been a cover for ongoing OSS or CIA surveillance because several of Ricardo's old OSS colleagues were involved. Ricardo used this time to build up a network of important contacts. Amongst his contacts was the Ullivarri family.

The more you look into the history of J&B Rare, the more you will realise that at each phase of the brand's development a significant portion of its success was generated by a small number of rather special individuals. Rafael Ullivarri was to become a colossal star within that firmament.

Ullivarri is a Basque name, and the family comes from Bilbao in the North of Spain. In 'our' Ullivarri family there were three brothers: Fernando, José Angel, and Rafael, the hero of this story, who was the youngest. In 1958 Rafael had been sent to America to learn about banking. He spent a couple of years in New York with Chase Manhattan. Then, in 1959, he returned to Spain and married Maribel. For a while he worked in Bilbao as the manager of an automotive distributor. Rafael has written his own excellent account of the J&B Rare story in Spain, and I must thank him for giving me a lot of information that would otherwise have been difficult to unearth.

Rafael recounted how in 1962, the three brothers, together with Ricardo Sicre, met and decided to create the GECEPSA company. Fernando was elected as the president and the other three were appointed as directors, with Rafael also taking on the role of general manager. The objective of the company was to look for import or export opportunities. One suggestion was whisky. Of course, the economy was still weak, and the importation of Scotch whisky was strictly limited by quota. However, there was strong demand and consequently margins were very high. Scotch whisky looked like a good opportunity provided they could first secure the rights to import a brand, and then get an allocation within the quota system. Ricardo, with his many contacts, agreed to see what he could do to find a brand. Thus, while the Ullivarris were hunting from one end, J&B were searching from the other.

J&B Rare was an unknown brand in Spain but when Ricardo told the brothers that he had a contact who could open a door for them at J&B, Rafael jumped at the idea. He had seen for himself how well J&B Rare was doing in New York. As I mentioned before, it was Ralph Sassoon who formed the bridge across which Ralph Cobbold and Ricardo Sicre eventually made contact.

Thus, on an auspicious day in 1963 Ricardo took Rafael to the J&B offices in Bond Street to meet Ralph Cobbold and Dorrien Belson. Ralph gave them a brief overview; it was the year that sales of J&B Rare to the USA first reached one million cases. However, sales to other markets were of no significance at all. Ralph then delegated the rest of the commercial discussion to Rafael and Dorrien while he and Ricardo settled down to chat about the prospects for the forthcoming grouse season. That's the way business was done in those days.

The meeting between Rafael and Dorrien was a success. Dorrien would doubtless have explained all about the 'Tiffany trade' marketing philosophy. When in New York, Rafael had, in addition to his training at Chase Manhattan, done a marketing course. The idea of pricing up to sell more (rather than less) instantly appealed to Rafael's newly acquired banking and marketing pedigree.

Within a short space of time the first shipments were made: 100 cases each to Madrid, Barcelona, and Palma de Mallorca. Work could then begin to seed J&B Rare in the best watering holes of these cities. I understand that in the early days Ralph Sassoon was also a shareholder in GECEPSA. He and the other four directors therefore each had 20 per cent of the equity. I only met Ralph Sassoon once. It was at a cocktail party in the early 1980s. By then J&B Rare was beginning to go like a train. Unfortunately, Sassoon had sold his shareholding in GECEPSA to the other four partners a few years before. He was quite grumpy when I told him how well the brand was now doing – thereby tactlessly reminding him that he had sold far too early.

Now before we get too stuck into Spain, we ought to make an important detour to Italy.

35

Intermezzo in Italia

In 1974 J&B had two agents who were given godlike status by one and all. The first was Abe Rosenberg, whose company The Paddington Corporation, was our agent in America. The other agent with top status was Nino Bandini. His first name was really Gaetano, but Dorrien and James called him Nino. Everyone else called him Mr Bandini. He was our first agent to make a success of J&B Rare outside America. He had proved that it could be done.

We did not find Bandini. He found us. In 1959, when his initial approach had been ignored, he had flown to London and harangued ET until he was allowed to place a trial order for fifty cases. From that very small start he never looked back.

I do not know a lot about Bandini's background. As a young man towards the end of World War II, he was, I understand, active within the partisan movement. After the War he set himself up as a wholesaler dealing in a variety of goods, including toys. When I first met him, his sole activity was the import and distribution of various drinks brands. Chief among these were J&B Rare, Grand Marnier, and Bollinger.

In the early 1960s, IDV had done some market research in Italy. The Gilbey side of IDV had another whisky brand called Black Prince that was to be distributed by Cinzano. IDV wanted to know which brand to invest in, and decided to find out if Italian consumers would prefer Black Prince or J&B Rare. The consumers they asked liked Black Prince. They did not like J&B Rare. They thought the off-yellow colour of the label revolting, the whisky too pale, and the name unpronounceable. Do not forget that in Italian the letter J does not exist. Giacomo Justerini, the man from Bologna who founded Justerini & Brooks in 1749, must have had his name anglicised. Originally, he was Giusterini.

Fortunately, Belson had his strategic vision: to make J&B Rare a global brand. He ignored the research, side-stepped the Gilbey faction, and placed the money on J&B Rare. After all, market research will only tell you what the consumer is thinking today: not what they might be persuaded to think in the future. For his part, Bandini was looking for a distinctive brand of whisky. He wanted something different, and of higher quality than the run-of-the-mill whisky from the DCL. His thinking dove-tailed with ours, and his timing was perfect. He got round the J problem by getting Italians to pronounce the brand 'Gee Bee'.

Sometime in the 1970s Bandini took me to meet a man who had helped him make J&B Rare fashionable.

Max Mugnani lived in a shabby bohemian flat somewhere near the centre of Rome. He was delightful, and Bandini was clearly fond of him. When Bandini was starting out, it was the time of *la dolce vita* and the Italian 'economic miracle'. Mugnani, although an impoverished aristocrat, was a man of great charm, who was much loved by many in high places. He introduced the brand to the top people; he also arranged for J&B Rare to be 'placed' as a prop, in those wonderful films that were pouring out of Cinecittà. In those days such 'placings' were a novel idea and cost only the few free bottles that Bandini was happy to contribute. Today 'product placing' in films is big business.

In January 1973 the UK had joined the EEC (the fore-runner of the EU). Until then, most EEC countries imposed various discriminatory taxes to hinder the importation of Scotch whisky. Italy was no exception. Once we were inside the EEC club, the British government complained politely about the Italian discriminations.

In 1946 Italy had abolished the monarchy, and their new Republican constitution had come into force in 1948. This constitution seems to have become a recipe for an ongoing cascade of ever-shifting coalition administrations. In the seventies and eighties each government rarely lasted a year. So, when the British government complained about the discriminations against Scotch whisky, one could summa-rise the diplomatic spiel behind the Italian response as follows:

'Your complaint sounds extremely logical, but you see we are a completely new government, and we shall have to study the case carefully before we can respond.'

They would then procrastinate enthusiastically until that particular coalition collapsed, only to be replaced with another. The next government would then play the same gramophone record all over again. And so it went on, and for several years. The Italians can be charmingly good at this sort of ruse.

It is easy to forget that the 1970s was a turbulent decade for everyone. In the UK we had the miners strikes and the Three-Day Week. Throughout Europe industrial action was a commonplace problem exacerbated by the repercussions of the oil crisis. In Italy they also had to put up with the Brigate Rosse (Red Brigades). For people like Bandini, kidnapping was a real threat. To get to the office he left his De Tomaso at home and climbed into a grotty old Fiat Uno, also taking care to vary his route and his timing.

Despite all this, by 1974 J&B Rare was a leading brand in Italy and Bandini was selling over 200,000 cases every year. He had 'arrived'.

Back in Spain things were very different.

36

Franco's Spain

Generalissimo Francisco Franco (1892–1975) was the Fascist leader who started the Spanish Civil War in 1936. After defeating the Republicans, he ruled Spain as a dictator until 1975. Unlike most dictators, he had created a succession plan so that after his death it was possible to establish the democratic constitutional monarchy that governs Spain today. Whether Franco was the saviour of Spain, or a major human rights criminal, is a debate that will run and run.

Nowadays when you travel to Spain, Portugal, or even Greece it is easy to forget that for many years after World War II these countries were all ruled by dictators. Although Hitler had helped Franco to win the Spanish Civil War (1936–1939), Franco had, during World War II, wisely refrained from returning the compliment. Nonetheless Spain had suffered hideously during her internal conflict. In the 1960s Spain was like a third world country. Franco would rule Spain with an iron grip for nearly forty years. He was the sort of chap who could nonchalantly munch chocolate while signing reams of death warrants. Order and discipline came at a price.

J&B's Spanish story began in the second half of the Franco era. Helped by a growing tourist industry and backed by the effective, but undemocratic, discipline of a strike-free economy, Spain was beginning to catch up with the rest of Europe. Consequently, import quotas for Scotch whisky were allowed to grow, albeit from a low base. But the quotas were allocated on the basis that an importer got the same share as the year before. This was all very well for the existing importers, but it made progress difficult for new brands like J&B Rare.

In the early years the brand leader for Scotch in Spain was Johnnie Walker Red Label. The sale of 12-year-old blends was of no significance, and malt whisky had not yet been heard of. Most Scotch was consumed in bars, discos, and restaurants. Supermarkets were still few in number, and hypermarkets had not arrived. These early days marked a golden era when well-marketed brands had real leverage.

When I joined J&B in 1970, I was presented with a copy of Malcolm Burr's *International Marketing and Advertising* manual. He had surprised us all when he switched to run IDV's wine division. But for many years, his manual continued to be our marketing bible. It was a slim booklet containing only four pages of concise and elegantly written text. These were the days when the whole of China was marching to the instructions contained in Chairman Mao's 'Little Red Book'. Malcolm's manual had a bright yellow cover; and so, the J&B world quickly responded by calling it the 'Little Yellow Book'.

Back in the sixties and seventies our agents were not sophisticated marketeers. The good ones were entrepreneurs with a fine understanding of their customers and a feel for what consumers wanted. They liked to be out and about selling, not sitting at home reading large, boring brand manuals. So, the four pages of sensible well-crafted text gave them just what they needed.

The manual explained the history of the brand, the character and style of the blend, and why the colour of the whisky is pale. It covered the pricing and distribution strategy, and how to go about setting up an advertising and promotional campaign. All in all, the 'Little Yellow Book' served us very well in those early days. Today it reads as well as it did then. Rafael Ullivarri was to prove exemplary in his adherence to the J&B Rare gospel as spelled out by Malcolm Burr.

Franco, the great Caudillo, died on 20 November 1975. Immediately all forms of censorship were abolished. This resulted in a welcome freedom for political expression. But also, and startlingly, pornography had a heyday. Rafael was quite shocked by it. General Elections were held in 1977, and the new democratic constitution was approved by referendum and sanctioned by King Juan Carlos I on 27 December 1978.

By the end of the Franco era, J&B Rare had established a firm foothold in the Spanish market. The brand had been well seeded in all the best places in Madrid, Barcelona, and the other major cities. But then we had our first crisis.

However, before I tell you about that, let us take a detour to nearby Portugal.

37

Portugal

Towards the end of his 'reign', Portugal's dictator may have heard about Harold Macmillan's 'wind of change' blowing through Africa. If he had, António de Oliveira Salazar paid no attention to it. Instead, Portugal continued a grinding series of campaigns to hold on to various colonies in Africa and Asia. These campaigns were expensive and damaging.

Then, in 1968, Salazar had a stroke and could no longer govern. Marcello Caetano became Prime Minister and took over the management of the *Estado Novo* form of government that had been created by Salazar way back in 1933. Caetano tried to initiate some reform. He was not successful. Six years later he was thrown out by the Carnation Revolution. The uprising was known as such, because the people rallied behind the military, who had spiked their guns with red carnations. Happily, the revolution was almost bloodless.

Between 1974 and the end of 1975 the *Processo Revolucionário Em Curso* (Process of Ongoing Revolution) took place. During this time there was much political turmoil and a severe economic crisis. And the country was swamped with colonial Portuguese coming back from territories that had been granted, or taken, independence. Finally, in 1976, elections were held, and Mario Soares was

able to form Portugal's first democratically elected government for nearly fifty years.

It was during the chaotic *Processo Revolucionário Em Curso*
that I made my first visit to Portugal for J&B.

Our agent in Portugal was a company called Sileno. They
were the domestic sales arm of José Maria da Fonseca.
Established in 1834, José Maria da Fonseca were, and
are, one of Portugal's great and respected family-owned
wine companies. They are based in Azeitão, in the Setúbal
Peninsula, across the Tagus and not far from Lisbon. Their
range of wines includes the superb red Periquita, their
luscious Moscatel de Setúbal, which is grown nearby, and
Lancers, a rosé that is widely exported.

Before he left J&B for Cutty Sark, Robert Cecil had
warned me that when I went to Lisbon, I should watch
out for a man called José who, according to Robert, was
extremely dangerous and much inclined to lead visiting
firemen astray.

I was met at Lisbon airport by three men. Their leader
was a middle-aged man called Álvaro. His 'number two'
was José, a younger man with a spectacular moustache,
much in the style of Dumas's musketeer, d'Artagnan. The
moustache coupled with his exuberant welcome, instantly
alerted me to Robert's warning. I vowed to myself to be
very careful when José was around.

This, as I have said, was a time of austerity for Portugal.
The Ritz and other big hotels had been taken over to house
homeless *retornados* who had come back from the colonies.
After I had dropped my bag at a family hotel, we squashed
back into the car (it was small and dilapidated) and were driven
off to dinner by the third man. He was old, spoke no English,
and his role, other than that of driver, I could not make out.

The four of us had a slap-up dinner in a delightful *taberna*. Towards the end of the meal, José excused himself saying he had to go, adding with the semblance of a wink that he had to meet someone. That, I thought, was a relief: the danger man now being out of the way.

We finished dinner with a glass of their glorious 20-year-old Moscatel de Setúbal and drove back to the hotel dropping Álvaro on the way. I was now relaxed and looking forward to a good night's sleep.

As we drove towards the hotel my driver, whose name I had not caught, asked me if I spoke any French. Having received a hesitant affirmative he said that just by the hotel was a famous bar that was a tremendous client for J&B Rare.

'So why,' he asked, 'don't we stop for a quick nightcap because the owner would be *enchanté* to meet someone from the J&B distillery?'

So in we went.

I don't speak any Portuguese, but as we went in, I got the feeling that my driver-cum-host was known in the establishment. Moreover, everyone seemed very pleased to see him, especially the girls who, in such places, are at hand to encourage out-of-town visitors to buy them expensive drinks.

To cut a long story short, and after doing my J&B Rare ambassadorial stuff in this bar, I was then prevailed upon to do the same in three more establishments. I finally got to bed at about 3 am.

It must have been around 2 am, in bar number three, when I and my companion were putting the world to rights in our best O Level French (his was as bad as mine) that I discovered that he was also called José.

183

Jorge Avilez is a member of the family that has owned José Maria da Fonseca since its foundation. In 1974 he was in charge of the Sileno subsidary. He was also involved in their export business and would visit me from time to time when he was in London. Jorge was always delightfully laid back. That, combined with his subtle humour, neatly camouflaged an astute brain.

During the years of the *Processo Revolucionário Em Curso*, when Sileno were doing a terrific job at growing J&B Rare, Jorge would tell me news of the terrible austerity raging in Portugal. The government were even threatening to expropriate his vineyards; and it was extremely difficult to finance Sileno's growing imports of J&B Rare. He wondered if we could possibly give him a bit more credit. It would, he said, be a tremendous help, to them and to J&B, if we could. Such was his eloquence and, knowing his company's balance sheet would be robust (not that I would have been able to 'read' it in those days in English, let alone in Portuguese), I allowed his payment terms to be extended: first, from 30 to 60 days, then from 60 to 90 days, and then yet again from 90 to 120 days. Desmond Clarke, our usually tolerant director of finance, was beginning to get rather grumpy about my largesse. But sales were going very well. So, I got away with it – just.

A few months later, on a visit to Lisbon I was allowed to spend a day in the trade visiting customers. My guide was Sileno's senior salesman for Lisbon, and he spoke English. In between meetings with his best customers, he complained about the economic crisis, and about how slow these customers were at settling their wine bills. This was not news to me. I had already heard all about it from

Jorge. But, when I said that it must be the same too for their whisky bills, he astonished me by saying:

'Oh no: whisky is restricted by import licence. Anyone who wants J&B Rare has to pay cash.'

A few weeks later when Jorge tipped up in London and asked, as eloquently as ever, if we could possibly extend their credit terms from 120 to 150 days, he was a bit surprised when I said: 'No.'

But they took 150 days anyway.

In due course Portugal became a very important market for J&B. In 1986 when the country joined the EEC, import tariffs were abolished and volumes rose dramatically. J&B Rare became the leader for Scotch whisky. José Mesquita (he with the moustache) did a fantastic job in managing the brand. And in the 1980s when we introduced our J&B 15-Year-Old Reserve, Portugal became its most successful market.

I have always enjoyed going to Portugal and always wonder why I have not gone there more often. Like their neighbours, the people have great charisma, but it is of a more subtle, and less revved-up variety, than in Spain. I find that of particular appeal. Also, cities like Lisbon and Oporto have an old-world charm. They function very well in the modern world, and without being 'blessed' with too much tourism.

38

Back to Spain in the Sixties

In the early days, the top priority for Rafael Ullivarri and his brothers was to obtain import licences. Thereafter they concerned themselves with managing and financing the importation and distribution of J&B Rare. Distribution was sub-contracted to a company called Enol, which was owned by Eugenio and José González Mayo.

Enol were appointed towards the end of 1963. To begin with they sold J&B Rare in Madrid, but gradually their territory was extended to cover Barcelona, the Balearic Islands, and then the whole of mainland Spain. Eugenio González Mayo was a great entrepreneur. He had many contacts, and these undoubtedly helped the early development of the brand.

Selling J&B Rare in the early days was not easy. The light colour and premium price were obvious barriers. But by dint of hard work and the expenditure of much shoe leather, the brand began to take hold. Scotch whisky was then an aspirational drink for the young and emerging middle classes. At the time the brand leader was Johnnie Walker.

Johnnie Walker Red Label is a powerful, full-bodied blend. So, for anyone who is not accustomed to Scotch Whisky, but who feels the peer group pressure to acquire a taste for it, trying a glass of Red Label can come as something of a shock. And in those days, you could not fudge it by mixing your whisky with Coca-Cola. You had to be brave and take it neat or on the rocks. Consequently, many aspirational consumers shied away when they were asked to jump this 'hurdle' for a second time. But, when they discovered the elegant, smoother style of J&B Rare, their problem was solved. Here was a brand of Scotch that they could enjoy. And by being premium it also satisfied their ego. Also, by pronouncing the JB initials in Spanish (hotter bay) it was supremely easy to call for – unlike many other brands.

In the first ten years (1963–1973), establishing J&B Rare was a bottle by bottle, bar by bar slog. But the job was done carefully and seriously. As demand expanded, Enol themselves started to set up a network of their own provincial sub-distributors. It was at about this time that Antonio Mendez was recruited by Enol; he would be instrumental in appointing some future stars.

Madrid does not dominate the Spanish market in the same way that London does in the UK. Consequently, it was important to seed J&B Rare in all the key provincial cities of Spain. In the early days supply was constrained by import quotas, so margins were very generous. This made it perfectly feasible for a brand like J&B Rare to be sold from an importer (GECEPSA) to a national distributor (Enol), and then onwards to a provincial sub-distributor, and finally to local wholesalers and retailers. All down that chain everyone could make a decent margin.

A typical provincial distributor would have had a portfolio of non-conflicting wines and spirits. He would represent these on an exclusive basis for his province. It was important to find dynamic sub-distributors who could handle a brand like J&B Rare.

When I started my involvement with the Spanish market in 1974, sub-distributors had been appointed in the seven major provinces. You could call them our 'Magnificent Seven'. They were to stay until IDV gradually set up its own network in the 1990s. They were all outstanding entrepreneurs. During their tenure they built the brand impeccably. It was John Rideal (our man for Eastern Europe during the Cold War) who coined the expression growing 'from bare feet to BMW in one generation'. To say that some of our sub-distributors did this is a bit of an exaggeration. But by the 1990s many of them were selling 250,000 cases per annum. In so doing they became the provincial barons of our industry.

But before we get properly stuck into Spain let us take a trip to somewhere very different: Norway.

39

A Cautionary Tale

As I have already mentioned, in 1973 James Bruxner came over from Gilbeys to become managing director of J&B. He was, in time, to become our chairman. James was also to be my boss for seventeen years. I was very lucky. He was the ideal boss, being very strong on strategic marketing and knowing how to strike the right balance between delegation and interference. With Messrs Belson or Bruxner as my superior for the greater part of my time at J&B, I was supremely fortunate. So was the company.

However, it was not all plain sailing: in 1973 the IDV board asked Tommy Barlow to spend some time with us. He came from a different part of the group and was anxious to find out how we operated. The best way for him to do this was to come with us on our market visits. I did several trips with Tommy, the most memorable being a visit to Norway in November 1974.

In the early part of the twentieth century, prohibition had existed in all the Scandinavian countries (except Denmark). After its repeal, a system was introduced wherein the sale of alcohol had to be made through a state-owned monopoly. In Norway this was called the Vinmonopolet. So, to sell J&B Rare in Norway, you first had to get a listing with the Vinmonopolet.

In the 1970s the retail shops run by the various Scandinavian liquor monopolies were tidy, antiseptic affairs totally lacking in any friendly 'caviste' ambience. Your shopping would be wrapped in brown paper because alcohol was still frowned upon. On top of that, prices were exceptionally high, whisky and vodka costing double the price back home. Consequently, there was massive 'infiltration' of supplies from duty free sources, and illicit home distilling was not unknown. In a bar, a measure of whisky would be tiny. They would get precisely thirty-two shots out of a bottle. In Spain they would get ten. The markets in Scandinavia were not like those in Spain or Italy.

Under the system, brand owners were allowed to appoint commission agents to promote their brands, albeit in a constrained manner. In 1974 J&B Rare was listed by the Vinmonopolet, but sales were weak. We had just appointed a new commission agent in the hope of generating some improvement.

I got to Oslo a day before Tommy to make sure that everything was set up for his visit. When he arrived, he said that my 'name' was all over the English newspapers. In fact, it was not my name in the papers, but that of my cousin's wife, Susie. It was the time that Lord Lucan had disappeared, and Susie was the last person known to have seen him.

Tommy was by nature hearty, entertaining, and extrovert. He and Engwald, our new agent for Norway, seemed birds of the same feather. They hit it off right away. We had a very jolly dinner in Engwald's house. Afterwards Tommy wanted to show Engwald a new trick he had just learned. I do not remember the game's finer points other than it required glasses full of water (or whisky), plus napkins and eggs. I think the idea was to place the egg on top of the napkin which itself was on top of the glass of water (or whisky): and then jerk the napkin away. If all went well the egg would drop into the water (or whisky) without making a splash. That evening it mostly did not go well. The result was a lot of broken eggs and much spilled whisky (or water). However, it was a very merry party, and greatly enjoyed by one and all, except perhaps for Mrs Engwald who had to mop up.

Eventually we took a taxi back to our hotel. Tommy was keen to have a nightcap before retiring but the bar was closed. Not to be outdone, he said we could probably find something acceptable in his minibar. So, we repaired to his room. Unfortunately, there was no J&B Rare in the minibar. Tommy seemed not to mind. Instead, we found an eclectic selection of brands from well-known competitors. Holding up miniatures of one brand after another, and under the pretext of: 'Gosh, I haven't tried this for a while. Let's see what it's like?' we worked our way through the entire contents of his minibar. It was a bit like that scene from *Our Man in Havana*, but without taking the trouble to play the game of draughts.

Working our way through miniature bottles of Smirnoff, Bacardi, Norwegian Aquavit, Gordon's, Johnnie Walker, Vat 69 and then on to Courvoisier, Martini Rosso, and Harveys Bristol Cream was hard going and took us into the wee small hours. During this marathon, Tommy confided in me some strategic ideas that he had been pondering for IDV's whisky portfolio. I found these somewhat eccentric but since he was very senior to me, I thought it wise to be polite. I also tried to avoid matching the velocity of his miniature-by-miniature steeplechase. At one point when he caught me tipping the Vat 69 into a wastepaper bin I was told: 'Don't be so bloody wet and drink up properly.'

After we had finished his minibar, Tommy suggested we remove to my room and have a go at mine. Fortunately, he didn't press this point and I escaped.

That night, short though it was, I could not sleep. Everything kept going round and round. The alarm went off just as I did get to sleep.

At 8.30 sharp Erik, Engwald's son-in-law, was downstairs waiting to meet us. We had a 9 a.m. appointment in the harbour with Engwald's Number One Duty Free Customer.

There was no sign of Tommy when I got to the hotel lobby. And I felt dreadful.

I rang Tommy's room. No response. Eventually I went up to his room. After some polite tapping which became increasingly less polite, he came to the door looking rather tousled and still in his pyjamas. But he promised to come downstairs pronto: which he did within ten minutes. Annoyingly, he looked better than I felt, saying that after our late-night 'tasting session' he'd swallowed a couple of Mogadon and slept like a bird.

Down in the harbour, the meeting with Number One Duty Free Customer went off pretty well, with Tommy being appropriately diplomatic, though somewhat less ebullient than on the previous evening.

On the way back into town we passed a number of fine-looking bars and cafés. It was now around 10.30 and Tommy wondered out-loud if any of them stocked J&B Rare? He was clearly anxious to stop for a 'distribution check'. As we passed from one area to another these hints became heavier and heavier. All the time Erik, at the wheel, paid no attention to them whatsoever. But eventually he gave way and said, 'Mr Barlow. I'm afraid it is illegal in Norway to serve spirits before 1 p.m.'

Short pause.

Then quick as a flash Tommy said: 'What about port and sherry?'

With some reluctance Erik admitted that port, sherry, wine, and beer could be had at any time of the day. He was then persuaded to pull into a friendly hostelry where happily we found that they stocked Croft Pale Cream, IDV's principal brand of sherry. A large tumbler of the stuff convinced Tommy that 'our sherry' was in excellent condition. It had travelled well from Jerez to Oslo (via Harlow in Essex where it would have been bottled) and we were allowed to continue for our meeting at Engwald's office.

Tommy left IDV in 1978. I had some mixed feelings about his departure. When I had left that bottling hall in 1970 to come across to J&B, he had written me a very generous letter of commendation. I still have it.

And since this is a cautionary tale, Tommy Barlow is a made-up name.

Around the same time, in Spain we faced a dilemma of a different nature.

40

Spain: The First Hurdle

At the end of 1975 they buried Franco in his specially prepared tomb at el Valle de los Caídos (the Valley of the Fallen). At the time, the effect of the first oil crisis was hurting. Inflation in Spain was running at 30 per cent, and the market was fragile. But Scotch whisky was an aspirational drink, and total shipments had crept up to a million cases. J&B Rare was becoming fashionable, and demand was growing. However, our actual sales were flat at around 60,000 cases, because getting a bigger import quota was proving impossible. Consequently, J&B Rare was put on ration to its key customers. We were frustrated not to be selling more, but with demand now exceeding supply the brand had established a healthy base for the future.

Enol (the Ullivarris' distributor) had also obtained the distribution rights for Croft Sherry and the Lagunilla wines from Rioja. Both brands were owned by IDV. To strengthen his ties with IDV, Eugenio González Mayo had persuaded Croft to take a shareholding in Enol. We, in J&B, were blissfully unaware of this arrangement, but at the same time Rafael himself was showing an interest in becoming more involved with the distribution of the brand. Sensing that one day the market might open, and that margins would fall, we encouraged him to do this.

We have seen that the quota system for Scotch whisky was bad for volume but good for margin. The same did not apply to local products. Spain had large surpluses of sherry and wine. Consequently, the margins available for Croft and Lagunilla were meagre. In fact, most producers of sherry, brandy and local wines sold their products directly to local wholesalers. So, having a national distributor such as Enol to develop Croft and Lagunilla did not make sense. However, Croft had promised to provide Enol with promotional support, and Enol were optimistic that they could achieve the targets that had been agreed.

Unfortunately, the promotional support did not quite live up to expectations, and achieving the targets proved extremely difficult. This is not surprising because both brands (though of excellent quality) were virtually unknown. To solve the problem Enol came up with the novel idea of forcing the sales of Croft and Lagunilla on the back of J&B Rare. This was not popular with the sub-distributors. They did not like being told that they would get no allocation of J&B Rare unless they also took sizeable quantities of Croft and Lagunilla. Matters came to a head in 1975 when the sub-distributors found themselves with dwindling supplies of J&B Rare and stacks of Croft and Lagunilla in their bodegas. They were so cross that they complained directly to Rafael.

It was only then that Rafael discovered Croft's shareholding in Enol, and he was not very chuffed. Towards the end of 1975 Antonio Mendez was becoming decidedly disillusioned by Enol's tactics. He told Rafael that J&B was getting a bad name in the trade. Rafael realised that something had to be done. After due consideration he came to us and sought our approval for him to fire Enol.

After examining all the evidence quite carefully we gave him that approval.

Then of course the balloon went up. Enol complained to Croft; and Croft complained to IDV; and our superiors at IDV complained to us. Dorrien Belson and James Bruxner managed the ensuing flack with massive aplomb. Croft suggested that we should fire Rafael and hand over control of the brand to them because if they, as an IDV subsidiary, managed the distribution it would add on another layer of profit for IDV. Of course, their maths was spot on, but it missed the wider picture. We argued that if we fired Rafael the decision would backfire because the Ministry of Commerce in Madrid would not like our heavy-handed approach; and they might reduce rather than increase future import quotas. Moreover, it would also send the wrong signal to our other independent distributors in markets like France, Portugal, Belgium, Greece, Switzerland, and Italy where the brand was performing well and where at that time IDV had no serious footprint. Fortunately, our argument won the day. Rafael then created Anglo Española de Distribución SA, and by the end of 1976 AED, as it became known, had taken over the role of national distributor from Enol. AED retained the old Enol sub-distributors and Antonio Mendez joined AED.

We were back on an even keel.

41

Franz v the Professor

Towards the end of 1979 James gave each of his three regional directors a pep talk. He reminded us that none of us had been to university. He said that if we should like to further our education by taking a few months off and attending a senior course at a reputable business school, then J&B would pay for it. Wyndham, who was in charge of Latin America, took up this offer straight away, and went to Harvard for their three-month Executive Programme. Derek and I ducked the offer for a while but after a bit of nagging from James I did some research into the various options and picked INSEAD, Europe's top business school.

I chose INSEAD because it appeared that those who attended their Executive Programme came from an interestingly diverse range of countries. Other attractions were that it was a six-week course, not a three-month one, and that being based in Fontainebleau, the food was likely to be better.

There were about a hundred of us on the course, and they did come from a wide range of countries. I recall fellow students from France, Belgium, Germany, Austria, Italy, Norway, USA, Australia, Singapore, and Mexico. The intake also included three from Poland which was still behind the Iron Curtain. There were only six from the UK.

The syllabus covered subjects such as leadership, corporate strategy, finance, marketing, HR, and macroeconomics: just what you might expect. We were divided into groups of about eight. I do not remember all the names in my group; but it included Randy, a very bright American banker, Patrick (who was Chinese and came from Singapore), Karin from Norway (the only woman on the course), Zbigniew (one of the Poles), an Englishman whose firm made sausages for M&S, a Frenchman who worked for St Gobain (they make glass), and Franz.

Every day we were given a mountain of reading to do, mostly case studies. I adopted the Jim Hacker technique and skipped to the key bits. We were supposed to do all the reading in the evening. Then the following day we would attend lectures on the relevant subjects. After each lecture we were sent off in groups to evaluate a particular problem and then, after due consideration, we had to return and report our conclusions. The subject I liked best was marketing.

The subject I hated was macroeconomics. I had thought it would be fascinating. But it seemed you needed a degree in higher mathematics to understand anything. For this subject, we had a professor whose name I forget, but he was obviously very clever. In fact, he was so clever that I could not understand anything he said.

One day this professor spent a lot of time outlining the problem that he was setting us by writing complicated equations across the large blackboard in the lecture hall. He then sent us off to consider his question.

Now, each group had its own little study room furnished with a table, some chairs, and a flip chart. There was also a nice supply of fresh coffee and a selection of chocolate biscuits. Normally, when set a problem, our group would get stuck into the subject (as well as the chocolate biscuits), and in due course come up with constructive answers.

On this occasion we just sat there looking blankly at each other. After a while Randy said he had a vague idea what the Prof was after. With encouragement from the rest of us he did a bit of work on the flip chart, but then he gave up.

It was at this point that Franz astonished us all when he said rather quietly that he thought it was quite straightforward.

Franz came from Vienna. He had a goatee beard, wore thick glasses, and had piercing blue eyes. He was genuinely modest but was probably one of the nicest and most intelligent people I have ever met. He was the technical supremo for a large company. I think it was Siemens.

With encouragement from the rest of the group, Franz set about demonstrating what he meant. He did this by writing some very exotic equations. They were all Chinese to me. Apart from maybe Randy, none of us had a clue what he was on about.

When we got back to the lecture hall, the Prof was there prowling up and down in front of his blackboard.

'How did you get on?' He asked, somewhat sarcastically.

Silence.

More silence.

Then someone from our group who was positioned on the deep square leg boundary, and on the far side of the lecture hall, spoke:

'Franz,' said our voice, 'show him what we have done.'

In terms of accuracy, I thought the 'we' was a bit wide of the mark. But Franz was persuaded to take a piece of chalk from the Professor, who was eying him in a rather condescending manner, and advance to the blackboard. It was about 3 yards wide.

Franz set to work. Under the Prof's own equations Franz began to extrapolate more equations. These were longer and filled with all manner of hieroglyphics that were totally beyond my comprehension. As he did this, he explained to the Prof what he was doing.

After Franz had covered the blackboard a couple of times, all the way across from west to east, the penny dropped. The Prof suddenly realised that Franz was better than him at this game. So, with bad grace he grabbed the chalk back and started to wipe the blackboard clean, muttering as he did so that we were falling behind our schedule and it was time to move on.

In our group we were mighty proud of our Franz.

I took my car to INSEAD, which was a real boon. It meant that I was not tied to the campus or hotel where we were staying. I even discovered a delightful bistro at Barbizon which had Château Smith Haut Lafitte 1971 on the wine list at the ridiculously attractive price of 32 Francs (about £3) a bottle.

But despite the occasional escape we did have to work extremely hard. I had always been sympathetic to people who said: 'If only I had more time to think' about this or that. After INSEAD, I realised that was all phooey. I discovered that when your brain is put under pressure it starts to work much faster. I suppose that is why so many breakthrough inventions happen during times of war.

At the end of the course, we had to play the 'INSEAD Business Game'. This was designed as a realistic exercise in corporate strategy. It was competitive, so our group was competing against all the others. Randy said it would be more fun if we adopted a highly leveraged approach; and this is what we did. On one occasion, our imaginary corporation was almost forced into an ignominious liquidation. But, in the end we bounced back and came second. I imagine that Richard S Fuld Jnr, the last CEO of Lehman Brothers, had never played the 'INSEAD Business Game'.

A year after INSEAD I visited Franz in Austria. I was staying at the Sacher Hotel. As I sat waiting on its marvellous Sachertorte-dispensing terrace, I was surprised to see an old pick-up truck arriving at the hotel entrance. I was even more surprised when the two figures who popped out of the driver's cab were Franz and his wife Susie. Furthermore, Franz was clad in lederhosen and Susie was looking as pretty as a picture in traditional Austrian dirndl. The doorman at the Sacher was a bit taken aback to find this battered tradesman's vehicle drawing up at his impeccable front door. But he took it well and solicitously held the door for me as I hopped up into the driver's cab. Franz and Susie then took me off to a splendidly noisy tavern in Grinzing where we had a hearty Austrian dinner washed down with the famous young wine of the parish.

Afterwards we went back to their flat. Franz and Susie had lots of small children who were all asleep. So, we had to tiptoe around as Franz took me on a tour. Much of the furniture and fittings had been beautifully made by him. We ended in the children's playroom where everything had been neatly tidied away. The one room we had not seen was their bedroom.

'But where do you sleep?' I asked, curious to know the answer.

Franz pointed to the ceiling; and when I still looked puzzled, he explained that if I looked closely, I could see that their bed was up there, attached to the ceiling. And indeed it was. Franz had engineered it so that every night they could lower their bed, and then in the morning winch it up again; and bingo, the same room served as playroom and master bedroom.

When they had picked me up from the Sacher in their lederhosen and dirndl, Franz had explained that he and Susie wanted to give me a typical Austrian evening. Typical of Austria in 1981? I'm not sure, but it was certainly a wonderful evening; and as I indicated earlier, it just showed that Franz was the sort of genius who could turn his hand to anything.

Franz and Patrick on an outing we did to Château de Chambord

42

Spain: Overtaking Johnnie Walker

By 1977 J&B Rare was firmly established as the fashionable brand in Spain. This was not all good news. Owing to the quota system, the increased demand for the brand could not be legally satisfied. So, considerable quantities were being smuggled in from Andorra, in the Pyrenees, and from Ceuta and Melilla, Spain's territories in North Africa.

Despite our fashionability, we could only ship 60,000 cases to Spain in that year. Johnnie Walker was shipping nearly double our volume. The trouble was that the peseta had just devalued, export prices for Scotch had risen, and the Spanish government were using import quotas as a bargaining tool before their entry to the EU.

By February 1979 Spain was in recession. Elections took place in March and Rafael reckoned that the new government would liberalise imports. Later that year, imports were indeed liberalised, but the Spanish government rather cunningly took the opportunity to raise duties. As a result of this, imports of Scotch did not increase; they declined for the next two years.

But liberalisation was good for J&B Rare. It allowed import volumes to reflect consumer demand. So, in 1979, shipments of J&B Rare doubled to 120,000 cases. We were now racing neck and neck with Johnnie Walker. Of course,

Johnnie was not going to take this lying down; and for a couple of years the leadership position see-sawed between the two brands. But, by 1982 J&B Rare was shipping 290,000 cases and Johnnie was trailing at 190,000. From then on J&B Rare accelerated away and Johnnie Walker disappeared backwards into the pack.

It was most satisfying.

You may wonder why overtaking Johnnie Walker was so important. After all, both brands were whiskies from Scotland operating in a foreign market against a wide range of Spanish spirits. That is true, but it was so. By the same token, I imagine that today brands like BMW and Mercedes compete against each other, in say Italy, just as aggressively as they do against Alfa Romeo and Lancia.

In other parts of Europe J&B Rare was also doing very well. This was the year that we first shipped 100,000 cases to France; and France was still well astern of Italy.

So, maybe we should pay due deference to Italy and return there for another intermezzo.

43

How to Catch a Condor

You will recall that Bandini was our agent in Italy. His office was in Milan, and over the years I was able to enjoy many visits to that marvellous city. His company was called Dateo Import and they had an office on the first floor of a large block in Piazzale Dateo, not far from the city centre.

In order to get into the Dateo office you had to negotiate your way past Gianni – a very large, Buddha-like concierge who, from his cubby hole just off the entrance hall, kept a brooding eye on everyone coming into or going out of the building. Gianni had two interests: food and football. I once had a very sticky time trying to distance myself from anything to do with Liverpool after a gang of their fans had behaved very badly, rioting just before a European Cup Final in Brussels between their team and Juventus. Several Juventus fans had been killed and Gianni seemed to think it was all my fault. But usually he was a pussycat. And, as you went past his cubby hole the most wonderful cooking smells would emanate from the kitchen tucked away behind his den. His wife, he would explain, was preparing his midday *collazione*. One could imagine his diminutive wife, for she was very small, slaving away over a tiny stove making a sublime slow-cooked ragout. It would eventually combine with proper homemade pasta. Meanwhile, resting in his den, big Gianni's dewlaps were already aquiver in salivating anticipation.

Bandini had a small but effective HQ. The key people were Alberto Antonelli, Giuseppina Tacchini, Gian Paolo Bugamelli, and Bandini's son, Massimo. Alberto, a lawyer by training, handled the advertising and administrative matters. Tacchini ran the accounting side with fierce vigilance. She was much feared by customers who occasionally 'forgot' to pay on time. Bugamelli ran the sales force. The atmosphere in the office was friendly but slightly feudal. Bandini was definitely *il capo*. I suspect that Tacchini and Bugamelli were referred to as such because they were more mature in years. On the other hand, Alberto and Massimo, being younger, were called by their Christian names.

In Italy there were strict employment laws. However idle or incompetent an employee might be, it was almost impossible to get rid of him, or her, without paying hefty compensation. Consequently, the sales were managed by regional agents who were contracted on a commission basis. Most of these represented more than one company. Many of Bandini's agents also worked for Antinori, one of Italy's most respected wine houses. This worked very well because both portfolios complemented each other.

Bugamelli had started his working life as a test driver for Lamborghini. Driving anywhere with him was quite some-thing. He once drove me from Milan to Rome in January, in freezing fog, and in under five hours. Much of the journey was spent tailgating cars going slightly slower than him in the fast lane. At one point, to distract him into going slower, I asked him a question. He didn't go slower. Instead, he looked at me when answering, which made it worse. Thereafter, I didn't utter a word. He was certainly a brilliant driver and has never, as far as I know, had an accident. Or, as Alberto once said: 'If he had he wouldn't be with us now.'

In his youth, Bugamelli had been sent to South America by his father on what nowadays would be called a gap year. Whenever there was a gathering of the Dateo sales force someone would inevitably provoke Bugamelli into telling some of his favourite stories. He was a great raconteur and some of his tales are famous throughout Italy. My favourite was to hear him recount how he hunted the condor. It went like this:

During his sojourn in Argentina, Bugamelli spent several months living rough with gauchos in the foothills of the Andes. In many ways, gauchos are like North American cowboys. But there is one important difference. To corral their cattle, gauchos don't use a lasso; they use bolas. These bolas are three weighted balls interconnected at the end of a rope. To catch a steer a gaucho whirls the bolas around his head (just like a cowboy with his lasso). He then launches them at a steer's feet. The bolas fly through the air, wrap themselves around the steer's ankles and bring the poor brute crashing to earth. A good gaucho can stop a running steer when he himself is at full gallop.

Now the condor is a wily bird, and if you want to catch one the first thing you need is bait. Condors are members of the vulture family: they feed on carrion. Bugamelli and his *compadres* used the carcass of a goat as bait. They laced the carcass with salt and parked it near a small stream. Then with their mountain ponies they retired to hide behind large boulders some hundred yards away. There they waited: and waited. The shadows began to lengthen. Still nothing. Then, just as they were beginning to abandon hope, Bugamelli looked up to see, soaring overhead, the vast silhouette of a lone condor. With its 10-foot wingspan, black body, and white ruff there was no mistaking what it was.

Crouching motionless in their hideout, Bugamelli and the gauchos waited. Fortunately, the condor had not seen them. After circling carefully, the great bird glided to earth. And before long he was tucking into a feast of *cabrón con sal* (salted goat).

Now your condor is not a tidy eater. And he was hungry. So he took some time to fuel up. After he had filled up, the salt kicked in and, being thirsty he waddled off to the stream, which you will recall was nearby, and had a nice long cool drink. After that he settled down for a gentle siesta.

That was a mistake. This was the moment for the gauchos to break forth from their hideout. Much in the vein of Lord Byron's biblical Assyrian, who 'came down like the wolf on the fold', they descended on the astonished condor. The gauchos' cohorts may not have been 'gleaming in purple and gold', but their bolas were whirling and there was much hallooing in Spanish (and Italian) as they closed on their prey.

As fast as he could, the poor condor galvanised himself for action; spreading his wings he attempted a vertical take-off but, overloaded as he was with *cabrón con sal*, he could not get airborne. With a terrified backward glance at his pursuers, he opted for a running take-off. So, he ran for it. Like that Boeing 707 taking off from the high altitude of La Paz airport in Bolivia, he gradually built up momentum until finally, with his wings flapping furiously, he clawed his way into flight. The condor was beginning to think that his troubles were behind him and below him when he was brought crashing to earth: by the bolas.

He was unharmed but extremely angry.

And that, according to Gian Paolo Bugamelli, is the proper way to catch a condor.

Somewhere in Scotland, 1975
DMS with (clockwise) James Bruxner, Mr Bandini and
Dorrien Belson

44

The Magic of Scotland

Knockando Distillery on Speyside
From a watercolour by Chloë Furze

Mike Vineall is a Yorkshire man. He lives in the Dales, loves football (Leeds) and cricket (Yorkshire, obviously) and is a marketing guru with an amazing insight into the psychology of consumer behaviour. His wise counsel was, for many years, a major asset.

'J&B Rare,' said Mike one day, 'is like a man-o-war sailing half a mile off the main flotilla.'

'What do you mean?' We asked, rather surprised by his non-sporting metaphor.

'Well,' said Mike, 'J&B Rare is not like other Scotches. It has no tartan, no pipers, no claymores, no little wee doggies, nor any of the bits of Scottish nausea [as I said, he comes from Yorkshire] favoured by other brands. Sure, with a blend stuffed full of top-class Speyside malts, J&B Rare is the genuine thing. But do not forget it was the brainchild of a very English wine merchant. So, its pedigree is quite different. It looks different and behaves differently.'

He was, of course, spot on in all of this. So, in our work of communicating to consumers we never tried to out-Scotch those brands that have a big Scottish pedigree. Nevertheless, we did have to respond to snide suggestions from competitors who tried to make out that because the blend is pale, it is not the real thing. The best way to do that was to take important trade customers to Scotland to see for themselves just how J&B Rare was made. Over the years we took battalions of customers to see the blending plant at Blythswood, and the bottling halls at Strathleven (both near Glasgow). But, above all, we ferried them up to our distilleries on Speyside in the Highlands where Jim Milne, our Master Blender, was frequently on hand to explain, in his inimitable manner, the pains he took to retain the high quality of the blend.

Talking of corporate hospitality, a competitor once said: 'All you need to do is get 'em pissed and give them a good time.' We did not agree. It was always our policy to entertain people to a level above that to which they were accustomed. This would confer prestige on the brand and the company. So, we chartered planes, boats, helicopters, and even whole trains. We served Scotland's best food, and we poured fine wine from our own cellars. I considered this valuable PR, but the accountants tended to be sceptical.

Knockando Distillery sits on a hill and looks down on a turbulent River Spey at an enchanting spot a mile or two upstream from Rothes. It was there that we converted an old warehouse into a reception centre. A grand ceilidh at Knockando was always the high point of any distillery visit.

At some point, someone said we should dress our guests in kilts for the ceilidhs. I was a bit nervous about this. My father, who had been brought up in the Borders, had always said that nobody should wear a kilt unless they were a proper Highlander. As a Borderer he, of course, did not qualify; though he did have a kilt which he had acquired when he fought with the 48th Canadian Highlanders in World War I. But that is another story. Anyway, the management on Speyside were not fussed by such qualms. They thought it a grand idea.

The first time we tried the kilt-wearing ploy was with a party of barmen. They came from the top night clubs in France. After their chartered plane had arrived at Inverness 'International' Airport, we gave them a briefing session to explain the programme for their three-day visit. I told them that the agenda would end with a typical Scottish party at our Knockando Distillery. Coming from a métier that exemplifies hospitality they liked the idea of the party. But when I said they would all be wearing kilts, they found this hilarious. They thought I was joking.

At five o'clock, I told them it was time for the kilt fitting. This caused first consternation, and then a mass revolt – until that is, a bloke from the back of the pack said: 'Oh come on, I'll give it a go:' or the French equivalent. Then they were all won round.

Now, they were a group of fifty, and we had hired fifty kilts, naturally. It took some time to get the party fitted.

Explaining to them the purpose and correct hanging positioning for the sporran was also a challenge. Some favoured it slung from the hip like a cowboy's Colt 45. But when we told them that their sporran should be positioned over their 'crown jewels' they got the message very quickly.

Another problem we had was the guest with a unique waistline. We did not have a kilt big enough for him. Then someone realised that you could buckle two kilts together and create one mammoth kilt of double girth. It worked brilliantly, though the flat bits and pleated bits did not fall quite where they were supposed to.

But this meant that we now had forty-nine kilts for fifty guests. I thought this would not matter because there was another guest who was extremely grumpy and was vowing that under no circumstances would he ever be seen in a 'skirt'; that is until someone told him that he would be the only person not wearing the kilt. At which point he became very angry and demanded that we find him one.

In time, the kilt-wearing ploy became a great success. So much so that guests sometimes 'forgot' to return their sporrans. But we had a solution for that too. It came in the form of one Suze Bower. She is an accredited Blue Badge guide for London and Edinburgh, fluent in French and Spanish. We recruited her when we needed someone to marshal boisterous parties. Whenever we had missing sporrans, Suze would team up with the baggage people at Inverness 'International' Airport. When the bags went through security, the missing sporrans would show up on the x-ray and could then be retrieved, much to the embarrassment of the thieving guest who, when the sporran was retrieved from his smelly laundry, would then swear on his grandmother's honour that it must have got there entirely by mistake.

The code of Highland hospitality is renowned, and rightly so, because the countless hordes of visitors to the distilleries were always received with great warmth and good humour.

On one occasion we had a friendly football match between our distillery workers and a team from Moët et Chandon.

Now, at this time Moët was already a part of the LVMH group (Louis Vuitton Moët Hennessy). When the two teams appeared on the field there were marked differences in their appearance. The squad from the distilleries were strapping braw lads of the 'rustic, haggis-fed' variety of which Rabbie Burns would have felt proud: the sort of chaps that could chuck cabers (or full barrels) around with equanimity. They were clad in good old-fashioned baggy shorts, the sort I had worn at prep school in the 1950s.

You will recall that, apart from Moët et Chandon, and Hennessy, the LVMH group also comprises a range of haute couture brands. The house of Christian Dior is one such. When the Moët team trotted on to the pitch it was plain to see that their kit could have come straight from the Dior HQ in the Avenue Montaigne. It was neat, trim, and beautifully cut, though definitely on the skimpy side when compared to the apparel of their adversaries.

Both teams eyed each other with a degree of disdain.

Then the referee blew his whistle, and the game was afoot.

For me, the referee came as a surprise: it was Innes Shaw, our distillery manager at Knockando, who strode onto the pitch clad in the authentic black uniform of a Scottish Football Association referee. I had no idea that Innes had this extra string to his bow.

I think the French must have brought a few ringers from Épernay because they danced circles round the Scots. The Scots tried to retaliate by using brawn against élan. But, as the score against the home team mounted, and as his lads tried using brute force to get back into the game, Innes did a tremendous job, racing up and down the pitch, and blowing his whistle furiously to head off mayhem, or even GBH, befalling any of our guests.

Innes exemplified that aura of true Highland hospitality. However disruptive those visits might have been, he clearly enjoyed them. His welcome was invariably warm and genuine. And his distillery was always spotless.

Mrs Thatcher was Innes's most famous guest. During my time at J&B the company won the Queen's Award for Export Achievement six times. Mrs T came to Knockando in 1985 for one of those award ceremonies. Innes took her on a comprehensive tour of the distillery. Having a scientific background, she was fascinated to know precisely how everything worked.

And, of course, at Knockando, Innes did make the best malt whisky in Scotland.

Mrs Thatcher at Knockando Distillery
September 1985

45

The Million Bottle Parties

In October 1980 I paid a call on Regine's Club in Marbella. At the time it was the smartest discothèque in Spain: a veritable playpen for the rich and trendy. In clubs like Regine's, regular customers would buy a bottle of whisky, and if they did not finish it at one sitting it would be taken and placed (with their name marked on it) in a 'Customers' Reserve'. To find out which brands were most in demand, all you had to do was check the reserve. I did this. There were 280 bottles of J&B Rare. The next best-selling brand was Johnnie Walker with a mere 47 bottles. This barometer gave a very good reading of just how strong the brand had become in Spain.

In 1983 we signed a ten-year contract with GECEPSA. This gave Rafael and his partners added confidence to invest for the future success of the brand. Between 1980 and 1985 the Spanish economy steadied as the country prepared to enter the EEC (now EU). Scotch whisky was in fashion and imports grew from a million cases to a million and a half. The growth might have been faster had the peseta not eroded at the same time. But none of this could stop the growth of J&B Rare.

Our sales grew from 100,000 cases in 1979 to over 500,000 cases in 1985. In the same period our share of market surged from under 15 per cent to over 30 per cent. J&B Rare was driving the market growth.

In 1980 Nielsen (an American information, data and market measurement firm that operates in all the major markets) did their first audit of the whisky market. Modern marketing techniques were beginning to arrive in Spain.

In 1979 we had, by shipping 120,000 cases, sold more than one million bottles. This was a milestone to celebrate. So naturally we invited GECEPSA and some of their key sub-distributors to come and celebrate in Scotland. At the time I rashly said that when they got to two million bottles, we would have another party. This was to happen much more quickly than I expected. And later, when the brand soared past one million cases the million bottle parties came thick and fast. It seemed unlucky to interrupt a winning formula. The celebration parties became an annual event.

In 1985 you could not import Scotch whisky into Spain unless you were licensed as the exclusive importer for a particular brand. On the other hand, in the EEC they believe in 'the free movement of goods'. This means that, if you are a wholesaler, say in France, and can get a lower price by buying in Italy, you are encouraged to do this. This practice is known as 'parallel importing' and is promoted because it has the effect of lowering consumer prices. But parallel importing disrupts marketing strategies and enrages distributors when they have been undercut.

So, when Spain joined the EEC on 1 January 1986 the Spanish market suddenly became vulnerable to parallel imports. We knew that our price structure in Spain was higher than in the rest of the EEC – considerably higher. This was not an attractive scenario, but the problem could not be ducked.

So, we sat down and explained all of this to Rafael. He was not happy about it, not at all. There was however a significant upside to Spain's EEC entry. The old import tariffs would be abolished, and J&B's price would reduce significantly. What the experts call 'the price elasticity factor' would then work in our favour. At the time we had no idea how to calculate the expected benefit. We just hoped that we could compensate for lower margins by selling more.

Rumours in the trade indicated that other importers did not see the need to reduce their prices. They wanted to pocket the tariff saving. We knew that if this happened chaos would ensue.

Confronted with these rumours, we felt that we had no alternative but to go it alone, and then manage our way, as best we could, through the ensuing competitive confusion.

In mid-December 1985 Rafael closed his warehouse and refused to accept any more orders until the New Year. Then on 1 January 1986 he published his new EEC price list. His new prices were reduced by the tariff saving plus enough to harmonise our Spanish and French price structures. This would eliminate any incentive to parallel J&B Rare into Spain from France. As he did this, it was a bit like lighting the blue touchpaper of a rocket and wondering what would happen when ignition took place.

But before I tell you what did happen in Spain in 1986, let's catch up on what had been happening in France, another increasingly important market.

46

Cooper Goes to Épernay

As the business in the markets outside America continued to grow, Dorrien's team also expanded. One of the best additions to the squad was Anthony Cooper. He was rarely called Anthony, sometimes Tony, or even Coops; but we usually just called him Cooper. He joined us from the London Stock Exchange, which he had found underwhelming.

Soon after he joined J&B, Cooper came with me on a trip to France.

I always preferred to visit Moët in Épernay rather than in Paris. Some people found this strange. I think I did it because of my ongoing love of wine; and because I am a bit of a country boy at heart. They put you up in a delightfully elegant, but rustic, hotel. When you opened the curtains in the morning you could look down over a sea of vines. And between discussions they would take you for lunch to their château.

Château de Saran was originally an eighteenth-century hunting lodge that, together with its vineyards, has been owned by Moët et Chandon for decades. A fine, elegant building, not far from Épernay, the château is set in a commanding position with vineyards slipping away on all sides. Back in the 1970s it was beautifully, but comfortably, decorated, rather like a grand English country house but with a splash of French élan. I understand that the château was closed between 2014 and 2019, and then completely refurbished. I imagine that Saran now stands at the very pinnacle of everything that is grand luxe.

After World War II, England was the principal export market for champagne; and Moët used Saran to entertain smart English wine merchants. Eddie Tatham and Ralph Cobbold were doubtless regular guests from J&B. It was still much like that in the seventies, though Moët were already also using the château to receive visitors from all over the world.

The running of the château was under the command of a châtelaine. The châtelaines retained by Moët were invariably elegant ladies of a certain age. They had impeccable pedigrees and were always genuinely charming and fun to be with. On this occasion our hostess was a Countess with a complicated Polish name that I cannot possibly remember. It was her job to organise the details of the lunch – menu, wines, flowers, placement, and so forth – and to make sure that everything ran smoothly. She was assisted by Albert, the friendly butler, and various other staff, all in white gloves.

Apéritifs consisted principally of champagne (served from magnums) and whisky (J&B Rare obviously). The French drank whisky to *faire plaisir* to us; and I suspect that for them, it made a pleasant change. We drank champagne. Cooper was on his best behaviour and mingled politely with our hosts and the other guests. Moët were represented by Claude Fourmon, Ghislain de Vogüé, Louis Haingerlot and James Guillepain: all very senior people. During the morning we had been discussing an extension to their distribution contract – an important meeting. There were also other people present at the lunch, including their agents from Venezuela and Quebec.

The dining room was magnificent. The first thing you noticed was the platoon of large Baccarat crystal glasses formed up in front of each place setting. These were for a range of different champagne cuvées that would be presented during the luncheon. Sometimes, in deference to *les Anglais* (when any were present), a small glass for red wine would be added to the line-up. I always found it amusing that these glasses were about a quarter of the size of those used for champagne. Usually, it is the other way round.

On the day of our visit, we were a group of a dozen or so placed around the large table. The Countess (with the complicated Polish name) presided; and whenever the talking flagged she would throw in a conversation igniter to keep things going. She seemed able to do this in all manner of languages, which at times was most helpful.

Now Cooper was positioned opposite me and next to the man from Quebec, who was called Pierre. After second helpings of an exquisite *suprême de volaille* had been offered, there was a very slight lull in the conversation. The Countess (with the complicated Polish name) turned to Pierre and asked him about whisky in Canada: 'Was there any?' she enquired innocently. Pierre, of course, then explained to the Countess (with the complicated Polish name) that whisky was a thriving business in Canada. The skills to make it had been brought there by the Scots. Furthermore, it had been a major revenue earner when Prohibition had ruled in the States because tons of the stuff had been bootlegged across the border from Canada. He then turned to Cooper and asked him if he had ever tried any Canadian whisky.

Cooper said he had once tried a Canadian whisky.

'And what did you think of it?' asked Pierre.

It was at this point that I began to panic. Cooper has always had a way of saying things as he sees them. He does it with great charm; but what can be taken as friendly banter on a boys' biking outing (he loves big motorbikes) might not go down well at a formal international business luncheon.

To warn him to be diplomatic, I could not kick him under the table because the table was too wide. Instead, I gave him a hard stare. The sort that Paddington Bear could give. What it tried to say was: 'I think I know what you are going to say Cooper but please, PLEASE don't say it.'

Cooper was sitting with three glasses in front of him: the first still held a few traces of Moët et Chandon Brut Impérial; the next, which was almost empty, still held a whiff of Moët et Chandon Vintage 1971; the third glass, with which he was toying, held some very pretty Dom Pérignon Rosé.

Cooper looked as if he was in Heaven.

Cooper met my stare with a confident smile, but his gaze was just a tiny bit glazed. Then swivelling to Pierre, he said:

'To be quite honest Pierre,'

'Cripes,' I thought, 'now we're for it.'

'To be quite honest,' Cooper repeated, 'I thought it was … absolutely disgusting.'

At this point all conversation stopped.

Everybody looked at Cooper.

Cooper smiled cheerfully back.

Then everybody started talking. All at once. About anything.

The French were appalled.

Now Pierre was a nice man. He was also a wise bird; and he could see exactly what had happened. So, he just chuckled, bless him, taking it as the piece of banter, which Cooper had intended, and told Cooper that probably he had not tried anything like the best of what Canada had to offer.

The Countess (with the complicated Polish name) then kept the rest of the conversation well away from whisky.

Cooper stayed with us for about ten years. During his time with J&B the markets under his management flourished. He was undoubtedly the best salesman we ever had. He could sell ice to an Eskimo. I was very sad when he left but, happily, I have kept up with him ever since.

And as for his faux pas, I thought of giving him a rocket but then remembered all the stupid things I had done as a new boy, out of sight in Latin America. So, I desisted: at least I hope I did.

Dorrien Belson and Ghislain de Vogüé signing the new distribution contract in the J&B hot air balloon at L'Abbaye de Hautvillers in 1976

47

Publicité Française

In France the Loi Évin regulations greatly restricted all forms of advertising for alcohol and tobacco. But James Guillepain, Moët's marketing director, compensated for this by contriving wonderfully creative PR initiatives.

James was on very good terms with Patrick Fourticq, a senior pilot with Air France. Patrick liked to fly, not just Jumbo jets, but all manner of aircraft. In the late seventies, when microlite planes first appeared, he and James teamed up and entered a J&B Rare branded microlite in an aerial Tour de France. Patrick won that. Then, moving up from microlites, they clad a Piper Malibu in J&B Rare colours and established a new record for the Atlantic crossing by a single-engine aircraft. All of this attracted a great deal of favourable publicity for the brand.

Peter Darbyshire, who had taken over from Cooper, was an enthusiastic supporter of these ventures. When I had wondered aloud whether they could be as successful as they turned out to be, I had been told that if we did not back these schemes the Moët board would be very upset. Their top brass were, I was informed, very keen. Not wishing to spoil our *entente cordiale* with Moët, I withdrew any slight misgivings that I may have had.

But after a while I twigged that, on the French side, James Guillepain was playing the same card, and telling his bosses that J&B were very enthusiastic about these initiatives, and that if Moët blocked them, it would spoil their 'special relationship' with J&B. It was clearly a case of boys having fun, but happily to very good effect for the brand.

And that was only the beginning.

Back in 1938, Howard Hughes had set a round-the-world record when he piloted a Lockheed 14 Super Electra from New York to Paris, Moscow, Omsk, Yakutsk, Fairbanks (Alaska), Minneapolis, and back to New York. He did it in 3 days, 19 hours, and 17 minutes.

One day in the 1980s, when he was flying for Air France, Patrick Fourticq had a stopover in the Bahamas, and there he spied a Lockheed Lodestar. She was parked in an aircraft scrap yard and was being used as a shed for chickens. Although the plane was in a terrible condition, she was undoubtedly very similar in style and vintage to the Howard Hughes plane. Patrick then conceived the idea of buying her, restoring her to operating condition, and then using her to replicate the Howard Hughes round-the-world flight – but hopefully in a shorter time.

The Guillepain, Fourticq, Darbyshire confraternity then swung into action, and within a short space of time J&B had bought the plane and she was back in France being restored under the supervision of Art Powell, a Canadian who was a professional aircraft engineer. She was renamed *The Spirit of J&B*.

Preparations for the flight were meticulous. In 1938 Howard Hughes had stuffed his plane full of table tennis balls in the belief that if she came down in the drink, they would create extra flotation. So, *The Spirit of J&B* was likewise loaded. This time the ping-pong balls were branded with the J&B Rare logo.

After she had been restored, Patrick took *The Spirit of J&B* on a tour to visit our major European markets. This created plenty of excitement for our agents and their favoured customers. For example, Philippe Meerte, the CEO of the J&B agent in Belgium, chartered a plane and took a hundred journalists on a surprise 'Mystery Tour'. After a short flight from the main airport at Brussels, they landed at a small remote airfield. Philippe and Peter then escorted their passengers to a hangar which had been decorated as a 1930s American speakeasy, complete with old cars and Tommy guns. There, the journalists were revived with canapés and glasses of J&B Rare. But they remained bemused – until, that is, they were taken outside to hear an approaching growl of old piston engines before witnessing *The Spirit of J&B* perform a (very) low-level flypast. Patrick Fourticq then piloted her around in a tight loop before landing and then taking her up again; but only after the TV crews had climbed aboard.

Across Europe, *The Spirit of J&B* attracted massive press and TV coverage. The plane was a real star. It was an excellent way to build momentum for our attempt to beat the Howard Hughes record.

The crew selected to fly around the world with Patrick comprised: Henri Pescarolo, Hubert Auriol, and Art Powell. Having Art on board, the man who had managed the plane's restoration, made sense as well as being a reassurance for the others. Henri was not only a qualified pilot but also a famous racing driver who had won the Le Mans 24 Hours on four occasions. Hubert was equally well known: he was the first person to have won the Paris-Dakar Rally on a motorcycle as well as in a car. *The Spirit of J&B* was blessed with a star-studded crew.

Getting permission to land at three Soviet airfields (Moscow, Omsk, and Yakutsk) had not been easy, but they had got it. So, everything was cleared for the take-off of our three French musketeers (plus one Canadian).

Then a young German threw a spanner in the works.

In May 1987 when Matthias Rust was only nineteen, he rented a small Cessna aeroplane. He had only fifty hours' flying experience, but on 13 May he took off from an airfield near Hamburg and flew to the Faroe Islands. From there he went to Iceland where he stayed for several days. Eventually he flew on to Helsinki via Bergen in Norway.

On 28 May Matthias took off from Helsinki with a flight plan filed for Stockholm. But after take-off he banked sharply and headed straight for the Soviet coast of Estonia: and then on towards Moscow. By a series of lucky breaks and Soviet incompetence he was neither forced down nor shot down. So, chugging innocently onwards, through one Soviet airspace after another, he eventually reached Moscow and spotted the Kremlin. He circled Red Square a couple of times. He was trying to shoo the promenading babushkas and their prams out of the way so that he could land safely. This ploy failed; so instead he landed next door, on the Bolshoy Moskvoretsky Bridge.

The Comrades were naturally appalled and deeply embarrassed by this uninvited incursion into the very heart of their heartland. But the rest of the world thought it a most wonderful lark.

Gorbachev used Matthias Rust's thrust through Soviet airspace as an excuse to fire his defence minister for incompetence. He also managed to get rid of some hard-line generals who were not in favour of his shift towards Perestroika. So, for him it was, though deeply embarrassing, not all bad news.

However, Gorbachev's air traffic control Comrades revisited the permission they had given for *The Spirit of J&B* to land at Moscow, Omsk, and Yakutsk, and issued an emphatic *Nyet*, or 'no way'.

This created a huge problem for the intended flight because it had been scheduled to coincide with the Paris Air Show. Some quick thinking was required.

The solution was to have a different flight path but with the same distance. So, on 17 June 1987, with Patrick Fourticq at the controls, *The Spirit of J&B* took off from the Paris Air Show at Le Bourget and flew to Spitsbergen, the Norwegian islands in the Arctic Ocean. There it refuelled before continuing onwards and over the North Pole to Fairbanks in Alaska. The crew then set a course for New York with further refuelling stops at Vancouver, Los Angeles, and Miami. It was in New York that the 35,000 J&B Rare ping-pong balls were loaded into the belly of the plane. From New York they flew on to Gander, in Newfoundland, before crossing the Atlantic and returning to the Paris Air Show at Le Bourget.

The journey had taken 3 days, 16 hours, and 48 minutes. Patrick Fourticq was able to declare: 'Nous battons Hughes' – we beat Hughes.

But now we must leave *The Spirit of J&B*, with the magical growl of her piston engines echoing in our ears and move back to our story in Spain, where the brand was destined to fly higher and faster than in France or even Italy.

Published in 1987 by Albin Michel in Paris, *Le Grand Challenge* was an account of how *The Spirit of J&B* took on and defeated Howard Hughes's epic round-the-world journey

48

Ignition in Spain

If you have ever flown on Concorde, you will know what it's like when you take off. One moment you are sitting on the runway. Across the aisle Nick Faldo is reading about himself in *Golf World*. Further up front you can hear Robert Maxwell being rude to the cabin staff. Other passengers are reading their FTs. Then the captain comes on over the intercom. He explains that he is just waiting for the TWA 747 in front of you to take off. Then it will be our turn. He can't resist telling you that the TWA Jumbo is also bound for New York, but that we will get there three and a half hours before her.

Finally, he is cleared for take-off. He slides the throttles forward. The four Rolls-Royce Olympus 593 engines roar into life. The whole plane vibrates with frustrated power because the brakes are still on. Then they are released. At that moment you are thrown back and pinned into your seat. An instant later you are hurtling down the runway. Seconds later, London, Windsor Castle and Slough are far behind and way below. A minute or two later one of BA's veteran stewardesses is cantering towards you with Dom Pérignon on ice, a mumsy smile on her face and promises of a hot lunch to follow. You are in a new world, high up and above the clouds. You may be blasting holes in the ozone layer, but it is exciting stuff.

Riding J&B Rare in Spain during 1986 was a bit like that. In that year our sales grew by an incredible 50 per cent to 770,000 cases.

Pat Connolly was the person who managed all those shipments to Spain. Pat was a quiet, meticulous, gentle Irishman. He spoke no Spanish; yet in all the years that he dealt with Spain there was never a single misunderstanding between him and them. He was the sort of person who epitomises what good customer service is all about. 1986 was to be a turbulent year for Pat; he managed it all with quiet efficiency.

In the first few months of 1986, chaos reigned in the Spanish whisky market. Other importers did not reduce their prices to EU levels. Consequently, their sales stagnated as ours accelerated and, as we had predicted, parallel imports started to appear. Learning the hard way, Rafael's competitors now realised the need to bring their prices in line with EU norms.

In 1986 Margaret Thatcher had not quite finished licking the trade unions into shape. The world of the 'just in time' supply chain had not yet arrived; we were still vulnerable to wildcat strikes. As a precaution against this we built a substantial reserve of bottled stock which was kept on hand in Scotland ready for immediate shipment if a strike threatened.

We also gave our production people in Scotland sales forecasts that were more ambitious than the targets we gave to group HQ. In this way we could be sure to meet a sudden demand for extra sales without running the risk of being pilloried for not meeting an over-ambitious forecast. Eventually head office started talking directly to Scotland and we had to abandon this ploy. However, during that testing period it served us very well. But even so, Pat Connolly's abilities were stretched to the limit to keep up with the demand.

The surge in sales did not end in 1986: the following year sales grew by a further 30 per cent, taking J&B Rare to over a million cases. Our sales had doubled in two years. By 1987 our market share had grown to an unprecedented 37 per cent. Johnnie Walker had fallen back to third position. However, in the previous two years Ballantine's had doubled its market share and was now lying in second place. Ballantine's was now the emerging threat.

It was around this time that we invited Rafael to try and do something he had always dreamed of doing: catching a salmon in Scotland.

49

Don Rafael's Fish

J&B Rare was blended and bottled at Strathleven, near Dumbarton, not far from Glasgow. Strathleven Bonded Warehouse Ltd was then owned by Michael Everist and his associated directors. It was Michael who very kindly invited James Bruxner, Rafael, and me for a day's fishing at Meikleour: one of the finest salmon beats on the River Tay.

Ronnie, the resident ghillie, was to be our mentor for the day. Ronnie was a very good ghillie, and rightly proud of his beat; but he liked his charges to be competent fly fishermen. He felt that a salmon beat of this calibre was for killing fish, not for learners to muck about on. If he had a fault, I would say that he was not very patient with beginners.

So, there we were, all lined up on the lawn outside Ronnie's bothy, suitably armed with rods, nets, and wading sticks. With all this kit, and clad in chest high rubber waders, we must have looked like a squad of Robert the Bruce's irregulars off for a day's Sassenach bashing down at Bannockburn.

Rafael had assured me that he knew how to cast a fly. From watching him warm-up with some rather tentative waggles of a 12-foot Hardy rod, it was clear that Ronnie did not agree. We were not off to a good start.

The usual technique on Ronnie's beat was for two rods to fish from the bank, and for the other two to go out on the river with him in a small boat. Clearly being with Ronnie was the premium slot. However, Ronnie made it clear that if Rafael was going in the boat there would be no room for a second rod: 'Too bluddy dangerous,' he muttered.

To be honest it was not a good day for fishing. The sun shone. The scenery was enchanting. But there was no sign of any fish. Still, it was very pleasant to be away from the office, out in the fresh air, and enjoying nature on a glorious summer's day. After working hard all morning we repaired, fishless, to the hut for a slap-up picnic lunch. Rafael seemed to have enjoyed himself in the boat. Clearly Ronnie had managed to stifle any urge to tip him overboard.

At the end of lunch Michael outlined the options for the afternoon. He hinted that the normal practice was for the boat people to swap with those who had spent the morning fishing from the bank. So, he asked Rafael if he would like to have a go from the bank; or (after a very long pause) perhaps he would like another go in the boat. Rafael looked him straight in the eye and said that yes please he'd love another go in the boat.

This was the moment for James to deploy his talent for delegation and instruct me to pass on the good news to Ronnie. Ronnie was not best pleased, but he took the news stoically and trudged off to prepare the boat. Michael, James, and I repositioned ourselves along the bank and set to work. The sun shone, the birds sang, we admired the scenery; and we diligently flogged the water: all to no avail. Not a single fish showed itself. We suspected that they were all lazing about in the river and laughing at us. Fishing had to stop at five o'clock; that was the rule of the beat. So, at the stroke of five we plodded back to the hut. We could not imagine that Rafael had fared any better.

We were wrong.

As their boat rounded the bend in the river, Rafael and Ronnie were both wearing smiles that you could see from 50 yards away. They had fished assiduously all afternoon; and, according to Ronnie, Rafael was beginning to cast well but they were having no luck. Then at five to five, and thinking about his tea, Ronnie said it was time to stop. 'Wait a minute,' said Rafael (rather in the mode of Jesus when he was in that boat giving fishing tips to St Peter and a couple of the Apostles), 'Can I have one last go in this pool?' He then launched into a titanic cast but, according to Ronnie, it all went horribly wrong. The line landed in a tangled heap about 5 yards out from the boat.

Now, fish are not logical beasts. If a fly is presented to them in a clumsy manner, they usually treat it with disdain. But not always: and this was a case in point. There was a fish idling in that pool, just off from their boat. This fish saw the fly and took it. Then shocked to find that it was not what it thought it to be, the fish raced across the river and, in a rage to get rid of the offending bait, leaped clear to shake it off. All of this straightened out the line very nicely and revealed a truly big salmon.

Surprised by the sight of this monster, and by the strong pull on his line, Rafael was all but yanked out of the boat. Fortunately, Ronnie caught him before he disappeared overboard. Then the fight began. With Ronnie urging him to keep the tip of the rod up, Rafael fought for a good twenty minutes. But in the end, he won. It was a fine cock salmon fresh from the ocean and carrying sea lice. When we weighed it, Rafael's salmon tipped the scales at over 20 pounds.

Rafael, of course, was ecstatic. So was Ronnie: and so were we all. Then the question arose; what should we do with it? Rafael wanted to take his prize fish home to Spain, but he was due to stay in Scotland for three more days and the weather was gloriously warm. So, the idea of taking home a large, fresh salmon did not seem sensible. Michael advised having it smoked, and that was what we determined. Michael said he would take care of the arrangements.

At around 5.30 our party broke up. James and Michael headed south. Rafael and I were due to join a group of his customers who were flying in for a visit to our distilleries. We were due to meet them that evening at the Clifton Hotel in Nairn. Owned and run by Gordon Macintyre, the Clifton was a wonderfully artistic and quirky hotel. Sadly, it no longer exists.

Since it was such a fine evening, I decided to take the back road. We headed north through Blairgowrie and past Balmoral. Then we turned west and went over by Cock Bridge and Tomintoul before coming down to Nairn by way of Grantown-on-Spey. Bathed in that soft northern light that is so special in Scotland, the scenery was pure magic. I thought Rafael would enjoy the ride, but he seemed to be sleeping the sleep of the just. Judging by the look on his face he was dreaming of more, and bigger fish.

We got a great reception at The Clifton. First by Gordon Macintyre, and then by a bevy of Rafael's senior lieutenants. Everyone knew we had been fishing, and everyone wanted to know the score. Rafael had no trouble explaining his triumph. In truth, he was quite happy to tell the tale several times that evening. Of course, they all wanted to see the monster salmon that he had caught; so, we had to explain that it was away being smoked.

It was at this point that some snake at the back of the pack said: 'But Don Rafael why didn't you have it made into a *trofeo*?'

Now none of us had thought of having the darned thing stuffed and made into a trophy. Rafael was quite cross at my lack of foresight. So, I phoned Michael Everist to see if it could be headed off from the smokehouse and sent to a taxidermist instead.

'It's too late.' He said, 'It's already in the smokehouse; and no, David, there is no way I can find a replacement 20 pounder to have stuffed in its place! Salmon that size are very rare.'

That night I had a nightmare. I was visiting Rafael in his *despacho*. It was an enormous room rather like the Oval Office. Rafael was sitting behind a very big desk, and the desk was flanked by the Spanish flag on one side and a J&B flag on the other. Displayed on the wall behind the desk was an enormous stuffed salmon. If only …

It was about the time that Rafael was learning how to catch a salmon that I started to learn Italian.

50

Learning Italian

I thought Bandini would be pleased when I told him I was learning Italian. He did pretend to be pleased, but he looked suspicious. Anyway, I persisted in my studies. These consisted in going to a language school in Oxford Street every morning for a two-hour session. Half the session was spent with headphones clamped on doing 'exercises'. The other half was spent with a tutor: mine was Michel Camilleri. A good teacher and extremely *simpatico*, Michel actually came from Malta; but his Italian credentials were impeccable.

After Michel had drummed the rudiments into me, I squared up to Bandini and said I'd like to practise my newly acquired skills by spending some time in the market visiting some of his agents and their customers. He thought about this for a bit before saying that, since it was cold and miserable in the north of Italy at 'this time of year', perhaps I would enjoy a visit to Naples?

I was very pleased with this proposal. I had never been to Naples but had read some wonderful accounts of it. Moreover, Bandini's commission agent in Naples was one of his best. He was always winning Bandini's annual award for best in class at selling. It seemed therefore, the perfect place to practise my Italian.

Bandini's commission agent in Naples was Commendatore Cucinella. I asked what being a commendatore meant. It sounded frightfully important. Bandini said it was like being a 'Sir' in England, and was granted, in Italy to distinguished citizens for outstanding services to their country.

I had been informed that Neapolitans are lean, olive-skinned, extroverts, much given to waving their hands around, especially when speaking: a sort of revved-up version of a bookmaker's tic-tac. I was told that, if you tie a Neapolitan's hands together, he will be quite unable to speak. These nuggets of information all added zest to my anticipation.

When I met the Commendatore, he was not like that at all. He was short, pale, and almost completely spherical. But he seemed friendly enough and took me off to dine at a swanky restaurant.

It was a fish restaurant.

Now it turned out that the Commendatore was the one citizen in town who was not a great talker. Moreover, when he did talk, he seemed to have an accent that I had not encountered with Michel nor from my language school's taped exercises. I tried hard but conversation was proving sticky.

For our main course we had some delicious local fish. I don't remember what they were called, but they were presented to us before being cooked so that we could examine them and see how fresh they were: not that I could tell a fresh fish from a stale one. But the Commendatore examined them closely and expressed satisfaction.

After being lightly, but perfectly, grilled they were deftly dismembered in front of us. I was then offered the heads, These I naturally declined. Who could possibly want to eat the head of a fish?

But, to my surprise the Commendatore indicated that he would like to have the heads. I assumed he must have cats at home and wanted the waiter to wrap them up so that he could take them back to his pet moggie. They do this sort of thing in America; maybe the custom had travelled to the States with early immigrants from Southern Italy?

So, to try and fan the dying embers of conversation, and out of sheer curiosity, I cranked up my awful Italian and asked the Commendatore if he kept cats?

The Commendatore clearly understood my question which pleased me. But he seemed much affronted by it, which did not.

It transpired that somewhere in the bony structure of the heads of this particular type of fish, there lurks some morsel of flesh which, when eaten, delivers the ultimate pescatarian delight. The Commendatore was therefore not amused by my quip. He spent the rest of our *secondo* course picking over the heads of his fish (and the heads of my fish) in almost total silence.

I did my best to explain that in England, being not very sophisticated in culinary matters, we don't eat the heads of fish but instead (I very foolishly confessed) we give them to our cats, if we have any. This explanation clearly confirmed the Commendatore's prejudices about our cooking culture, or lack of it, in England. After a while he relented, doubtless consoling himself with the fact that he'd just managed to land, for himself, a double helping of his favourite delicacy.

In the ensuing days I visited several Neapolitan customers with the Commendatore. His best customer, a major whole-saler, had a cavernous medieval warehouse. There seemed to be no order or method in the way his stock was stored. But the Commendatore assured me that this customer kept all the information in his head. For example, he knew, and showed us that he knew, exactly how many cases of J&B Rare he had in stock, and where different batches were stored. And, not trusting banks, he kept bundles of cash hidden in various parts of this warehouse. But he didn't show us where.

It was all very different from Northern Italy.

Although communication was a problem, I enjoyed my first visit to Naples; and I got the clear impression that our Commendatore was a greatly respected figure in the local trade.

Before I went to Naples, what I had not appreciated, but what Bandini had known perfectly well, was that in Naples they speak Neapolitan which is not really Italian at all. The poor Commendatore had been trying hard, but he was not comfortable in proper Italian. Bandini must have known this too. My trip to Naples was therefore, for him, a splendid practical joke: a bit like sending someone to the Gorbals to learn English.

51

Modern Marketing

Strangely, some of the new marketing disciplines that we deployed in the 1980s stemmed from the teachings of Leonardo Fibonacci da Pisa, a famous thirteenth-century mathematician. It was Fibonacci who had introduced the Arabic-Hindu decimal system into Europe; he had also rediscovered an ancient mathematical rule that had been much used by the Greeks and Egyptians.

It all began with rabbits. While observing their breeding habits, Fibonacci had noted a rhythmic ratio in the way that rabbits could increase and multiply. Moving on from rabbits, Fibonacci discovered that this mathematical rule also seemed to fit naturally with many aspects of architecture, music, and even nature.

The rule in question is known as the golden mean, or the golden ratio. To find it you begin by adding a sequence of numbers. So, you start with 1+1 and get 2. Then 1+2 = 3. Then 2+3 = 5. Each time, you are adding the last number to the one before. So next comes 3+5 = 8, and so on. But when you get to higher numbers (say 34+55 = 89), and instead divide the total (89) by the previous number (55) you invariably get an answer close to 1.62 (or 1.618 if you wish to be more precise). Try it. It works.

It is this ratio of 1 to around 1.62 that is known as the golden ratio or the golden mean; and it crops up all over the place. When constructing their pyramids, the Egyptians recognised that these great monuments would look just right if the height of the pyramid had a ratio of 1 to 1.62 with the external slope. Funny thing this: but it fits. Even in nature the formation of florets in a cauliflower and seeds on a sunflower are said to conform to this rule.

Nowadays, Fibonacci's discovery is even used to measure stock market volatility.

When Paul Curtis joined IDV as group marketing director in the mid-1980s, I was invited to tell him all about the amazing success that we were having with J&B Rare in Spain. I suspect that if there had been a fly on the wall at our meeting the fly might have concluded that neither of us quite understood what the other was talking about.

Coming from Mars (the confectioner), Paul had a very thorough understanding of FMCG marketing. FMCG, of course, stands for 'fast-moving consumer goods'. These 'goods' being brands that get most of their sales from super-markets. They are usually driven by heavy conventional advertising such as you see on TV.

Our approach to marketing had always been different. We had built the brand in the 'on-trade': that is to say places like bars where you consume 'on' the premises. Only later was J&B Rare allowed to emerge cautiously into the land of super and hypermarkets. We had a natural aver-sion to adopting a supermarket-led strategy. However, it was clear that as the market got bigger, supermarket sales were going to become increasingly important. So, we did need to improve our expertise in that field, even if it was through gritted teeth.

At the end of our chat Paul suggested I call David Turtle. He had known David at Mars and thought he might be able to 'help'. Since leaving Mars, David had set up Strategy in Focus, his own marketing consultancy. Paul probably wanted David to take a look at what we were doing, and then send him a 'translation' so that he could understand what we were up to. Naturally, I was deeply suspicious of this suggestion. However, turning it down didn't seem to be a very smart career move.

So, I dutifully called David. I was concerned that J&B might find itself coerced into a supermarket-led strategy. At the time our old enemies at DCL (by then owned by Guinness) had adopted just such a model; and we had managed to benefit considerably from their sudden disinterest in the on-premise trade.

I need not have worried. From the start David was fascinated to discover what was, for him, a new experience. He quickly appreciated that consumers acquire their drinking habits in the on-trade. Furthermore, the on-trade is of much greater importance in Southern European markets where people are more accustomed to socialise outside their own homes. He demonstrated that the Spanish market would continue to grow for some time, and that the opportunity was there for J&B Rare to drive that growth. He said that he could help us achieve this and he managed to convince me that he really could.

In the next few years David was to use Fibonacci's golden ratio in a number of ways to enhance our marketing campaign. Key amongst these was pricing. He demonstrated that in a free market (with no fiscal constraints or quotas) the market for any product would cluster its volume around four price points. He defined these pricing categories as *cheap, standard, premium*, and *deluxe. Cheap* was at the commodity end of the scale and was mostly occupied by own-label brands. *Standard* would be for big local brands. In Spain that meant brands like Larios Gin or Whisky DYC (a huge brand of Spanish whisky). *Premium* was for fashionable imported brands like J&B Rare. And *deluxe* was for brands like Chivas Regal or Johnnie Walker Black Label.

The greatest volume would come from *standard* brands. The highest margin per bottle would come from *deluxe* brands; but the greatest combination of volume and profit would come from *premium* brands. J&B Rare was therefore positioned in the sweet spot.

David explained that if you started with the *cheap* category, the optimal price points for each superior category would rise in steps of around 62 per cent (or exactly in line with the golden ratio). He showed how this norm worked for markets as diverse as cars, beer, restaurants, and dog food. We therefore monitored our price position against the big local *standard* brands as well as against our direct competitors.

DYC, a Spanish whisky, was the benchmark *standard* brand. When our differential rose above 62 per cent, we would lose share. When it dropped below that premium, we would be losing margin without gaining sufficient extra volume to compensate. It was all very precise: and to our astonishment it worked.

In all of this, David became a tremendous asset to us.

Ever since my J&B days I have been fascinated by the concept of the golden ratio. It pops up in an unexpected manner all over the place. When I was about eighteen, my parents were given a book called *The World Mine Oyster* by Matila Ghyka. They didn't read it. My mother dismissed it as: 'Another of Matila's books.'

'You won't understand it,' she said, 'Matila is frightfully brainy; and his books are always about mathematics. Only about four people in the world can understand them.'

So, I didn't read it. Not then: but recently I found it and did.

Matila Ghyka was a Romanian prince; his great-grandfather was the last Prince of Moldavia. We knew him because he was married to a distant cousin. *The World Mine Oyster* is only in part, about mathematics. It is really his memoirs, which are fascinating.

Born in1881, in the Moldavian part of Romania, he was educated first in Paris and then in Jersey, where he attended a Jesuit school. When he was sixteen, he joined the French Naval Academy; he would later join the Romanian navy.

In 1910, when Romania bought four gunboats from the Thames Iron Works, Matila's boss thought it would be more amusing to sail them up the Rhine, across the Ludwig Canal, and down the Danube to Romania, rather than via the Med. Matila was put in command of the gunboat flotilla for this voyage. Some two years later, he took a year off to travel, first to America, where he worked as a labourer under an assumed name; he didn't want them to know he was a prince. He then continued west to Hawaii before moving on to the Far East.

During World War I, he briefly served as a liaison officer to a Russian naval squadron in the Black Sea. The Russian admiral, to whom he was attached, and who was actually French, rounded off all his meals with bumpers of green Chartreuse to the tunes of a hussar's galloping song. After the Russian naval force retreated to Sebastapol, Matila was back to manning his English gunboats on the Danube. He received several decorations, including the MC, for his service during the Great War.

Between the two World Wars he served as a Romanian diplomat in a number of European capitals. But, at heart, Matila must have been a polymath. His real interests were mathematics, science, architecture, art, and poetry. His book, *Le Nombre d'Or*, was published in Paris in 1930. *Le Nombre d'Or* was of course the golden ratio.

Matila never went back to Romania. When I first met him in about 1960, I found him to be a charming, gentle, quiet old man. I recall playing piquet with him and being able to talk to him about anything. His curiosity had been prodigiously eclectic, but not at all commercial. In his old age Matila had little in terms of worldly assets; yet his memoirs demonstrate how varied are the disciples of Leonardo Fibonacci da Pisa and how varied are the applications of his teaching.

Before we return to Spain, I feel that a visit to Greece is well overdue.

Leonardo Fibonacci da Pisa (c1170–c1250)
In the Camposanto Monumentale, Pisa (very near the Leaning Tower)
1863 statue by Giovanni Paganucci

52

Lunch in Greece

When I took over responsibility for the Greek market, democracy had just returned to its birthplace.

It is easy to forget that between 1967 and 1974 Greece was ruled by the Regime of Colonels, a military dictatorship. Then in 1974 the Turks invaded Northern Cyprus. This precipitated a political crisis and the collapse of the junta.

Our agents in Greece were S & E & A Metaxa. The company had been founded in 1888, and at one time had owned branches in Piraeus, Alexandria, Constantinople and, I think, the Crimea. Their brand of Greek Koniak had won numerous medals from across the globe. Then, after some international agreement about denominations of origin, they had to stop calling their spirit Koniak. It sounded too like Cognac. Thus, by the time of my first visit to Greece it was called brandy; and Metaxa Brandy was the leading brand in its category. The company also owned Ouzo 12, which was the top ouzo. Metaxa was undoubtedly the leading spirit company in Greece.

The company was run by Spyros Metaxa and his brother Elias. In 1968 the business had moved from its original premises in Piraeus to an impressive modern distillery, bottling plant, and office block in Kifissia, a suburb to the North of Athens.

Rather unexpectedly, behind the plant there was a chicken run and some fig trees. Spyros told me that the chickens were his mother's pride and joy. One day a fox got in and assassinated the lot. Spyros contrived to keep his mother away from her chicken run for a couple of days while he had the place cleaned up and new chickens installed. Unfortunately, when Mrs Metaxa came back to feed her chickens, she was dismayed when they failed to greet her with their customary enthusiasm. Mrs Metaxa was a formidable woman with a magnificent head of jet-black hair. Spyros said it kept its colour because she washed it in a mixture of eggs and Metaxa Brandy. He went on to suggest that if I tried her recipe, it might stop me going balder. I did try but the experiment was not a success.

Spyros and Elias each had an office on the first floor of the main building. Between their offices was a private dining room where a sweet old lady, in a hair net, served excellent home-cooked Greek nosh.

At the time of my early visits, all production matters and sales to the Greek market were run by Elias. Spyros took care of the growing export market. He was often abroad when I visited but would occasionally turn up in London. The brothers were, I believe, the grandsons of Spyros, the founder.

Occasionally, when I was talking with Elias, an old man would potter in and out offering us cups of delicious grainy Greek coffee.

'Who's that?' I asked one day.

'Oh, that's my father,' replied Elias.

It was all rather confusing.

Spyros and Elias were quite different. Elias was very efficient and methodical: a stickler for detail. Spyros was a man for the big picture and the big decisions. Eventually, as the elder brother, Spyros pulled rank and took over control of the entire business. I am not sure what the father made of this, but when I next visited Kifissia, Spyros had installed a splendid statue of the old boy on the steps leading up to the entrance of the Metaxa HQ. He had also created a deluxe cuvée of Metaxa Brandy in his honour.

It was certainly more fun dealing with Spyros than Elias, though sometimes less predictable.

For the Greek market, Metaxa had their own sales force to cover Athens and the Attica peninsula. The rest of the country was covered by a network of sub-distributors. These were highly effective local entrepreneurs. They did a tremendous job for J&B Rare. So, one day I suggested to Spyros that I ought to do a tour of Greece. I could then see for myself what they were doing for our brand. Spyros said this was a very good idea. But I'm not sure that he meant it.

Spyros informed me that my guide and driver for the Greek tour would be Paris Tsiatas. He explained that Paris was the shop steward at Metaxa and therefore represented the unions. He was also, said Spyros, part of the management team. This perplexed me. How could he do both? But Spyros did not like to be cross-examined about such matters; so, I put it down to a quirk of the patriarchal culture that seemed to exist very happily at S & E & A Metaxa.

On the first day of my tour, when Paris came to collect me at the Hilton Hotel in Athens, I found him to be a large, genial, and well-nourished looking man. He came in a very small car. He also spoke no English. Since I speak no Greek, I assumed he might speak French. He did not. I tried Spanish. Not a word. In desperation I tried the Italian that I had just started to learn.

To my astonishment, and relief, Paris could speak a little Italian. Not much. About as much as me. So off we set,

with Paris's Fiat 500 listing heavily to port, on account of
his superior ballast, as we chuntered away in a westerly
direction over the Corinth Canal, and towards Patras for
our first stop.

That week we took a clockwise route, of about 1,000
miles, around the Greek mainland. After Patras we struck
north to Corfu, then east to Thessaloniki before turning
south and returning to Athens past Mount Olympus and
via Volos.

In those days, the roads were not good, but they weren't
crowded either. It was early summer, and as we chugged
along in Paris's noble Cinquecento, more slowly uphill on
account of his weight and always listing to port for the
same reason, I was able to admire the countryside, which
was wonderfully green and alive with springtime colour. I
also noted a lot of tortoises. They must have been emerging
from hibernation and seemed to be playing Russian roulette
as they crossed, or just sat on, the nice warm tarmac. Greek
drivers must have kept a kindly look out for them because
I did not see any squashed ones. The other thing was the
cherries. It was the season for them. They were quite the
best cherries I have ever eaten – better than the best from
my native Kent.

Conversation with Paris was a bit stilted. But we
managed. He was a lovely man, and the sub-distributors
went out of their way to be as hospitable as they could.
Greek hospitality is famous, and rightly so.

Each morning the programme began with a long and
intense discussion between Paris and the local sub-distributor. It was all in Greek. I assumed that Paris was cross-
examining the local man to make sure that he had a good
display of J&B Rare (and Metaxa Brandy) on display in his

store, and that we would be visiting only those customers of his who were enthusiastic clients for J&B Rare. In other words, that our sub-distributor was all revved up to give me a favourable impression of his tireless efforts on behalf of my brand. So, during these morning prologues it seemed best for me to tactfully pay no attention to what might be going on. Which is what I did.

Spyros Fakalos was a typical Metaxa sub-distributor. He was based in Patras and covered the surrounding area. He and his wife Rubini ran a thriving wholesale business as well as a very smart patisserie in the town centre. He was wonderfully convivial and a great ambassador for J&B Rare. But the most successful sub-distributor was Basil Ioannides who, with his business partner Petros Kefalas, was based in Thessaloniki. They controlled Macedonia and the north-east of Greece. And, like all the Metaxa people, their hospitality was exceptional. We were always taken to the best restaurants in town. I had had no idea that Greek cooking could be so good. As well as marvellous fresh fish, and delicious salads, I recall spring lamb, kid (as in goat) and boar being on the menus, and an abundance of cherries everywhere.

Few of the sub-distributors spoke English. Mr Christou at Volos was one who did. Volos was our last port of call. The morning prologue in Greek between him and Paris seemed to go on for longer than usual and to be of a greater intensity than on previous days. So, I decided to break with my usual feigned indifference, and when Paris was not looking, I asked Mr Christou what it had all been about.

'Oh,' replied Mr Christou, 'Mr Tsiatas wants to know where we are going for lunch.'

53

Dinner in Las Vegas

Whenever I visited Rafael in Madrid, he would always pick me up from the hotel at *las diez menos quarto*. Literally, that means 'ten minus a quarter' or, as we might say, 'a quarter to ten'. In the evening, he also came at *las diez menos quarto*, because of course, no self-respecting Spaniard would ever be seen dead dining in a restaurant before 10 p.m. The *las diez menos quarto* thing became a bit of a tradition between us: rather a lucky one I thought.

I was reminded of this when writing the piece about all those splendid lunches I had with Paris Tsiatas in Greece.

Every year, as our sales in Spain were soaring upwards, Rafael would reward his key sub-distributors by inviting them and their wives for a holiday jaunt. This would take place in the quiet trading time of the year just after Christmas. These trips were to far flung and exotic places. In 1981 Rafael invited me to join the group. That year their itinerary would take them to the USA and Mexico. It was to be a two-week trip.

It was a very convivial group that I met up with in New York. Rafael was there with his wife Maribel, as well as with his brothers and their wives. Antonio Mendez, the sales director, and his wife Tita made up the team from HQ. Then there were his top sub-distributors or, as I was wont to call them, Rafael's provincial barons.

They came from Barcelona (Carlos Olmedes and Vicente Estruga), the Costa del Sol (Juan Lara and Manuel Becera), Andalucía (Miguel Merino), Seville (Rafael Noriega), León (Eduardo Bartolomé), the Asturias (Alberto Cortina), and last, but by no means least, Pedro Tejada from the Basque country. And their wives came too. They all got on very well with each other.

From New York we flew to Las Vegas. Since J&B Rare was such a big brand in the States, I thought that it would be an appropriate place for me to let J&B buy them a night on the tiles. The idea was to have dinner and go to one of the shows for which Las Vegas is famous.

It was the Lido de Paris, at the Stardust Resort, that I chose for this jolly. So, I went along in the morning to book and make the necessary arrangements. When I got to the venue, I met up with a very slick individual who was the Maître d' of Reservations. He explained that I had two options. I could either book for the dinner show at 6 p.m., or for the after-dinner show at 8 p.m. This was much earlier than I had expected. It seemed that in the States they like to dine at around 6 p.m., a hangover perhaps from the habits of the time when they were George III's top colony. At first, I could not see how this might fit with the customary feeding timetable of my guests. But, after a moment's reflection I had a brainwave; I booked the after-dinner show. The Maître d' of Reservations then explained to me that the price of the tickets allowed each guest to order two 'cocktails' for consumption during the show.

A bizarre conversation then ensued. It went roughly as follows:

Me: 'Can the cocktails be J&B Rare?'

Him: 'Yeah.'

Me: 'Please can we have a bottle of J&B Rare on the table?' The Spaniards would expect that.

Him: 'No.'

Me: 'Why not?'

Him: 'Cos it's dispensed from a tank in the roof.' (This was true. They had a contraption up aloft with half-gallon bottles of J&B Rare being tipped into a tank which had dispensing pipes leading down to a tap in the bar, like draught beer in a pub in England, except that would come up from the cellar, not down from the attic.)

Me: 'Oh. When do you serve the two drinks?'

Him: 'When the show starts, yer guests will each get two glasses of J&B Rare.'

Me: 'What both at the same time?'

Him: 'Yeah.'

Me: 'Does it have to be like that?'

Him: 'Yes sir. It do.'

Me: 'I see. But can we have a good table please?'

Him, now distinctly surly: 'Look buddy; are you sum kinda lawyer or summit? Why d'ya keep asking me deez questions? I ain't seen the colour of yer oiyz yet.'

At this point the briefing from our US agent's local man kicked in. He said I would have to give a big tip to secure a good table. He had recommended $100, which was a lot of money in 1981.

I had therefore prepared a discreet wodge of five twenty-dollar bills for this eventuality. I took the wodge of readies out of my pocket and passed it surreptitiously to the Maître d' of Reservations. I expected him to trouser it discreetly. Now the Maître d' of Reservations did not do 'discreetly'. Instead, he took my wodge, scrutinised it carefully, and then peeled back each note in turn. I could see his lips counting:

'Twenty, forty, sixty, eighty, and a hundred.'

Beach, the stately butler at Blandings Castle, and Alfred, the top waiter, at the Mirabelle, would have been appalled by such vulgarity.

But, as far as this Maître d' of Reservations was concerned it did the business. He refolded my (now his) wodge of cash and stuffed it in his pocket saying as he did so:

'Sure buddy, I'll get ya a real good table.'

His attitude had switched from grumpy and hostile to best friend in a nanosecond. Since the Maître d' of Reservations was now an ally I ventured to ask him one last question:

'Where,' I said, 'can we get a decent dinner after the after-dinner show?'

This threw him for a moment but, warmed doubtless by the hundred bucks in his pocket, his brain cells clicked into motion, and he gave me the name of a restaurant, Château Vegas, which was patronised by leading artists after their performances.

And he did give us a splendid table.

As the show started a platoon of waitresses marched up and delivered our 'cocktails'. Bang, bang they went as they plonked down two glasses of J&B Rare for each of us: all lined up neatly in a line astern formation.

The show itself was excellent: very Hollywood. We had comedians, conjurors, crooners, and of course, lots of chorus girls whose legs seemed to go up to their armpits; and who could kick higher than I had ever seen anyone kick before.

The Provincial Barons loved it all, especially the chorus girls. Their señoras eyed them (the chorus girls) in a mumsy sort of way. Begoñia Tejada, from Bilbao, said that the big blonde, second from the end on the right, had a hole in her tights.

256

The dinner in the after-the-show restaurant was also a success; until that is, one of our group went off, loaded with a pocket full of quarters, nickels, and dimes, to make a call home to Spain from a pay phone at the back of the establishment, this being many years before the arrival of mobile phones.

Now the date of this great outing to the Stardust Resort was 23 February 1981. What my party did not know, until the phone call, was that at 6.23 p.m. (Spanish time) on 23 February 1981, Lieutenant Colonel Antonio Tejero had marched into the Palacio de las Cortes in Madrid at the head of 200 armed officers of the Guardia Civil. His intention was to stage a coup d'état so that democracy in Spain could be overturned and the country returned to a Falangist dictatorship, albeit under the titular control of the king, Juan Carlos.

For a while confusion had reigned. Shots had been loosed off in the Parliament building as Tejero and his men sought to wrest control. They held the MPs hostage for nearly a day, but after Juan Carlos went on TV and rejected the coup, and after other military units stayed loyal to the government, the coup collapsed, and Tejero ended up in prison for the next fifteen years.

All of this was going on at the time of that phone call. The effect on our dinner party was electric: akin perhaps to that on the hens in Mrs Metaxa's chicken run when the fox got in. Everybody wanted to get back to the hotel as quickly as possible so that they could phone their families in Spain and get the latest news.

Happily, by the following morning, the news had filtered through of the rebels' surrender and we got back to normal.

But it had been an interesting day.

54

Travelling with Great Uncle Bulgaria

That morning there was a tremendous racket going on in the office. I had got in early – very early: it was before 8 a.m. and the noise was coming from a small room on the ground floor. It sounded like a Prussian drill sergeant at the top of his game. In fact, it was John Rideal, in his den and on the phone in his best Hochdeutsch, haranguing one of his customers in Eastern Europe. The year was 1975 and John had just been recruited to develop J&B's business in the Soviet Bloc. Eastern Europe is two hours ahead of London and John liked to catch his customers first thing: their time. His habit of fortissimo early morning calls to the Comrades became legendary.

The Comecon countries behind the Iron Curtain and in Eastern Europe were small markets for Scotch whisky, but Dorrien felt that J&B should put down a marker. He predicted that the Iron Curtain might one day rust away. John was recruited because he was an Eastern European specialist. Later, West Germany (as it then was) and Scandinavia were added to his territory.

John was born in 1925. He was therefore considerably older than the rest of the team. When he joined us, it was the era of the Wombles: those delightful furry creatures that enthralled small children and were said to live in burrows under Wimbledon Common. Given that Bulgaria was part of John's territory, and since he was portly of build and with a kindly nature, John was sometimes given the moniker Great Uncle Bulgaria: GUB being the oldest and wisest of the Womble clan.

John had spent his childhood in Berlin. His father had been based there as the European representative for the Eaton Company. Eaton's had major department stores in Canada, and a global catalogue business.

John used to tell me how he saw the Reichstag burning. And how three years later, in 1936, his family had two tickets for the Berlin Olympic Games. He and his brother went most days. They carved their names on the wooden seats and, many years later, John was able to rediscover their graffiti. Then just before Christmas in the same year, the British Ambassador invited the family to a gala performance of Humperdinck's *Hansel and Gretel*. From his vantage point in the Ambassador's box, the eleven-year-old John spent most of the time using his opera glasses, not to watch the performance, but to scrutinise Hitler, and Goering who was resplendent in an exotic cream uniform. The family's dentist, Dr Hugo Blaschke, also did the gnashers of Goering, Goebbels, Himmler – and yes, Hitler too. When the War started Dr Blaschke was made an SS General.

The Rideal family was just able to scramble back to the UK before the outbreak of hostilities in 1939. By then John was a naval cadet at Dartmouth. Towards the end of the War, he served on various ships doing convoy duty in the Far East. He also took up flying. By the time he left the Royal Navy in 1959, he had flown over twenty different types of aircraft. He told me that landing on carriers was particularly hazardous because the instruments on some of the Fleet Air Arm's planes were unreliable. John's solution for this was to have the instrument panels covered with brown paper, and touch down by flying in 'by the seat of my pants' – an expression he was rather fond of.

After leaving the Royal Navy, John had gone on to represent several British companies in Eastern Europe. However, the 1973–74 oil crisis disrupted his business to such an extent that we were able to recruit him to join J&B.

So, as I said, John's background, when compared to the rest of the team, was different. None of us could have shared a dentist with Hitler; spied on Goering at the opera; gone to the Berlin Olympics; and flown twenty-four types of aircraft: all before joining J&B. But the team warmed to his avuncular nature.

John's era at J&B lasted until his retirement in 1990 and covered the last fifteen years of the Cold War. It is easy to forget how tricky that time was. For instance, my Aunt Ferga rented a house in The Little Boltons in Chelsea from Greville Wynne, a businessman who travelled frequently to Eastern Europe. In 1962 the KGB arrested Wynne for spying. He was sentenced to eight years in the notorious Lubyanka, but in 1964 he was exchanged for Konon Molody, a KGB agent. Molody was known here as Gordon Lonsdale; he was the mastermind behind the Portland Spy Ring.

Some of us thought that John might also have been working for British Intelligence's MI6. He thought this a huge joke but said that sometimes he did get the impression that MI6 thought he was spying for the KGB, and vice versa.

John's markets were tough. Scotch whisky could only be sold to diplomats, airlines, and the special hard currency shops that the Comrades established in the Soviet Bloc. The only people who could use these shops were high-ranking members of the Party and those who, for various reasons, had access to hard currency. The favoured denominations were US dollars and deutschmarks. It was a system not very different from the military *cantinas* whose existence I have mentioned in various Latin American countries.

Getting 'listed' in those hard currency shops was difficult. Layers of idle, slow motion bureaucracy had to be penetrated. The process usually culminated with a tasting. Samples would be sent out in advance. There would have to be enough to taste on the night, and more for the participants to take home. The proviso for this was 'as much as they could carry'; the Comrades were clearly extremely diligent about carrying out a very thorough assessment of a brand's quality before accepting it for a listing.

At J&B we had a wonderful array of P.O.S. material, P.O.S. being 'point of sale'. Our P.O.S. stuff included everything you could think of from pens, tote bags, golf umbrellas, and aprons through to bar material such as ice buckets, water jugs and, of course, ashtrays, because everybody smoked in those days: especially in Eastern Europe. All our P.O.S. items were elegantly decorated in the logo and colours of J&B Rare. For the tastings, the heavier P.O.S. stuff was shipped with the whisky, but since it was prone to pilferage en route, John liked to carry with him as much as he could when travelling out to host a tasting.

One other item of P.O.S that we had was matches: elegant little boxes they were too. Being flammable, they were prone to extra controls. John liked to get round that by carrying as many as he could in his capacious briefcase.

I was on a trip with him to Warsaw as we passed through, into the departure zone at Heathrow Airport, when John was stopped by a squat, square, officious-looking security lady. She demanded to see inside his briefcase. Of course, when it was opened up, all those matchboxes were revealed:

'You aren't allowed to carry all those matchboxes,' declared the fierce guardienne of Heathrow security.

'Why not? Who says I can't?' declared John, who always loved a battle with petty bureaucracy. It explains the 'hate' bit of his love-hate affair with Eastern Europe. The Comecon era abounded in petty bureaucracy.

The exchange between John and the squat, square security lady went on in this vein for some time. It ended when the squat, square lady accepted a challenge from John to get her boss and tell him to come back with a proper copy of the rules to prove her point. Otherwise, John was not to be persuaded. I could see this was going to take up some time, so I wandered off to check out the duty free shop, leaving John to look after my own bag while I was away.

When I returned, I found John standing there, legs braced and jaw jutting in a defiant Churchillian posture: he was even wearing a bow tie. The scene made me think of Horatius on the Pons Sublicius as he awaited the attack from Lars Porsena of Clusium. In the event it was not L P of Clusium who bore down upon him but a posse of Heathrow security's finest. There were about four of them and they were led by the squat, square lady who was gesticulating and pointing at John. She was addressing her comments to a chap in uniform with some gold stuff on his cap. He must have been the boss. Anyway, as they approached, John whispered to me:

'I've put the matches in your bag.'

The boss-man then asked John, quite politely, if he would mind opening his bag. John was happy to oblige because by now it contained only two boxes of matches. The small, squat, officious lady was much put out by this and protested to her boss that she was sure she had seen at least twenty boxes of the offending matches on her first inspection. John invited the boss-man to examine the evidence. He even offered to be frisked. By this time, the boss-man was looking bored. Maybe he thought the matter too petty to warrant intervention by a man of his rank. This was just as well because I'm sure I heard minion number three mutter to minion number four:

'I bet his mate [meaning me] has got them.'

During the various exchanges I was standing next to John endeavouring to look as innocent as possible – just like Paddington Bear at the Underground station after he had secreted that aromatic slice of bacon in his satchel and was being pursued by hungry dogs, and who had feigned ignorance when being cross-examined by the ticket inspector about the ensuing mayhem and the 'queer smell'.

Fortunately, the boss-man did not overhear the comments between minion number three and minion number four. So, after cautioning John that, strictly speaking, he was only allowed one box of matches and not two, he and his posse withdrew, with the squat, square lady member of his team muttering darkly to herself as she went.

John, of course, was triumphant.

Things like that happened when you travelled with Great Uncle Bulgaria.

I had never been to any of the Comecon countries. So, over a period of several years, I contrived to visit most of them with John. Apart from the three Baltic states, and Albania, I saw them all.

During the Cold War, it was an eye-opener to visit capitals such as Prague, Budapest, Bucharest, Moscow, Sofia, and East Berlin, the latter via Checkpoint Charlie. There were no bright lights and none of the glitzy advertising that you normally see in major cities. They were all drab, and the traffic was invariably sparse. On the other hand, the buildings in the city centres were much as they had been a hundred years before, although they were much shabbier. That was depressing.

Many years later, in 2010, Isabel and I went to Berlin. At the end of the War, Berlin had been bombed to ruins. So, it was interesting to see how the two sectors of the city had been rebuilt. What had been West Berlin had a gamut of modern buildings, some merely functional but many impressive. In the former Eastern sector, most of the historic buildings had been faithfully rebuilt. This had been normal Soviet policy.

But in all the Comecon cities you would also find massive architectural expressions of Socialist Classicism. The Palace of Culture in Warsaw was a typical example. 'Donated' by the Russians and standing nearly 800 feet tall, it looked like a giant wedding cake plonked down in the wrong place.

Occasionally John would take me to see one of the historic churches; St Vitus's Cathedral in Prague was one that I recall. Usually they were empty, but on one occasion when I was in Warsaw on a Sunday, I asked at the hotel if Mass was being celebrated at the local church. I was offered options at 7, 8, 9, 10, or 11 a.m. When I arrived at 8.55 for the 9 a.m. Mass, a tsunami of parishioners was leaving the 8 a.m. Mass. At the end of the 9 a.m. Mass there was a crowd waiting outside to get in for the 10 a.m. Mass. The Catholic Church was clearly flourishing in Poland. I suspect the faithful enjoyed being able to combine practising their religion with giving a quiet two fingers to the Comrades.

During the years that I travelled regularly to cities such as Madrid, Milan, Munich, Copenhagen, Lisbon, Athens, and Paris (or Épernay), I was invariably lodged in grand hotels and our agents always entertained us at very good restaurants. Consequently, I put on weight: in my prime I weighed in at over fifteen and a half stone. But it was not like that in Budapest, Belgrade, Bucharest, Prague, Warsaw, Sofia, or Moscow. In all those places the food was dreadful and the hotels grim. At the Intourist Hotel in Moscow, which was just next to Red Square, there really was a big babushka seated at a table at the end of the corridor on every floor. If you wanted to take a bath you had to go to her and 'borrow' a bath plug. She was actually quite friendly.

Once, in Sofia, we could not go to the best hotel because the Comrades were holding a Peace Conference there for the Soviet Bloc, and all the usual hotels were taken. So, we had to make do with a hotel for local tourists. It was awful. In the morning when I turned on the light in the shower cubicle, a battalion of cockroaches ran for, and disappeared through, various holes in the skirting.

In Moscow we were given an official car to take us to our appointments. Whenever we got to the car, the driver would have the radio switched on. It was invariably tuned to a station that sounded just like the BBC. But it wasn't. The English was perfect, but the news would be all about wonderful things that the Comrades were doing in places like Cuba, coupled with snide reports about the latest industrial disputes taking place in England, France, or Italy.

Of course, the Comrades did do some things extremely

well. We never saw the Bolshoi but, one evening, John and I went to the Moscow State Circus. Before the performance, there were queues of people lined up outside in disciplined groups waiting for the doors to open. The groups came from individual state factories. It smacked of school outings on a grand scale. But, inside, the performance was outstanding.

John did a wonderful job at planting a J&B presence in Eastern Europe as well as managing Germany and the Scandinavian markets.

In the early 1990s I did go back to Moscow. By this time John had retired, so I was travelling with Richard White, a brilliant new star in the J&B firmament. The Berlin Wall had fallen, and Boris Yeltsin's chaotic privatisation programme was in full swing. They were even having problems making glass bottles. This meant that in Russia, of all places, there was a shortage of vodka. Consequently, our sister company, Smirnoff, was shipping trainloads of the stuff into Russia from our bottling plant in Scotland.

At the time there were some very unsavoury characters in Moscow who were involved in the newly privatised wholesale liquor trade. There was open war amongst some of them. We were told that a few days before our visit, one of the major dealers had returned home one evening and gone to his fridge in search of a refreshing bottle of beer. Instead of beer, he found his wife inside. She was chopped up in little bits.

Although John had done a great job at planting the J&B flag in most Comecon countries, J&B's sales in Russia were still tiny. However, at this point Smirnoff's exports to Russia were huge. Because of our connection with Smirnoff, it was deemed prudent for us to be accompanied everywhere by a team of four bodyguards.

Having not one, but four, bodyguards was a new experience. They spoke no English but seemed friendly enough, though we were told that they were all ex-KGB. They wore identical blazers that were rusty red of hue and very shiny.

Richard and I did go to the Bolshoi. What we saw I don't recall, but we struck up a friendly conversation with a retired American couple who had just done the canal trip from St Petersburg to Moscow and were seated next to us. Our bodyguards waited outside. When we came out, our new American friends were quite taken aback when our bodyguards emerged from the shadows to form a protective ring around us.

Our Smirnoff hosts took us to a couple of the top night clubs. To get in you had to pass through a metal detector. As we left one club, we witnessed one of the mafiosi bosses come swaggering out. He looked neither right nor left but strode directly towards his bulletproof Mercedes. As he did so, his entourage closed in around him. One of them ran up behind him to drape his overcoat around his shoulders, Al Capone style.

We were staying at the recently opened Kempinski Hotel, just across the river from the Kremlin. It was extremely comfortable and a far cry, in style and quality, from the old Soviet Intourist Hotel that I stayed in with John.

Restaurants were now divided into two sorts: local or hard currency. The local ones were awful, and reminiscent of the Soviet era. Hard currency restaurants were excellent but very expensive, even by hard currency standards. At one such we had our bodyguards with us, but they were sitting at a nearby table. The huge menu was written in English, French, Italian, and German, but strangely not in Russian. Our poor troopers could not understand a word of it, until, that is, they spied the word *steak* which they recognised and pointed at because, bizarrely, the waiter also spoke no Russian. What they had not noticed was that the word next to *steak* was *tartare*. They were therefore quite shocked when their order arrived. Their steak tartare was presented in the customary form: looking like an elegant pile of gunge heaped into the shape of a small volcano with the yolk of a raw egg placed artistically in the crater. A far cry from the steak and chips they were doubtless expecting. At first, our lads were clearly perplexed by this, but once they had worked out that the main ingredient was raw meat their KGB pedigree kicked in and they attacked their grub with gusto.

Sitting in that entirely faux restaurant was surreal. It made me nostalgic for the good old days of travelling to the Soviet Bloc with Great Uncle Bulgaria.

55

Return to Go

In 1983 I was given the responsibility for all our R.O.W. markets. Since the USA still accounted for over half the business, the rest was classified as R.O.W., or Rest of World. I therefore took charge of an area management team that reported to me, and I acquired the splendid title of commercial director. James Bruxner continued to manage the business in the States, and he was still my boss. It was a very happy arrangement.

One of the things I did that year was to travel back to my original territory: Latin America. I flew out to Santiago in Chile to meet up with Bob Bedloe who was our area director for the region. Later, when I became the managing director of J&B, Bob took direct control of Spain during its most successful era.

Chile was now under the firm control of General Pinochet. The economy and its market for Scotch had greatly improved since the Allende era. From Santiago we flew to Bogotá with a stopover in Lima. The last two markets we visited were Venezuela and Mexico, which we flew to via Miami. I was away for ten days.

During my travels I sometimes took a duplicate notebook with me. This enabled me to send notes and reports back to the office as well as letters home. The carbon copies were retained in the notebook. I kept most of those notebooks.

The following is a letter I sent to my sons James and Charles towards the end of that trip. James was then twelve and Charles eight. So, it gives a different perspective.

Wednesday 9 November 1983

Dear James and Charles,

This morning we had to get up at 5.a.m. to get the early flight to Miami. When we drove out of town [Caracas] we could see all the ranchos on the outskirts. The ranchos are where the poor people live. They are very small huts on the steep slopes of the hills. Some are made of wood and some of brick. There are no roads between them, but they get electricity by connecting themselves to the main electricity lines. They don't pay for this electricity.

When we got to Miami everything was suddenly very American. The porters were all black: very efficient and very cheerful. We got served coffee in the drugstore by a little lady in a mini-skirt and shoes with 2-inch soles. She was about sixty but as bright as a button. Mr Bedloe had cream in his coffee which was squirted out of an aerosol can. When I asked for some 'nice Florida orange juice.' She said: 'Sure honey, straight from California.'

Before we left, we gave her a J&B lighter [from our P.O.S range]. She was frightfully chuffed and showed it to everyone.

Well, we got to Mexico alright. Mexico City is a vast sprawling town with a population of sixteen million. It is situated 7,000 feet up so is a bit like Bogotá. Most of Mexico City is rather ugly but there is a nice area in the middle of town called the Zona Rosa. We had dinner there.

270

RETURN TO GO

Mexico City, Thursday 10 November 1983
Our agents here are Domecq Mexico – a huge company
that sells millions of cases of Mexican Brandy. They also
do very well for J&B Rare. We went to their offices and
met all the important people. I don't know why, but
they all speak [Spanish] at nineteen to the dozen and I
have to concentrate very hard to understand everything.
The president of the company has a canary in his office
and the more they rabbited on the more the canary sang.
I was beginning to think I was in a mad house.

In the evening we went to the Plaza Garibaldi. It
is very colourful: lots of Mexican Indians try to sell
flowers, rugs, and other handmade things. There were
also many groups playing mariachi music. We had
dinner there in an old inn. It was typical Mexican food
which included pigs' trotters, black beans, avocado, and
chilli sauce on everything. I don't think you would like
it.

We drank Tequila which is a spirit made from cactus.
You first put salt on the back of your hand then squeeze
lemon juice into your mouth, then lick the salt, then
knock back the Tequila: that is one way of drinking it.
The other is to all raise your glasses saying: 'arriba,
arriba'; then lower them, 'abajo, abajo'; then clinking
them together in the middle of the table you cry, 'a
centro, a centro'; then with a final shout of, 'a dentro, a
dentro, a dentro', you swallow the whole lot in one gulp.
I suppose it makes a change from J&B on the rocks!

Lots of love,
Daddy

56

Game Fishing off Cape Town

During my exporting years I managed to visit over a hundred different countries, and in so doing touched every continent (except Antarctica). Admittedly many of the visits were short and therefore superficial; and I was there for business, not to see the tourist sights. So, I did get a different perspective from that of a holiday visitor. I also travelled with many J&B colleagues. In those days we had around eighteen people in our area management team. They were, without exception, a talented and convivial bunch.

Peter Prentice, or Prent as he was habitually called, exemplified that trait. South Africa was his favourite, and one of our best markets. Our agents were Gilbey South Africa: a group company. This was unusual because most of our top agents were independent businesses. The team at Gilbeys in Cape Town had done a magnificent job at building J&B Rare into one of the top whisky brands in South Africa. Their sales activities were supported by creative advertising as well as classy PR. The latter included sponsorship of the J&B Met: Cape Town's equivalent to the Derby at Epsom.

Game fishing was another activity that they used to promote the brand. They even had a fishing boat in J&B colours for entertaining key customers and opinion leaders.

One spring in the late 1980s I flew to Cape Town at the time of the annual game fishing event. Prent was already there. On the evening of my arrival, we were invited to dinner at the house of local J&B enthusiasts. It was a noisy and boisterous affair. Our host spent a lot of time messing around with a french fry inserted into each of his nostrils. I think he was trying to impersonate a walrus. It was that sort of party. They usually are if you travel with Prent.

The next morning, I had to get up early to go down to Hout Bay. The plan was for me to go out in the J&B boat and see, at first-hand, how the game fishing sponsorship worked. When we got to the Atlantic Boat Club the water in the harbour looked calm and I had no qualms about tucking into a fully fried-up South African breakfast.

Big mistake.

The harbour at Hout Bay is sheltered by its extended harbour walls; and the wider bay itself is also well shielded from the ocean. When I got onboard the good ship J&B I discovered three things. The first was that Prent wasn't coming.

'Too much real work to do,' he said somewhat uncharacteristically.

The second bit of news was that the game fishing tournament would last thirty-six hours.

I only discovered the third 'thing' when Bob Busby, our skipper, took HMS J&B out of the harbour and out from the bay. As we steered straight for the South Pole via the Roaring Forties, I discovered that the sea was not calm. In no time at all our vessel was being tossed up and down in a most unfriendly manner. On one particularly downward lurch my breakfast opted to defy gravity and come up. I felt awful.

Being the only Brit on board I felt a terrible wimp for letting the side down. Fortunately, Bob and his crew were very decent about it: albeit with a touch of smugness built into their commiserations. They gave me a pill which helped. There were about five of us on board; some were crew, others were trade customers.

Once we got further out, the sea eased a bit, and we ran into a shoal of tuna. Fishing rods were quickly issued to all on board. Tuna are torpedo-shaped, muscular fish; and although only about 12 pounds in weight, they fought like hell. We managed to land a good few before coming out of the shoal and continuing our course.

Our direction was bound for the waters above Cape Canyon, which lies about 10 nautical miles off the South African coast. The size of the Canyon is akin to that of the Grand Canyon: only below water and even deeper.

We would be fishing there for broadbill swordfish: and at night.

The broadbill swordfish is a mighty beast that can weigh up to 600 kilos. It likes to lurk in deep waters such as those in the Canyon. To hook one, Bob paid out a long, deep line. There was a float set on his line, about 30 yards off from the boat. The float had a small balloon attached to it; and inside that balloon was a light.

It was a very dark night. The sky was heavy, and the sea was black. All you could see was this light bobbing up and down with the swell. If the light disappeared it meant that way down below a broadbill swordfish had taken the bait and would be trying to break free. At which point the fight would begin. Meanwhile patience was required.

As the boat rose and fell with the swell, I must have dozed off. When I awoke, I found Bob tightly strapped into a 'fighting chair', with legs braced, and a tight grip on his rod. He had a determined look on his face. He was clearly battling a big 'un. At times the line would run out, hissing as it went. Then Bob would tighten the ratchet and try to wind it back. The fight went on for some considerable time. Again, I dozed off.

When I awoke for the second time, I found the crew manning the side of the boat. They were armed with gaffs. In the water lay a very large but exhausted broadbill swordfish. With consummate teamwork it was gaffed and hoisted aboard.

I had never seen such a big fish. It had a magnificent, ugly, primeval beauty: like a marlin's prehistoric ancestor perhaps? It was about 12 feet long and took up a lot of space in the small boat.

After catching this monster, the sun was coming up and it was time to head for port. Bob was confident that our fish would win the prize. But as we headed for home there arose much boat-to-boat radio chatter. It became clear that another boat had also caught a big 'un. Tension mounted.

At this point I rather pompously suggested that, since J&B were sponsoring the event, it was not very sporting for the J&B boat to win. So, shouldn't we stand back and let the other boat claim the prize even if our fish was the biggest? This suggestion was not popular: not at all. There was even talk of chucking me overboard if I persisted. I didn't.

As we chuntered back to harbour the weather cleared, the sun came out, the sea calmed down, and we hit another shoal of tuna. It was the perfect culmination to an epic trip.

Back in Hout Bay there was a gantry on the quayside from which a very large swordfish was already suspended.

It weighed over 500 pounds. Would ours be bigger? Slowly ours was winched up beside its rival, and weighed.

Our fish was heavier, but by a mere 20 pounds. We had won. Prent was there to meet us. He was chuffed, and not remotely embarrassed, that HMS J&B had been victorious. But when he drove me back to the Mount Nellie, he kept the car windows wide open.

The Mount Nelson Hotel in Cape Town has always been one of the world's great hostelries. I believe it is now owned by LVMH so feel sure that it still is. But it is not the sort of hotel you want to enter when your clothes are disgustingly dirty, blood stained, and emitting a pungent, fishy aroma. Fortunately, I entered at a quiet time of day and collected my key in a manner that was as unobtrusive as I could muster. The concierge, bless him, didn't bat an eye.

'Been fishing,' I said rather lamely as I shot for the lift.

57

Musical Chairs

At risk of being too serious, it might be helpful to paint a brief picture of the corporate scene as it was in the 1980s.

When I joined J&B most of our successful markets were run by independent 'third-party' agents. As I said at the beginning, in the 1970s it was the DCL (Distillers Company Ltd) that had the best operators. Thus, it was not easy to find good ones. But over time we built up a first class network. In the early days we did not have long and complicated contracts with our agents. We told those that we had that their best job security was to succeed. They accepted that was how we worked.

However, as time passed, this attitude began to change. The DCL became Guinness, and IDV (our parent company) became the wine and spirit division of Grand Metropolitan (a major conglomerate). IDV found itself competing in international markets with three other leading players: Seagram, Allied Distillers (who later became Allied Domecq) and, of course, Guinness. These four companies were all competing for supremacy. Today those 'big four' companies have morphed into two: Diageo and Pernod Ricard. But in the 1980s, the original four were striving to increase their competitive positions. The easiest way for them to get bigger was for each company to take over its independent agents in major markets. IDV was to embrace this strategy quite vigorously in the 1980s.

In 1987 Anthony Tennant, the CEO of IDV, moved to Guinness. The year before, in 1986, we had celebrated a twenty-five-year relationship with Moët et Chandon. To mark the occasion, we had a grand dinner at one of the City livery companies. We presented each of our Moët guests with a silver 'J&B Crusader'. I had been to a local shop that special-ised in toy soldiers and bought one of their crusader knights. Laurence Bauer, who was in charge of sourcing our promo-tional material then took the knight to a friendly jeweller who had it reproduced in solid silver. The Moët bigwigs were bowled over by their personalised J&B Crusaders.

Unfortunately, that celebration with Moët was to be short lived because, after switching horses to Guinness, Anthony Tennant promptly negotiated a deal whereby Guinness acquired a 34 per cent share of Moët Hennessy. This meant that Moët Hennessy would now be required to distribute Guinness's brands in France and other countries. Moët therefore had to give up J&B Rare and take on Johnnie Walker: a nightmare.

J&B Rare's business in France was then transferred to Sovedi, IDV's French distribution company. It was not a happy time because we had many friends at Moët. Ironically, Jean Bourland, the Sovedi CEO, had previously headed up the agent in France for Johnnie Walker. So, it really was a case of musical chairs. For his part Jean did a fantastic job. The transfer went smoothly, and the brand did not suffer. Blessed as he was, like James Bruxner, with the right initials, how could he have done otherwise?

Everyone will admit that it is much more fun dealing with an independent third-party agent than with a sister company. I suppose the chief reason is that with independent agents you can negotiate normally. You are free from internal politics. And you can also fire them if they do a bad job.

That was how we felt about it in J&B.

However, the IDV strategy did make sense. In the EU, a brand owner cannot dictate a pricing policy to an independent agent. It is illegal. Thus, if you have a string of third-party agents across Europe there is always the risk that one of them will adopt a rogue pricing policy. This can ruin your co-ordinated marketing strategy.

During the 1980s IDV took over a number of J&B's agents in Europe. I think Sileno, in Portugal, was the first. Italy was a tragic case. Bandini died very suddenly in 1983. He was only sixty. The business was then run by his son, Massimo but a few years later, Massimo himself died in a car accident. Eventually IDV acquired the Bandini business and merged it with Cinzano, which they owned. Alberto Antonelli managed this very well for a while, then left. I suspect he did not take to the new corporate life.

As various J&B agents were changed, it was with something of a heavy heart that we had to accept the logic of the IDV policy. It is not easy giving up dealing with a successful organisation that you like and respect, and then having it replaced with something new and unknown. Fortunately, in some instances, such as Portugal we were able to continue the relationships with the same management team as before.

58

The End of the Ullivarri Era

By 1988 Rafael Ullivarri knew that he was on the 'transfer list'. The discussion between him and IDV's European division began that year. The negotiations were to drag on for thirty-four months and put a lot of pressure on the J&B team as well as on Rafael's organisation. When this sort of thing happens, it is the management on the ground that has to take the brunt of the pain; and will get the blame if it all goes wrong.

It did not go wrong.

At this time Bob Bedloe was the J&B director in charge of Spain. Together with Javier Barretabuena, Rafael's sales director, and Carmelo Ruperez, the brand manager, they worked together to manage this uncomfortable period. It was a significant contribution to the ongoing health of the brand.

Meanwhile back at HQ I got an invitation to see Tim Ambler. At the time Tim was, I think, the deputy managing director of IDV and thus second only to George Bull on the corporate totem pole. Tim had a cunning plan. Apparently, the negotiations with Rafael were not going quite as smoothly as he had hoped. Tim suggested that I organise a mini-conference for the core European agents. Rafael would be the guest of honour at this conference and should be made to feel that he was the star of the show. If the ploy worked Rafael would then feel better disposed towards IDV when the next round of negotiations took place. This was Tim's thinking. Château Loudenne was chosen as the venue for the conference and, throwing fiscal caution to the winds, Tim told me that no expense need be spared. These were my instructions. So, the guests were invited, the arrangements made, and Rafael assured me that he was coming. Of course, astute as he was, he must have guessed what it was all about.

Then, two days before the off, and with impeccable timing, Rafael threw a sicky.

It was too late to cancel the event. So, somewhat on the basis of *Hamlet* without the Prince, we went ahead. Naturally, three days of sunshine and lavish hospitality at Château Loudenne went down very well for all those who came. We had a series of cosmetic discussions. As usual the agents from the most successful markets made the most enthusiastic but chaotic presentations, and vice versa. The highlight of the conference was a stupendous lunch at Château Lafite.

During this anxious period the sales in Spain continued to boom. In October 1988 Rafael and his partners hosted a party at a famous bull-breeding *finca* in Andalucía. The party was to celebrate twenty-five years of collaboration and the sales achievement of one million cases in the previous year. The guest list included Dorrien and Mary Belson, James and Carol Bruxner, Wyndham and Shona Carver, and George and Tessa Bull. It was a fantastic weekend. The local hospitality was outstanding. Naturally, it was spiced from time to time by some coy comments about what might happen in the next twenty-five years.

In 1989 our sales in Spain jumped to 1.3m cases, and then again in 1990 to 1.7m cases or over twenty million bottles.

But with it came the end of the Ullivarri era.

On 20 October 1990 Rafael and his partners signed the agreement by which IDV took over their business in Spain. Rafael stayed on as honorary president of his old company for one year and then served on the board of IDV Europe for a further five years. The previous three years had been very difficult for him. However, his commitment to the brand never wavered. And in the end, he negotiated a very fair deal for himself and his partners.

Rafael Ullivarri ranks up there as a giant for J&B. He took the brand from nothing in 1963 to sales of over a million cases in 1987. And by then J&B Rare also held an astonishing 40 per cent share of the Scotch whisky market in Spain. During his tenure he was ably backed by his partners, but it was Rafael who masterminded the business. He was not an extrovert like Abe Rosenberg or Bandini. Instead, he managed his company and his network of sub-distributors with quiet ability and firm authority, but not without humour.

At heart, Rafael was also a family man. Once, when flying with him to Barcelona, in the row in front of us there was a baby that was bawling and howling like a banshee at the top of her game. I found it really irritating. But Rafael just smiled and said that, for him, the sound of a baby crying was like music to his ears. Maybe that is why he and his wife, Maribel, were blessed with six children.

59

Emerging Markets, The Third Wave

Have you ever watched a film in a language that you don't understand, and without the benefit of subtitles? It can be quite confusing. I found myself doing just that one evening in Istanbul in the late 1980s. I was with Andrew Highcock, our star manager for Africa and the Middle East, and we were with George Lutikov, our agent for Turkey. The occasion was a film festival, and George had organised a VIP reception to take place during the interval. As we emerged from the auditorium George asked us if we should like him to tell us what the film was about.

We said: 'No, don't tell us. Let us see if we can guess.' Which we did.

As far as I can remember, it was a lively plot about a nice country girl torn between a good boy and a bad man: a Turkish take, perhaps, on *Tess of the D'Urbervilles*? At the half-time interval, the bad boy was winning.

George said our guess was spot on; but maybe he was just being polite.

At the time we were developing our 'Third Wave Strategy'. Put simply it meant that we should defend our strong position in the Americas (Wave 1), continue the growth in Europe (Wave 2), and invest for future growth in emerging markets (Wave 3). J&B Rare was beginning to do well in several African, Asian, and Middle Eastern markets. Turkey was becoming a particular star amongst our emerging markets.

George's family came from Macedonia, but they had been in Turkey for two generations. Like many of our best agents, he was a natural entrepreneur. He had started as a journalist before becoming the agent for various tobacco and liquor brands. J&B Rare, Ballantine's, and British American Tobacco became his principal agencies.

In those days, all imports of liquor and cigarettes had to be imported and distributed by the Tekel: a government monopoly. Thus, it was not unusual to have commission agents, such as George, representing both booze and fags. George was a brilliant promoter who knew all the key people. J&B Rare was rapidly closing on the leading brand: Johnnie Walker.

During the late eighties and early nineties I visited many of our Wave 3 markets. India and Vietnam were two that I particularly enjoyed, even though my visits to them were few and brief.

They love whisky in India and produce millions of gallons of their own stuff. But they do hanker for the real thing. So, their aspiration for good Scotch whisky has always been high. That being so, and having as they do a population of well over a billion souls plus an emerging economy, India was, and still is, a market with gigantic potential for Scotch whisky. But back in the eighties the market for real Scotch in India was tiny because import duties and quotas were ferociously restrictive. Of course, there was a fair amount of Scotch that was also smuggled in, mostly from the Gulf.

Nonetheless, as a market for us, it was very undeveloped, rather like Spain in the sixties, but with even greater long-term potential.

Peter Prentice was a star architect for our 'Third Wave Strategy'. And Prent was the man who got J&B Rare going in India. He made some key trade contacts, and appointed Sammy Malik as an ambassadorial representative for J&B. It was an inspired appointment and somewhat akin to that of Max Mugnani by Bandini in Italy in the early sixties. This was because Sammy, a Sikh, was well connected to the top echelon of society in Delhi. He could introduce J&B Rare to all the right people. Here again we were following Eddie Tatham's 'Tiffany trade' strategy.

On my first visit to India, I was lucky enough to play golf with Sammy at the exclusive Delhi Golf Club. I had a caddy and a ball boy to help me on my way. That splendid golf course is set right in the heart of New Delhi. The ball boy was in fact a grizzly old chap with a broad smile, but few teeth and no shoes. His technique was to patrol ahead and search for my ball when I hit it in the rough, which was frequently. I thought it extravagant to have a ball boy as well as a caddy, but Sammy explained that in India the cost of hiring a ball boy was less than the cost of one new golf ball. Furthermore, whenever I hit the ball astray, he always found it. And when I arrived to play it, there it would be, not in the deep rough which is where I saw it go but sitting prettily on a nice tuft of grass and in a clearing. Sammy said that the ball boys did it with their toes.

Then just as Cartier now sponsor polo at the Guards Polo Club near Windsor, so we sponsored the Baroda Cup in Delhi. To do this we had help from Jim Edwards. Jim was the founder of Tiger Tops in Nepal and was a leading light in the creation and development of wildlife safaris. He was also our agent for Nepal. He was an accomplished polo player and well connected with the top players in the subcontinent.

During that first visit I attended a final of the Baroda Cup. It took place at the Polo Ground in Delhi. The cup was presented by the Rajmata of Jaipur, a splendid lady with whom Prent had developed a great rapport. For him she became like Aunt Dahlia of Bertie Wooster fame; and Prent always made sure that she had a constant supply of whisky. The Rajmata liked to have a miniature bottle of J&B Rare in her handbag at all times.

After the final chukka and the prize giving, Jim had organised an Indian barbeque. It was a partridge curry cooked in a rusty old cauldron over a small open fire. It was quite the best curry I have ever had. After that we did a tour of the stables. Having dashed up and down a large field chasing a small ball all afternoon, the polo ponies had had their oats and were looking relaxed and comfortable as they dozed in their stalls. But in one stall there was no pony. Instead, high up on the wall was a tiny black-and-white television set. And below, on the floor there squatted two neat rows of grooms and stable lads. They crouched there, perfectly still, but gazing upwards, mouths agape as they watched a Bollywood soap opera. That scene was pure magic.

The relationship between Prent and Jim had also blossomed.

Back in 1982 Jim Edwards had met James Manclark at a dinner in St Moritz. In addition to being a Cresta Run afficionado, James was also a polo player. So, when towards the end of a lavish dinner he heard that Jim had a herd of elephants at Tiger Tops, he conceived the idea of playing polo on elephants. A few months later he was in Jaipur and sent Jim a telex saying:

'Have long sticks, get elephants ready'

Since the telex was sent on 1 April, Jim paid no attention. So, he was taken by surprise when James duly turned up, fully armed with said 'long sticks'.

That is how elephant polo was invented.

At first, they tried to play using footballs, but the elephants seemed to find it amusing to tread on the balls and make them burst. So, they had to revert to ordinary polo balls, which worked perfectly well.

Before long J&B Rare was sponsoring the World Elephant Polo Championship at Tiger Tops. It took place every year just before Christmas. Sadly, I was never able to see elephant polo in action. It is usually played with teams of four elephants on each side. Each player sits behind a mahout who must direct the elephant so that the player can get a good shot at the ball. Apparently, the elephants enjoy it immensely. Sadly, Jim died in 2009 but elephant polo continues. Indeed, today Prent is the chairman of WEPA (World Elephant Polo Association).

These wonderfully eccentric ways of introducing J&B Rare to what would now be called 'opinion leaders' worked well and by the time I left J&B in 1996 the brand had planted a firm foothold in India.

Although the Vietnam War had ended back in 1975 it was not until much later that the Vietnamese market began to reopen for Scotch whisky. I went twice to Ho Chi Minh City, or Saigon as it used to be called. It is easy to forget that Saigon was known as 'The Pearl of the Orient' when Vietnam was part of French Indochina. But, in the hotels and restaurants that we visited some of the older staff still spoke French. And you could see fine French colonial buildings such as the Opera, and the Hotel Continental which had been much frequented by journalists during the Vietnam War.

Prent first went into Vietnam in 1989. He was probably the first whisky man back since the last American chopper took off from the American embassy fourteen years before. He quickly made some good contacts and set about planting the brand.

David Jacobson's *Q Bar ~ Saigon* was one of our first key accounts. Situated by the old Opera House, and sandwiched between the Continental, and Caravelle hotels, it was in a perfect location. The *Q Bar* was owned and run by David Jacobson, an American from New York who had given up his profession as a photographer to embark on this different career. I recall him showing me a Nikon camera that, he said, was indestructible. He proved this by throwing it onto a concrete floor. His bar became the stuff of legends. He was a tremendous supporter of J&B Rare. I still have a black *Q Bar ~ Saigon* baseball cap that he gave me.

On my first visit to Ho Chi Minh City there was remarkably little traffic. The humble bicycle was the principal mode of transport. One afternoon we spotted a throng of teenage girls emerging from their school. They were dressed in the traditional white *áo dài* uniform, and they were riding old-fashioned bikes with high handlebars. The *áo dài* is a long tunic worn over pyjama trousers. It is buttoned demurely up to the collar but has slits to the waist on either side. As they pedalled, very upright, but slowly and serenely past us, it was akin to watching a sea of swans gliding down a placid stretch of the River Tay.

IDV were quick to follow Prent's lead and open an office in Ho Chi Minh City. It was run by Simon Barstow, a Yorkshire lad from Bradford, who did a champion job at creating a platform in Vietnam for J&B Rare and other group brands.

The second time I went to Saigon the place was abuzz with motor bikes. I suspect that if you go there now the city will be gridlocked with cars and choking with pollution.

But you may be asking: 'What happened in the second half of that Turkish film?'

Well, I'm afraid we didn't go back for the second half, so I don't know. But my encounter with Turkey had a romantic twist of another sort.

After the millennium, the Tekel was privatised and the companies that George Lutikov represented set up their own subsidiaries in Turkey. George then moved permanently to England. He had, for many years, owned property in London and his children were being educated here. He now decided that he wanted to create his own whisky brand and I helped him do that. It was during this period that my son met his daughter. Tragically George died in 2017 but by then James and Anoushka had been married for fourteen years.

60

The Old School Tie
at Work in Monte Carlo

One day Jean Bourland asked me if we should like to hire a terrace in Monte Carlo for the Grand Prix. Jean, you will recall, was the CEO of SOVEDI, our group company in France. He had therefore been responsible for our sales in that market ever since we parted company with Moët: and a very good job he was doing too.

The terrace in question was on the roof of an apartment block that overlooked the racing track's starting grid and pits. It was the perfect spot for entertaining VIP customers. I jumped at Jean's offer because at the time we had begun to hold an annual marketing forum for our key agents; and we were looking for a suitable venue for the next one. The prospect of an invitation to a marketing forum in Monaco at the time of the Grand Prix would have any of our hot-blooded agents killing to earn a place. It was the perfect incentive; and so much so that we returned to Monaco for our annual marketing 'do' every year thereafter until I left J&B. After that they cancelled the arrangement.

During the Grand Prix week, you could not book a hotel room for just two nights. So, we had to book all the rooms that we needed for four nights: Thursday through to Sunday. We held the marketing session on Thursday and Friday. Then we kicked out the junior staff to make their rooms available for VIP trade customers who arrived in time for the racing on Saturday and Sunday. We booked most of our rooms at Loews Hotel, but also a few at the top-notch Hotel de Paris.

I always stayed at the Hotel de P.

Our guests loved the Grand Prix racing. Indeed, they loved the whole Monte Carlo experience. The view from the terrace was spectacular. We even had special permits to visit the pits. The Grand Prix track at Monte Carlo is laid out like an untidy bicycle chain. At the halfway point of the chain's haphazard circuit, the returning track runs very close to the outward starting straight. The pits are situated in a narrow space just between these two sections of the track.

The viewing platform for the pits was in a sort of cage suspended above them. Since the cars were roaring past both sides of the pits and in opposite directions, the noise from their engines, at full throttle, was gigantic. You needed ear plugs, but they hardly helped. And if a car pulled into the pits, it was mesmerising to watch the team of mechanics change all four wheels of a Formula I car in just six seconds. The teamwork was astonishing.

Back on the terrace, Jean had recruited a top local chef. He was a jolly roly-poly character with a proper Anatole moustache. Not surprisingly, he served wonderful French nosh. There was plenty of it too – *abbondante* as it was described to me by an appreciative guest from Milan. And although they had been kicked out of their hotel rooms on the Saturday morning, the junior members of our staff would reappear, as if by magic, to help out on both Saturday and Sunday. Where they slept in between, I have no idea: on the beach perhaps?

The Monte Carlo Grand Prix always took place the weekend after Ascension Day: thus, sometime in May. The atmosphere during that week was electric. There were Ferraris double parked at every corner, and with number plates registered from all over Europe. Anyone who owned a red Ferrari seemed to think it imperative to make a pilgrimage to Monte Carlo for the Grand Prix fiesta. One year Isabel and I drove down to Monaco, but alas with no prancing horse on the bonnet of our modest Lancia. However, there were two red Ferraris with us on the cross-Channel hovercraft. Sure enough, their drivers confirmed that Monaco was their destination.

And, in downtown Monte Carlo, I really did spot a small, round, bald, rich, middle-aged Italian impresario promenading out of a famous couturier's boutique with a tall, busty, blonde bimbo on each arm.

Of course, the concept of holding a lavishly expensive marketing forum for four days in Monaco during its most fashionable spring weekend had the accountants at head office gagging on their abacuses, and muttering darkly about the profligate expense, and whether it could possibly generate a sensible return on investment.

It has always been difficult to evaluate investment in the different fields of promotion. Financial people are often happy to sign off massive investments in conventional press or TV advertising. They feel that the effect can be 'measured'. Yet quite often the results don't justify the cost. When it comes to PR, which includes trade hospitality, the accountants find this an area much harder to monitor: they tend to be sceptical. This is understandable. Yet at J&B we did a lot; and we became rather good at it. Early on we realised that you can't do PR on the cheap. It doesn't work. So, to pre-empt adverse comments from our group HQ, every year we invited one of the main board directors to attend as a guest of honour. The idea was that if we got him to see for himself the value of what we did, he would tell the accountants to shut up. This ploy worked beautifully: until I left J&B.

And so it was that one morning as I was waiting outside the Hotel de Paris for our London taxi (in J&B colours) to come and pick me up, the following conversation took place between me and the Hotel de P's splendidly uniformed head doorman.

Head Doorman, in perfect English: 'Good morning, David, how are you today?'

Me, a bit surprised that he seemed to know me, and by my Christian name too: 'Fine thanks. How are you?'

HD: 'You don't remember me, do you?'

Me, trying not to sound pompous: 'No, I'm very sorry but I don't. Have we met before?'

HD: 'Of course we have. We were at school together. I'm John Grant.'

I did then recognise him – just. It was a long time since we had been at Stonyhurst together. I was about to ask him how he had got to be Head Doorman at the Hotel de Paris, when Paul Curtis appeared. Paul, you will recall, was the marketing director of IDV, our parent company. He was our guest of honour at Monte Carlo that year.

So, after giving Paul a friendly: 'Good morning,' I continued by saying: 'May I introduce you to John Grant. We were at school together.'

Paul then eyed John in his splendid uniform. He then eyed me. I could see that he was wondering whether or not I was taking the piss? Eventually he realised that I was not, and after exchanging a bit of friendly banter he and I climbed aboard the J&B taxi and headed off for a morning of honest toil down at Loews Hotel.

61

The Power of the Label

In my early days at J&B we were, I suspect, sometimes a little embarrassed by our label. Of course, it has amazing impact. If you go into a dark, smoky night club it is one of the very few brands that you can recognise at ten paces. We acknowledged that, but secretly felt that its bright red-on-yellow livery was just a little bit vulgar. Consequently, the point-of-sale material that we produced, although very elegant, was only branded with timid little J&B initials. Then one day we asked Howard Waller to take a look at our packaging. We wanted him to see if he could find a way to tweak and refresh it. This is something big brands need to do every five years or so.

Howard was a designer with a touch of genius. He told me that our label was the most extraordinary thing he had ever seen:

'It must have evolved,' he said. 'Nobody could design a label like that. Not in one go. And look at the writing on it,' he added. 'There are seven different fonts being used. Then there are those daft old kings and queens [Justerini & Brooks have held the Royal Warrant for every monarch since the days of George III. Their names are listed on the label]. It's completely crazy but it works, and it works brilliantly. So, don't be so bloody coy about it. Use it in spades and go for it.'

So that is what we did. Howard, with Paul McPherson, his partner in design, did a brilliant tweak to the pack. They then went on to redesign our point-of-sale material. When it was finished, we called it the 'flooded look' because it reproduced the full impact of the label with all its detail. The result was a veritable tsunami of umbrellas, ashtrays, ice buckets, pens, sports bags, and other must-have items that surged out of our stores into every bar in town. All of this was orchestrated by Laurence Bauer. With her flair for style, and her Swiss efficiency (Laurence hails from Geneva) our P.O.S. range became the envy of the industry. To cap it all, Bill Bullard's wife ran up a nice little cocktail frock in the flooded material. She stole the show when she turned up wearing it for the first night of our marketing forum in Monte Carlo. At the time Bill was running IDV's company in Venezuela.

This newfound confidence in our label led, not unnaturally, to our adopting it as the principal prop for our new advertising campaign. Clive Holland, from Young & Rubicam in London, helped us to develop the campaign for Spain. Our 'Label' campaign was launched there in 1989.

So, it is entirely appropriate that the leading player in this chapter should be Howard Waller: not an advertising guru but a designer who taught us to believe in the power of the label.

62

On Tipping and Practical Jokes

The biggest tipper I ever met was my much-loved cousin Ian. He was a gambler. The habit had started at school where he had run a book. His mother, in an attempt to nip the addiction in the bud, had sent him to see a psychiatrist. The ploy had not worked. It was said that his one and only appointment with the mind doctor had ended with Ian giving the consultant a red-hot tip for the 2.30 at Ascot that afternoon. At Oxford he had been in John Aspinall's gaming set. Later, when running a casino became legit, he joined Aspinall at his famed Clermont Club.

It was in the 1960s that Ian had a winning streak with the horses. The apotheosis of his purple patch came when he landed a Yankee. A Yankee is a series of eleven bets on four horses. It comprises six Doubles, four Trebles and one Accumulator. If all four horses win, the reward can be astonishing. Ian won £40,000 on his Yankee. In those days you could have bought a town house in Mayfair for forty grand.

The Clermont Club was, and is, situated in Berkeley Square. It is an exquisite Palladian house, built in about 1740, and designed by William Kent for Lady Isabella Finch. Lady F would probably have been astonished to learn that her London pad had been converted into a casino. But she would have approved the impeccable taste with which it had been refurbished.

Now, the Mirabelle restaurant was in Curzon Street, which is just round the corner from the Clermont. The Mirabelle no longer exists; but in those days, it was one of London's very top restaurants. The food was sublime. Their Omelette Normande was to die for; and their wine cellar was impressively 'deep'. Being, as it was, a dogleg par 5 away from the Clermont Club, Ian was a regular customer: especially during his purple patch.

It is always good to watch old pros in the waiting business massage a good tip. The waiters at the Mirabelle were top jockeys in that respect. They had Ian sussed out to a T. Every so often, but not too often mind, if they wanted to earn an extra-large tip from him, they would adopt a counter-intuitive ploy. They would ignore him. This would come as a shock to Ian because they usually treated him as their Number One Customer. And so, as the meal progressed and as the service got worse, Ian would begin to simmer. Eventually he would lose his temper: something he very rarely did. At this point they would be all over him: grovelling, apologising, and answering to his every whim. At the end of the meal Ian, who was by nature kind, generous and polite to a fault, would be so ashamed of himself for losing his temper that he would give them a truly gigantic tip.

The first time I went to the Mirabelle on J&B business, my guest was Spyros Metaxa. You will recall that Spyros was our agent in Greece. When I booked and gave my name, I detected a sharp intake of breath at the other end of the line. Then when I arrived, I noted a distinct look of disappointment on the face of Alfred, the Maître d'. He must have been hoping I was Ian. Ian's purple patch had by then ended. So, Alfred had probably not seen him for some time.

Spyros used to like the Mirabelle. He never drank wine, preferring a glass or two of J&B Rare to go with his food. And at the end of lunch, he liked to puff on a large cigar to go with coffee – and with his balloon glass of Metaxa Brandy.

For our first lunch at the Mirabelle, I had got there a bit early to brief Bob, the bartender, about Spyros. Consequently, by the time Spyros arrived Bob had a bottle of Metaxa Seven Star in pole position on the shelf right behind him. And as the coffee was served, Alfred appeared with an armful of cigar boxes from which Spyros selected a Churchill by Romeo y Julieta. Back then, the smoking of cigars was much encouraged in such establishments, and especially so when you consider the gigantic margins applied to the sale of each and every one of them.

As the cigar was being prepared for ignition, Bob the bartender approached, and with much deference poured out two large measures of Spyros's Seven Star Brandy. It was not often that Bob had the opportunity to serve the owner of an important brand with a shot of his own stuff. So, he did it with great reverence. I suspect that, along with the aroma of fine Havana, he also smelled, as only an old pro can, the whiff of a potential tip.

His instinct was not misplaced.

When we got up to leave, after I had paid the bill and had added a decent but normal tip, I found that our departure was to be honoured by a waiters' guard of honour. About five of them were lined up to wish us a safe departure. Bob was at the head of the platoon with Alfred covering the rear. Spyros was now in an excellent mood, and full of largesse (as well as Omelette Normande). Putting his hand in his pocket he brought out a fat roll of crisp new £20 notes. Back then five quid was a five-star tip; so, twenty was way above that. As we made for the door Spyros proceeded down the line of waiters, rather in the manner of Prince Philip inspecting a proper guard of honour except that as he proceeded, he peeled off a fresh £20 note and pressed it into each outstretched hand. I had to restrain myself from joining the line-up.

Spyros was famous for his generosity. In 1989, after he sold the Metaxa business to IDV (J&B's parent company), he gave each of his employees a personal gift of three months' salary.

In her heyday, Regine Zylberberg ran an empire of twenty-five night clubs. They stretched across the globe from Paris to New York, Marbella, London, and beyond. Famed as the 'Queen of the Night', she is credited with inventing the modern discothèque. Jimmy'z in Monte Carlo was one of her best. She was a great supporter of J&B Rare; so, whenever we held a marketing forum in Monte Carlo, most evenings ended at Jimmy'z.

The first time Prent went to Jimmy'z he drew the short straw. At the end of the evening, he was the one stuck with paying the bill. Recently he reminded me how astonished he was by its size. He also reminded me that he had sought my advice on how much to add as a tip. Apparently, I had asked him to suggest a figure, which he did. I had then pointed out that the amount he proposed was too low because it was less than 10 per cent of the bill and that we were likely to return during the weekend when the place would be chock-a-block, and we wouldn't get a decent table unless he upped the ante. I don't remember any of this, but Prent assured me that I eventually nudged him into paying a tip nearer to 20 per cent. But he also reminded me that on every subsequent visit to Jimmy'z, they always miraculously provided us with the best tables in the joint; even though the place was swimming in Grand Prix glitterati.

One year, on the final night at Jimmy'z, Prent, having got our last guest safely back to the hotel, finally made it to bed at around 4 a.m. He had to catch an early morning flight from Nice. So, his alarm went off a mere three hours later at 7 o'clock sharp. He got out of bed, went to the bathroom, put the plug in the bath, turned the taps on, and went back to the bedroom for a moment's respite. He sat down on his bed and promptly fell asleep.

A little while later a member of the hotel's staff, who was delivering fresh croissants and coffee to a nearby room, spied water flowing out from under the door of Prent's room. The alarm was raised. Prent was roused, and the taps turned off leaving Prent to exit as only he knows how when in a sticky situation.

The incident was reported to the hotel manager, who fortunately took a lenient view of the episode. After all, in the hidden life of any hotel, this sort of incident would not normally feature high on the Richter scale of earth-moving events.

However, it came to pass that Julia Thorold heard about it. It was Julia whose PR department was responsible for organising everything at Monte Carlo. Now, when it comes to PR, Julia is up there at the top of the totem pole. But she also has a penchant for practical jokes. In truth she is dangerously good at them. And here she spied fertile ground. She was also on good terms with the hotel manager, so procured from him some of Loews Hotel stationery.

A few days later Prent received a fax 'from' Loews. It said:

Dear Mr Prentice,

I regret we have to write to you on a very sensitive matter.

Our housekeeper has informed me that during your stay, which I understand was rather more 'jolly' as I believe the English say, than is usual for our clients, you attempted to make a swimming pool in room 5212.

This is unfortunate as we have a very nice pool on the roof of the hotel.

The extent of the damage was considerable, and we have to replace the carpet in the room. Unfortunately, the water also seeped through the floor and entered into the cupboard of the room below, damaging an entire couture collection of clothes.

The total damage is FF 1,000,000. I would ask you to reimburse this to us without delay.

Should you wish to stay in our hotel again, we will put a tent for you by the swimming pool.

With kind regards,

André Piscine
André Piscine

Hotel Manager

Now, Prent had begun to think that his episode at Loews was behind him, so the arrival of the fax came as a shock.

After a quick skim of the contents, he felt an inclination to panic. A million francs was a lot of money: around £100,000 in those days. He then read the letter again, more carefully this time. He noted it was signed by a Mr Piscine. Now Prent is by no means a chump; and, as I have already mentioned, he was our top man for developing J&B Rare in emerging markets. Sensing a wind-up Prent went over to Julia (big mistake) and as casually as he could asked her if she could remember the name of the manager at Loews. At this stage of his career with J&B, Prent was unaware of Julia's pedigree in practical jokes.

Julia responding to Prent's enquiry, pretended she did not know but proceeded to leaf through her address book until she 'found' the answer.

'Ah!' she said. 'He's a Mr André Piscine,' before adding brightly, and with the feigned innocence that Paddington Bear was wont to deploy when he was being somewhat less than truthful: 'Gosh, that's a funny name. Isn't piscine French for swimming pool?'

Prent did not find this at all reassuring. But he was still suspicious. He was aware that the hotel had been housing a lot of fashion people for the Grand Prix weekend; but he found it difficult to believe that a 'couture collection of clothes' in the room below his could be worth anything like a million francs. So, he phoned his friend Hughie who had a tailoring business in Saville Row. Hughie would be sure to know.

Hughie did not help. In fact, he told him that a couture frock could easily cost £10,000. And, of course, if a lady has one, then she's probably got lots. So, it would make eminent sense for a flashy dame, who was attending the Grand Prix, to have as many as ten couture outfits in her travelling wardrobe.

The situation was getting worse.

Finally, Prent rang Jim Edwards at Tiger Tops in Nepal. By now Jim was like an uncle to Prent. You will recall it was he who got us into elephant polo. Jim was always very quick on the uptake. He also knew Julia, and instantly put two and two together and decided to play along with the joke. He told Prent that he was in the mire, big time, and had better work out what he was going to do when the news broke.

While all of this had been going on my brilliant PA, Sue Cavanagh, had been keeping me informed of 'developments'. I think it was when Prent started saying: 'Do you think I should tell David about this?' that someone put him out of his misery and told him he had been thoroughly Thorolded.

Prent took it all frightfully well. And still does; even to the extent of sending me a picture of the fake fax which as you can see is framed and, I believe, now hangs in prime position in his downstairs loo.

But now, I fear, it is time to end such frivolities, return to Spain and tell you about developments in that market.

63

The Barons Get the Sack

I never knew where the expression 'getting the sack' came from. Then I discovered an intriguing take on the subject when I came across a character named Ropes McGonnigle in *Sense of Humor* by Damon Runyon.

According to Runyon, what Ropes would do to take out a Mob competitor, was whack him over the head with a blackjack, and then put him in a sack but tied up in such a manner that when he woke up and tried to straighten out, he would strangle himself. Eventually when someone came along and opened the sack, they would 'find the guy dead'.

This system of taking over a rival's territory in the big American cities during the years of bootlegging and Prohibition was undoubtedly effective. But it was also brutal. When seeking to enlarge their own distribution network, IDV would never have resorted to such drastic measures. However, after taking over Rafael Ullivarri's business, the accountants at group HQ were naturally keen to find more ways to enhance profit. By this time some of the top sub-distributors in Spain were selling two or three hundred thousand cases of J&B Rare and other group products. Their margins on this business were still substantial. By building these businesses so effectively, they had become veritable barons of our trade in their provinces. It therefore seemed relatively easy to replace them with a more cost-effective network that could be wholly owned by the group. This was the proposal. It was very simple, and they could start by firing some of the lesser sub-distributors and then work their way up to the big guys.

This plan was first broached to Jean d'Amécourt. Jean came from the IDV corporate HQ. He had been put in to run Spain before they found a permanent CEO for the business. So, he was there for around a year before Alan Cordery was appointed. At the time, the market was still growing at a fast pace. However, margins were beginning to slip. So, in time the traditional role of the sub-distributor was going to become vulnerable. At J&B we recognised this. We also recognised that IDV were determined to integrate the sub-distributor network. The question was how to do it in a manner that would not damage the business? We suggested to Jean that, for good commercial reasons, an orderly and gentlemanly approach would be best.

Being astute (and French), Jean completely agreed that we should pay due deference to the Spanish pride that our barons deserved for their achievements. So instead of starting the programme by firing a few of the minnows, we began by taking over Pedro Tejada's business in Vizcaya. Pedro was based in Bilbao and his territory was an important one. He was nearing retirement age and was happy to be bought out for a fair price. This sent a strong signal to the other barons. They now realised that if they did get fired it would be done fairly: provided of course they were still managing an effective business. By and large they responded very well to this.

This policy of integration was gradually rolled out after Alan Cordery took over. It meant that IDV could properly digest each new province as they acquired it. Many of the sub-distributors stayed on in an alternative role. For instance, in Málaga, Juan Lara's firm continued to provide the company with warehousing and physical distribution.

Accountants are great at telling you how to cut costs and improve the bottom line. However, if you take all their recommendations at face value you run the risk of strangling the business. Then it will be you, not them, that gets the sack.

64

Operation Dunkirk

When asked the question: 'Which is more important, short-term profit or long-term growth?' one great captain of industry is reported to have said: 'Both.' His reply is understandable because the City imposes huge pressure on big corporations to do just that. They want both. Grand Metropolitan, the conglomerate that owned IDV and therefore J&B, was constantly under such pressure. So, there were times when this pressure was passed down the line and had a big impact on us at J&B. I became increasingly aware of this after I became managing director of J&B in 1986. What happened to us in Spain in 1992 was a prime example.

In Spain, the one brand that had grown to become a serious threat to J&B Rare was Ballantine's. In 1989 our share of the Scotch whisky market had achieved an incredible 42 per cent. At the time Ballantine's had risen to second place with 24 per cent. Ballantine's was Allied Domecq's flagship brand. They were also accustomed to promoting their brand very heavily. Looking back, we were in a most unusual position. J&B Rare was a very strong leader. Yet we had got there with comparatively modest levels of advertising investment.

We saw the danger signals when the consumer research began to show Ballantine's in an increasingly favourable light. Their market share continued to grow and ours began to wobble. David Turtle advised us that it was now essential to outspend Ballantine's. He argued that if we called their bluff and outgunned them, they would eventually have to back down. J&B Rare, as the brand leader, could then expect to outsell the number two by at least 62 per cent (Fibonacci's golden ratio again). All of this would happen provided we kept up the pressure and did not do anything stupid.

We then did something really stupid.

To put it in a nutshell, we raised our price; and for once Ballantine's did not follow. Moreover, they increased their advertising spend, and we didn't. All of this was driven because IDV was under tremendous pressure to deliver more profit.

Alan Cordery, the new CEO in Spain, was tearing his hair out. J&B Rare was beginning to lose share in a dramatic fashion. Things came to a head in the autumn of 1992 when we received the Nielsen audit and discovered that in the previous two months Ballantine's had overtaken us.

Something had to be done.

Alan and I decided to ask for a war chest with which to fight back. The opportunity came when I had to present J&B's business plan for the following year to the IDV Board. Alan had done his sums and said he needed an extra £4m to solve the Spanish problem. That was a big sum in those days: but I got it.

So, in 1993 we went to war with Ballantine's and won. It was an exciting period. We drafted in the whole J&B team to visit different provinces and help with the campaign that had been drawn up. We called it Operation Dunkirk. Having the J&B team swarming over different parts of Spain probably had little practical use, but it did send out a clear message. That message was: we meant business.

Then, as David Turtle had predicted, we regained the leadership position and Ballantine's' share of market slipped back to below 30 per cent. But it had been a close-run thing. Operation Dunkirk was not just a battle between J&B Rare and Ballantine's. It was also a battle between long-term brand equity and short-term profitability. If we had not taken on Ballantine's, J&B Rare would have lost the leadership position and in the long run delivered much less profit.

Getting the balance right between long- and short-term objectives is one of the great tests for a brand owner. On that occasion we got it right – just.

65

Spain: Was it Just Luck?

It doesn't matter if you are looking back at J&B Rare in Spain, Baileys in the UK, or Absolut Vodka in the USA: when a brand like one of these takes off in a major market it all looks terribly easy. People forget that several years of groundwork has been put in when not much seems to happen. Then suddenly the brand catches fire and it seems that nothing can stop it. When this happens there are usually several favourable elements that are in place.

For us there were simple things like the brand name. If you are Spanish, it is very easy to pronounce the J&B initials (in Spanish). Then there was the label that by pure coincidence is in the colours of the Spanish flag. Did this help? Who knows, but it can't have done any harm?

In the 1960s Spain was still emerging from the dark period of the civil war. But the economy was growing and by the 1970s there was an emerging middle class. This was ideal. David Turtle once did a study of demographics. He noted that countries with a high birth rate were invariably poor. But when the birth rate decelerates you get a period when the proportion of people who are of productive working age is greater than usual. In Spain that twenty-five-year window of 'birth control economics' coincided perfectly with the development of J&B Rare.

The management of the brand and the consistent application of the brand strategy was nothing to do with luck. It was all to do with good leadership. Moreover, making the transition from a niche brand to one with mass market success took some skill. Having people like David Turtle, Mike Vineall, and Howard Waller to advise us was an enormous help. But in the end, we succeeded because the extended J&B team had a very diverse mix of characters and skills.

J&B Rare in Spain was the apotheosis of the strategy to build the brand beyond America. But the brand also became a major player in many other markets. Italy, France, Portugal, Belgium, Greece, Brazil, Mexico, South Africa, the Philippines, Vietnam, Turkey, Israel and the Lebanon are a few I could mention. Indeed, when I left J&B in 1996 the brand's global sales had been second only to those of Johnnie Walker for over ten years.

To achieve something like that you do need some luck; but you cannot put it all down to Lady Fortune. Napoleon was always anxious to appoint marshals who were lucky. He knew that luck is not obtained just by accident. It is underpinned by application, dedication, and flair.

Now, before I close this story, I've got one more country I'd like to tell you about …

66

The Lebanon

In 1984 Hassan got a call from Harry. Hassan Zantout was our Lebanese agent, and he was in Beirut. Harry Langley was in Cyprus, and at the time he was the J&B area manager for Africa and the Middle East. The Lebanon was part of Harry's territory.

Harry was in Cyprus visiting his father who was the Commander of the British forces at our Sovereign Bases in Akrotiri and Dhekelia. Harry said that he was getting bored in Cyprus and had booked himself onto the overnight ferry and would arrive in Beirut the following morning. He was looking forward to seeing Hassan.

Hassan did not think the visit a good idea. Definitely not. The Lebanese Civil War (1975–1990) was in full swing, and Beirut was a very dangerous place to visit. His own family had moved to France, leaving him in Beirut to conduct what business he could as best he could. Moreover, to collect Harry from the ferry, he would have to cross the Green Line, a dangerous demarcation zone that ran north–south along Damascus Street, and that separated the warring factions of Muslims in West Beirut from the Maronite Christians to the east. There were checkpoints on each side of the line, and up on the rooftops there were snipers perching, like a committee of vultures, and waiting to take random potshots whenever it took their fancy.

Stiffened doubtless by his father's warrior genes, Harry was not remotely put off by Hassan's warning. He said he already had the ticket and was coming anyway.

I only learned about this escapade several years later, but Hassan said that Harry's visit, 'Thanks God,' had gone off without incident. He said that throughout, Harry didn't turn a hair. But afterwards he realised that during the day they had, between them, consumed an awful lot of J&B Rare. There had been several anxious moments, particularly when they crossed and recrossed the Green Line.

The history of the Lebanon stretches back to Phoenician times. Over the centuries the country was subjugated by Persians, Greeks, Romans, and the Ottomans. But their great trading culture had always endured, and today the Lebanese diaspora is truly international. In my travels I came across many traders of Lebanese descent in Latin America, the Caribbean, and West Africa.

After World War I, and the collapse of the Ottoman Empire, the Lebanon and Syria were put under a French Mandate. We got Palestine and the oil fields of Mesopotamia. This was done under the Sykes-Picot Agreement, a deal that had been struck between Britain and France in 1916.

Today the population of the Lebanon has a Muslim majority. The Muslims are themselves divided almost equally between Shia and Sunni with an additional small block of Druze (a Shia offshoot). The Christian population is mostly Maronite or Melkite. Both look to Rome. There is also an Orthodox presence of some size.

In the fifties and sixties the Lebanon was an attractive place to visit and was popularly known as the Switzerland of the Middle East. But Beirut was its Paris.

314

In the early seventies the PLO (Palestine Liberation Organisation) was trying, by force, to build its own state within the kingdom of Jordan. King Hussein did not like that. After considerable strife and the shedding of much blood, the PLO were thrown out. Many of them relocated to the Lebanon, including their leader Yasser Arafat. He based himself there until 1983.

The arrival of the PLO in the Lebanon was akin to throwing a lighted match into a box of fireworks.

To unravel the saga of the Lebanese Civil War (1975–1990) would be a nightmare. This is because there were so many factions and shifting alliances in play during its fifteen-year duration. The cost of the civil war, in terms of human lives and economic damage, was gigantic.

I visited Beirut several times between 1990 and 1996. The first time I went, Beirut was a wreck. If, as a child, you ever built houses with playing cards and then shook the table on which they were built, many of your houses would collapse, some completely and some in part. The buildings in downtown Beirut were like that. And those that were still standing had broken windows, gaping roofs and tottering walls. The masonry that stood bore pock marks and holes from bullets, shells, and rockets.

The second time I went, Hassan was very excited. The first traffic light was back in operation. I was taken to see it. Beirut was rising, phoenixlike, from its ashes, illuminated as it rose by symbolic flickers of red, amber, and green.

Hassan also explained a plan that was being introduced to speed up the reconstruction of Beirut. It was called Solidere. The idea was to knock down all the ruins in the Central District and sweep the rubble into the sea. The reclaimed land would itself create a new prime location. I believe that the Solidere project was very successful and has been trading since its creation in 1994.

As I mentioned before, the Lebanese are great traders. After the end of the civil war, the market for Scotch whisky began to grow. Patrick Millet, who was our area director at the time, sensibly suggested to Hassan that, since business was now picking up, he should recruit a marketing manager.

I should mention that Patrick had joined J&B in 1981. At the time Bombay Gin had been acquired by our parent company. The gin was distilled in Warrington and sold modest volumes, mostly in the States. We at J&B had been tasked to manage it, and Patrick was recruited as the brand director. It was he who was asked by the American importer to produce a premium version of the brand. Patrick did that: he created Bombay Sapphire. At the time gin was a tired and moribund category. Sapphire reignited the sector. Since then, gin has grown and grown, and today you can spot Bombay Sapphire everywhere. But that is a digression, albeit one with a nice sparkle.

So, Gilbert Ghostine was taken on by Hassan to do the marketing. It was to prove an inspired choice. The management makeup of Hassan's company was wonderfully eclectic. One of his partners was a Sunni and the other a Shia. And Gilbert was Christian. During the civil war Gilbert had been a special forces officer in the Maronite militia. Sometime later, at a clay pigeon jolly in Scotland, the instructor asked a group of our guests if they had shot before, and if so, what? Some had handled a gun: some had not. Gilbert said that he had, but admitted that he had never shot any pheasants, partridges, rabbits, hares or even grouse.

'So, what have you shot?' Asked the instructor: with just a touch of sarcasm. 'Only people,' replied Gilbert.

Some of the marketing initiatives that Gilbert came up with were truly astonishing. There is a highway that runs north from Beirut to Jounieh. Beside the highway there ran a line of electricity pylons – big ones. Carrying, as they did, high-voltage cables they were not very attractive. But they were, roughly speaking, shaped like giant conifers. For the festive season one year, Gilbert had them decorated as Christmas trees; each pylon bearing cheerful J&B baubles. The impact was spectacular: especially at night. Moreover, the location could not have been better because Jounieh lies by the sea ten miles north of Beirut and was both a fashionable resort, and a centre for the Maronite Christians.

After the end of the civil war, Hassan and his team made rapid progress with J&B Rare and within a short time our brand was threatening the leadership of Johnnie Walker. It was at this point that our parent company, IDV, decided that it would be a good idea to take over Hassan's business. IDV could then establish its own foothold in the Middle East. It was a region that was becoming increasingly important. J&B had for some time been a leading brand in Israel, and, as I have mentioned, in Turkey George Lutikov was doing an amazing job at taking J&B Rare to the number one slot.

John Hall, from corporate HQ, was tasked to join me on a visit to Beirut so that the negotiations could begin. I had first met John back in 1968. At the time I was garbed in a white coat and employed as a lowly bottling hall supervisor at Brown & Pank in South London. John was also there, and also in a white coat. He was the time and motion chap who, armed with his stopwatch and clipboard, would work out how we could bottle our plonk more efficiently.

It was amusing to think that having clawed our way up different sides of the corporate totem pole, here we were together on a plane bound for Beirut. On the way John explained that the price that we should pay for Hassan's company should be based on the multiple of a specific financial indicator. I forget which one it was, but he emphasised that we should not pay more than times two that of the chosen indicator. Not having a clue how to conduct such negotiations, I agreed to support his lead as best I could.

Hassan and his partners seemed shocked, appalled, and insulted by John's opening offer. They said that they were worth at least nine times the chosen indicator. There was clearly a huge gap in expectation between them and us. An uneasy silence seeped across the meeting room. To break the impasse, Alli, who was one of Hassan's partners, said he had observed that John had a slightly different accent from me. He asked John, very politely mind you, if by any chance he was Irish?

Now John is a good Scot. He did not take to this at all. Not one little bit. In fact, I could see smoke coming out of his ears as he grappled for a response. At this point I could not control my mirth. Happily, John then saw the funny side, and the ice was broken but not quite in the manner that Alli had intended.

An amicable deal was eventually struck and IDV Lebanon was born. I was its first chairman. Unfortunately, my tenure did not last long because it occurred just before I left J&B. I was particularly sorry to give up that role.

In 1997 Diageo was created. IDV Lebanon then became Diageo Lebanon. Consequently J&B Rare and Johnnie Walker, the two arch-rivals, were united in the same portfolio. I'm glad I wasn't there at the time. My feelings would have been rather mixed.

The native population of the Lebanon is around five million, almost the same as Scotland. Yet today she is host to around a million and half refugees from the civil war in Syria. Added to that are a further 300,000 Palestinian refugees, many of whom have been there for over forty years. Imagine what Scotland would be like if she were host to two million assorted refugees. It does not bear thinking about. Yet that is what the Lebanon must endure.

Towards the end of 2020 I spoke to Hassan on the telephone. In August there had been a monumental explosion in the dock area of Beirut. It had been caused by illegally stored fertiliser. The blast was so strong that it was heard 150 miles away in Cyprus. Many lives were lost, and swathes of property destroyed.

Hassan told me that he and his wife were fine, but his daughter and her family had an apartment in the area that had been badly damaged. His daughter had been seriously injured but, 'Thanks God,' would be OK. He lamented the disintegration of the government and the increasing influence of Hezbollah.

Happily, Hassan is still involved with the business. He told me that Diageo had been very helpful to customers whose businesses had been affected by the explosion. That was good to hear. He also told me that J&B was still in demand. That too was heartening.

But my heart bleeds for the Lebanon, a wonderful country but in dire distress.

You may wonder, that after the big *Beamonesque* story of J&B Rare in Spain, why should I end this book with a chapter about a small market like the Lebanon?

The reason is that this amazing little country encapsulates much of what the global whisky trade is all about. It shows how volatile a market can be. How it can turn on a sixpence from disaster to success: and alas back again to chaos.

It demonstrates the raw entrepreneurship that you can encounter in the most unexpected circumstances.

It demonstrates the wonderful diversity of people that you can meet.

And above all it demonstrates the colour and fun you can have when you are lucky enough to work in the whisky business.

Lebanese ceilidh at Knockando
Isabel is the only lady not wearing trews. Hassan is on her right.
During that visit Hassan planted a cedar of Lebanon at the distillery.
Innes tells me that it has grown considerably in the last 25 years

Acknowledgements

I should particularly like to thank those friends, old colleagues and other contacts who appear in the book and who have very kindly vetted, and in some instances corrected, what I have written. In order of first mention, they are: David Cossart, Robert Cecil, James Macadam (in Buenos Aires), Diana Diaz de Espada (for her father Raul Diaz de Espada in Asunción), Stanley Motta (in Panama), Polly Preston (for kind permission to use her story about Ronnie Lambert), Hew Blair, José Mesquita (in Lisbon), Franz Voggenberger (in Altenmarkt an der Triesting near Vienna), Mike Vineall, Innes Shaw, Suze Bower, Anthony Cooper, Peter Darbyshire, David Turtle, John Rideal and his daughter Joanna, Richard White, Peter Prentice, Tim Ambler, Julia Thorold, Ksenia Lutikov (for her husband George), Laurence Bauer, Paul McPherson, Cathy Maxwell Scott (for her father Ian Maxwell Scott), Harry Langley, Hassan Zantout (in Beirut), Patrick Millet, and Gilbert Ghostine (in Geneva).

I am also grateful to the following whose assistance has been invaluable:

Laurence Meehan and Hannah Reed at Diageo for permission to use anecdotes taken from Bob Lisle's *Recollections* (Chapter 27) and the extract from Dorrien Belson's 1966 report on the Dominican Republic (Chapter 31).

ACKNOWLEDGMENTS

Giorgia Ceccherini at John Lobb Ltd, Bootmakers, St James's, London.

Daniel Knight and the Born Group for their support with the typesetting. Because of my efforts with this book to raise funds for CAFOD's Humanitarian Appeal for Ukraine, they very generously reduced their normal tariff by a substantial amount.

Likewise, Isabel Hinchin and Clays for help on the technical side and for also reducing their normal tariff.

Paul McPherson who, in like manner, very generously designed the cover on a pro bono basis.

Jane Simmonds for her invaluable help with the copy-editing.

Theo Jones at the Society of Authors who was a great help with all matters concerning copyright regulations, and Wikipedia which I have used to check and refresh my memory about much of the geopolitical background material.

Elly Pace, my sister-in-law, and Patricia Roach for their helpful advice. Also, my nephews, nieces and my fraternal sister-in-law, who have provided much encouragement during the writing process. They are Mike Williams, Anne Rzyzora, Andy Williams, Sheila Van Der Merwe, Amanda Kay, Fiona Douglas, Jo Wschiansky and Moyna Maxwell Scott.

And last but by no means least, Isabel for her constant support, advice, and encouragement; likewise, our two sons James and Charles.

Image and Photograph Credits

Cover design by Paul McPherson.

Inside cover. Reproduced by Paul McPherson from one of the author's old passports.

Map of South America. *Peter Hermes Furian / Alamy Stock Photo.* (Chapter 10)

From a watercolour of the Plaza Major, Bogotá by Edward Mark. *With thanks to the Banco de la República for providing a high-resolution copy.* (Chapter 11)

Map of Central America. *Peter Hermes Furian / Alamy Stock Photo.* (Chapter 26)

Map of Africa. *Ingo Menhard / Alamy Stock Vector.* (Chapter 28)

Map of the Caribbean. *Peter Hermes Furian / Alamy Stock Photo.* (Chapter 30)

From a watercolour of Knockando Distillery by Chloë Furze. *Reproduced by kind permission of Chloë Furze.* (Chapter 44)

IMAGE AND PHOTOGRAPH CREDITS

The cover of *Le Grand Challenge* published by Albin Michel in Paris. *With thanks to Rosa Nascimento at Albin Michel.* (Chapter 47)

Every effort has been made to trace copyright holders. The publisher will be happy to make good in future editions any errors or omissions brought to their attention.